Retail Inequality

Retail Inequality

REFRAMING THE FOOD DESERT DEBATE

Kenneth H. Kolb

UNIVERSITY OF CALIFORNIA PRESS

University of California Press
Oakland, California

© 2022 by Kenneth H. Kolb

Library of Congress Cataloging-in-Publication Data

Names: Kolb, Kenneth H., 1975– author.
Title: Retail inequality : reframing the food desert debate /
    Kenneth H. Kolb.
Description: Oakland, California : University of California Press,
    [2022] | Includes bibliographical references and index.
Identifiers: LCCN 2021021914 (print) | LCCN 2021021915 (ebook) |
    ISBN 9780520384170 (cloth) | ISBN 9780520384187 (paperback) |
    ISBN 9780520384194 (epub)
Subjects: LCSH: Food security—Social aspects—South Carolina—
    Greenville. | Grocery trade—South Carolina—Greenville. | Food
    consumption—South Carolina—Greenville. | Equality—Social
    aspects—South Carolina--Greenville.
Classification: LCC HD9000.5 .K588 2022 (print) |
    LCC HD9000.5 (ebook) | DDC 338.1/975727--dc23
LC record available at https://lccn.loc.gov/2021021914
LC ebook record available at https://lccn.loc.gov/2021021915

Manufactured in the United States of America

30 29 28 27 26 25 24 23 22
10 9 8 7 6 5 4 3 2 1

Contents

Figures

Acknowledgments

This project began with a fight to stop the South Carolina State Department of Transportation from tearing down a bridge in 2012. I offered to help the Southernside neighborhood association, and they welcomed me with open arms. Mary Duckett and René Vaughn were the first to tell me the story of Southernside, and this book would have been impossible without their help. The list of other Southernside champions is too long to do justice here, but I will start by listing those who helped me at crucial stages of my research: Lillian Brock Flemming, Rev. J. M. Flemming, and Chandra Dillard. After a few years in Southernside, I branched out to the adjacent West Greenville Neighborhood Association. The leadership there was especially kind and patient. Rev. Vardrey Fleming, Rosa Byrd, and Inez Morris helped me in numerous ways. I will always be in their debt. And to the one hundred people who sat down with me to talk about food and the state of their neighborhoods, I am honored that you allowed me to listen to your stories.

The City of Greenville Community Development Division helped me in multiple ways. The former administrator, Ginny Stroud, was always available by phone when I needed help parsing through the minutia of bureaucratic policies. I also owe a debt of gratitude to the various other food-related groups and organizations in Greenville that I document in chapter 6 of the book. They are filled with hardworking and thoughtful people. I am especially grateful to Chad Bishop, Amy Bishop, and Roddy Pick at Greenbrier Farms for allowing me to muddle through their fields and roam among their livestock.

My own institution, Furman University, provided the resources and time necessary to conduct a multiyear project of this scope. My colleagues in the Sociology Department were always a great source of feedback, particularly Claire Whitlinger, Joseph Merry, and Kyle Longest. The Shi Institute at Furman helped fund early stages of this project through a Duke Endowment Food Systems and Farming Grant. And the staff at the Center for Applied Sustainability Research, headed by Mike Winiski, was a constant source of help. The Research and Professional Growth committee provided the financial support for me to secure the services of Letta Page, wordsmith extraordinaire, who gave the final draft of the manuscript a good scrubbing. Furman also provided summer research fellowships to a number of extremely bright and talented students who helped me conduct surveys and collect data cited in the book. Many thanks to Alex Bailey, Madison Allums, Lauren Bixby, and Mary Pauline Sheridan-Rabideau.

My academic friends and colleagues far and wide deserve much credit for the strength of any ideas in this book (and none of the blame for any errors). To Sherryl Kleinman, who taught me how to do ethnographic research; to Martha Copp, who offered great advice over ramen in New York City; and to the rest of my great sociology friends dating back to grad school (including, but not limited to, Matt Ezzell and Amanda Gengler): you have all helped me become a better thinker. And to my new friends in the Consumers and Consumption section of the American Sociological Association (especially Sarah Bowen, Jennifer Smith Maguire, Michaela DeSoucey, and Richard Ocejo), I sincerely appreciated your openness to a newcomer looking to start from scratch in a new subfield.

Some material in chapter 6 was published previously in "Feeding the Cultural Omnivores," *Contexts* 19(1) (2020), and is reprinted with permission from Sage Publications.

Of course, no book is possible without a press. My second time working with the University of California Press has been as smooth and seamless as the first. Although I missed working with Maura Roessner again, she

was very helpful connecting me with my new editor Kate Marshall. Kate offered some excellent advice at the right moment that really strengthened the book. Enrique Ochoa-Kaup was also a great help facilitating reviews and production, especially under the difficult work conditions posed by COVID-19.

But I am most grateful of all for the love and support of my family. My parents and my sister were constant sources of support. As were my spouse's extended family. But in the end, the most thanks go to Sarah, for always believing in me. And to our daughter, Vivian, who brings such great joy to my life.

1 What We Got Wrong

In the mid-1990s, a term was born. Areas without grocery stores would be known as "food deserts." Tucked into a British nutrition task force report in 1995, the food desert concept reached American shores a few years later, laden with an embedded argument: lack of access to healthy options was the cause of poor health among the residents of primarily poor neighborhoods. If "we" could shorten "their" distance to better food, they would eat healthier. If we failed to act, far closer convenience stores and fast-food outlets would push rates of obesity and diabetes even higher. The concept was so intuitive and persuasive that it would go from nascent public policy idea to major US federal program in less than two decades. A rare crossover, it captured the attention of both the scholarly community and the wider public. We had cracked the code of diet and geography in America. There was only one problem: We were wrong.

We were wrong because people in food deserts weren't really complaining about their diets. They weren't asking for help to improve *what they ate*; they were asking for help to improve *where they lived*. And we missed that. By "we," I mean the scholars, the media, the policy advocates, and the politicians who decided that we knew best what people in urban food deserts needed. (To be clear, I am on this list. I was wrong.) We heard people in poor, predominately Black neighborhoods complain about the lack of "healthy food" in their neighborhoods and we assumed that closer, more nutritious options would lead them to change what they bought and consumed and ultimately improve their well-being. We provided the evidence to support food desert interventions—primarily recruiting and subsidizing companies to build and operate healthy food retail—as well as the emotional anecdotes to promote them, the plans to execute them, and the funding to make it all happen. We focused on remedies that reflected *our* tastes and interests, without considering just how deeply people's dietary practices and preferences are grounded in the other aspects of their lives. We heard what we wanted to hear. This book will explain how and why we missed what people in food deserts were actually trying to tell us.

This is a book about *retail inequality*. For better or worse, to be an equal member in American society is to have an equal ability to shop at the same venues and for the same goods as everyone else. Political fights over what can be bought and sold in a community may seem trivial, but in a capitalistic society like ours, they are not. For decades, Black communities in poor urban areas have pleaded for the sorts of retail options available in other neighborhoods and towns. They asked for help when the grocery stores left, when the pawn shops and liquor stores took their place. Yet "we" ignored "them" until the problem was reframed in terms of health and food. *That* caught our attention.

This is also a book about *race in America*. Retail inequality is not random. It is the legacy of public and private sector abandonment of poor Black neighborhoods across the country. To demonstrate this link, I document the slow degradation of retail options in adjacent neighborhoods in Greenville, South Carolina. These communities were the front lines of the civil rights movement, and their leaders helped organize some of the nation's first lunch counter sit-ins (ironically, another battle over food access). Long-simmering tensions were exacerbated when the textile jobs began to disappear in the late 1960s. Decimated by the urban decline of the 1970s and '80s, these communities were hollowed out by the "urban renewal" programs meant to rescue them from decades of blight and administrative neglect. Meanwhile, the government shifted its focus toward suburban development. Whites fled. Retail followed. Residential segregation and concentrated poverty became entrenched. Today, the fight is over the future. Gentrification is "revitalizing" these once forgotten communities. But for whom?

This is also a book about understanding how and why we *mis*understood the issue of retail inequality so that we don't make the same mistake again. Had we listened closer, we would have heard that the food desert fight wasn't really about food. It was about fairness.

THE UNSEEN GREENVILLE

Revitalization was also a term used only among public policy makers. It also crossed over into the common vernacular. I heard it at least a half dozen times in the course of a single Southernside neighborhood association meeting in October 2014.

This meeting was special. It was being held in a historic church situated on the very edge of Greenville. Mountain View Baptist Church, a pillar of the Black community, was founded in 1908. Its pastor, the Reverend Stacey D. Mills, was just the third to hold the title in all that time. Geographically cornered by the Reedy River and the Norfolk Southern railroad tracks, the church isn't the sort of place you could just happen upon. You have to seek it out. In those days, the local paper had begun calling this area the "Unseen Greenville." And given the heavy downpour that night, I had to assume the thirty-five people in attendance were awfully motivated to have their voices heard.

A sleepy ex-textile town no longer, Greenville's property values were going up and high-end retail stores were moving in. The city center was thriving, but this neighborhood felt left out. The meeting's agenda featured a question being asked in similar communities across the United States: "When is *our* side of the city going to be revitalized?" At this forum, "our side" meant the poorer side of town. The Black side of town. As rain beat down on Mountain View Baptist Church, neighborhood residents pressed elected officials and municipal representatives on what it would take for the green shoots of prosperity to sprout where they lived, for this bit of Greenville to remain unseen no longer.

The meeting began on a hopeful note. The pastor informed the crowd that his church had acquired a sizable amount of land and wanted input from the neighborhood association about how it should be developed. A local community organizer stood behind the pastor with a flip board and a Sharpie, ready to jot down the residents' ideas and needs. When Reverend Mills opened the floor to suggestions, Shirley's hand shot up.[1] "What we need is a grocery store!"

A Black woman in her seventies, Shirley was not a native, but a transplant to Greenville. She grew up in New York, visiting Greenville to see her relatives over the years. Then she retired here. She lived in a senior housing project in Southernside and was the president of its tenant association. A few months later, I would interview her at her kitchen table. I came to learn that she walked two miles a day for exercise and, when her car was in the shop, took the bus to the grocery store. She loved to prepare meals and lamented the way southerners cooked their vegetables—*overcooked* in her opinion. Shirley's dissatisfaction with the food options near her apartment was formed by her past experiences: she knew another way was possible.

The pastor listened with the patience and compassion cultivated by his profession. He clasped his hands and lowered his chin to his chest. Others in the room nodded. Calls for a grocery store on this side of town were common at neighborhood meetings like these—especially since the closure of the nearest one a few years earlier. As local media outlets had been reporting, the west side of Greenville was officially a "food desert" (Callum-Penso 2014). Journalists and local news features documented the distances poorer residents of Greenville would have to travel to get healthy food, and just a few months before this meeting, the city's hired consultants returned a "Economic Development Analysis" recommending a "public-private" partnership to recruit a grocery store to the area. Seeing "NEED GROCERY STORE" in bold, capital letters at the top of the flip board here at Mountain View was hardly a surprise to anyone.

Reverend Mills acknowledged Shirley's concerns, but also noted the facts working against them: Compared to the city center, this area of town was sparsely populated. Vacant lots were common. People were starting to return to the neighborhood after decades of leaving it, but density (and a viable consumer base for a sizeable grocery store) would take time. Enticing a national chain grocer to the "other side of the tracks"—literally and metaphorically—would be a difficult task. Shirley seemed momentarily satisfied with Reverend Mills's response. But after a pause, she asked, "But what about the City, why can't they do something about this?"

The administrator of the City of Greenville Community Development office, Ginny Stroud, stood to respond. The City, Stroud said, had been trying for over a year to lure a grocery chain to the west side. It had even purchased a run-down strip mall in Southernside some years before, hoping it could be their bargaining chip: land as leverage. The City put out a request for proposals from developers across the country (City of Greenville 2014). It cleared the land to make it cheaper to build on. It dangled tax incentives. Not a single proposal had come in. With a hint of exasperation, Stroud stated that she *wished* a grocery store would contact her office. And then she sat back down.

All eyes then turned back to Reverend Mills, who clearly wanted to move on. By 2014, I had been attending neighborhood meetings in Southernside for two years. I knew that talk about grocery stores—or lack thereof—could take up the entire meeting; Mills seemed to know this, too. He had invited people to the forum to discuss other uses for the land the church owned: affordable housing, job training, youth mentoring, recreational activities. When he asked the audience to think of other ideas, the poster sheet began to fill with bullet points. The man holding the Sharpie flipped to a clean sheet. Again, Shirley's hand popped up.

Reverend Mills tried to appease Shirley by raising the idea of a small sundries store, staffed by local residents. This would increase nearby purchasing options, keep money in the neighborhood, maybe even provide a few jobs. He framed his suggestion as a more practical and reasonable goal than a fully stocked grocery store, but Shirley wasn't having it. "If not a grocery store, then a supermarket!" Laughs rose from the audience. It wasn't the first time Shirley had spoken out about this issue, and everyone knew it wouldn't be the last.

There were (and are) lots of problems facing the west side of Greenville and similar poor, Black neighborhoods nationwide. They need a lot of help. The items on the flip board gave me a visible sense of the cumulative downsides of uneven growth and redevelopment in urban areas. Gentrification was well under way in Southernside. Signs emblazoned "WE BUY HOUSES! FAST CASH!" shouted from utility poles on quiet residential streets. Rising rents threatened to displace long-time residents.

Good-paying manufacturing jobs had disappeared, and few people here had the training to apply for newer jobs (or the transportation to get to them if they were hired). The list goes on and on.

Yet I learned something from Shirley that night. At that early stage of my research, I had come to the meeting seeking evidence that bringing a nutritious food option to the neighborhood would help the residents on this side of town eat better. But I sensed I wasn't seeing the whole picture. Shirley's persistence hinted that *something else* was going on in the Unseen Greenville. No matter how hard Reverend Mills had tried to steer the discussion away to other projects or ideas, the topics of health and food had traction. Demanding "We need a grocery store," caught the attention of the public officials in the audience. It got them to act. Neighborhood residents knew that getting a grocery store was a long shot, but they could sense that they had stumbled on a powerful talking point.

The concept of food deserts has had a consistent presence on community agendas across the country for over a decade at this point. But why exactly did *this* problem attract so much attention? Past efforts to get people to eat better have clearly failed, so what is the real reason food deserts keep coming up in the national conversation? These are the questions that *Retail Inequality* aims to answer.

THE FOOD DESERT PROBLEM

It's still remarkable that the term *food desert* made the jump from policy forums to neighborhood meetings. Scan today's headlines and you'll find heartfelt accounts of people living in geographic areas that lack easy access to healthy foods. In 2014, the term was most often applied to urban areas with high percentages of Black residents, like Detroit and Philadelphia. Yet the concept was reportedly coined by a resident of public housing in Scotland in the early 1990s, then picked up in a 1995 report, issued by a UK Department of Health nutrition task force (Cummins and McIntyre 1999, 2002).

At the time, Britain and the United States were each decades into a dramatic transformation in how food was sold; specifically, neighborhood grocers had disappeared, as superstores on the edges of cities came to offer astonishing arrays of products at cut-rate prices, with parking as far as the eye could see.[2] The reasons for this "suburbanization of large-scale retail food outlets" (LeDoux and Vojnovic 2013: 2) are grounded in the changing nature of the industry. Innovations in transportation and distribution enabled supermarkets and "big-box stores" to sell a wider range of products on a much larger scale. Lower profit margins per item could be offset by higher volumes of overall sales. Suburban locations offered cheaper land, lower insurance rates, and affordable utility costs. Their locations were more easily accessible to highways and could feature loading docks suitable for tractor trailer deliveries (Martin et al. 2014). Consequently, smaller stores in urban centers with higher real estate costs found themselves unable to compete and began to close their doors.

This transition was especially painful for people living in small cities like Greenville.[3] Big cities may grab the most headlines, but the combined population of all small cities in this country (those with populations between fifty thousand and a hundred thousand) equals the combined total of people in the biggest ones (with populations of seven hundred fifty thousand and above).[4] And these plentiful small cities were particularly ill-equipped for the arrival of big-box stores. First, these municipalities, often dependent on single industries, had been particularly hard hit by the loss of manufacturing employment in the 1970s and '80s. Not a lot of capital was left, especially when it came to household budgets. Second, small cities lacked the population density to support the smaller food retail venues like bodegas and green grocers that still thrive in megacities. And third, as retail moved outward in search of bigger lots, small city residents without cars found themselves unable to access that retail. Their local governments, as cash-strapped as many residents' families, could not readily scale up accessible, economical, and efficient forms of public transportation.

These three factors, combined with this country's history of discriminatory housing and transportation policies, crushed many small cities' Black communities. Their lack of "consumer buying power" today is inexorably linked to state and federal disinvestment trends that began decades ago. Segregated and ghettoized, these communities watched as urban decline pulled down their property values and cut off opportunities to build intergenerational wealth. Urban renewal projects intended to ameliorate the situation resulted instead in widespread depopulation and displacement.

Dilapidated homes were cleared to make way for government-funded housing and roadway projects. Public monies were siphoned away to suburban development, fostering an era of "white flight." New subdivisions offered a fresh start to build equity, but only for those allowed through the gated entrance of neighborhood covenants and discriminatory home-lending practices.

This is how there came to be widespread blight in urban Black neighborhoods across the country. We have yet to undo—even effectively come to terms with—its consequences. Even though the civil rights movement did yield many legal victories that prohibited outright discrimination, racial inequality persists in these parts of town. How? "Color-blind" racism still operates under the surface (Bonilla-Silva 2014).

Even though explicit and overt racism is now illegal and, to varying degrees, politically untenable, the public and private sectors still manage to produce unequal outcomes by race. Unlike Jim Crow–era edicts, the policies that ultimately created food deserts were written in race-neutral language. The business decisions to abandon these neighborhoods were explained away as being decisions about profit, not race. And the people defending these choices and practices may have firmly believed their intentions were good and unbiased—*color-blind*. But racism doesn't hinge on what people say or personally believe. The real-world effects of race and racism don't disappear because people say, earnestly, that they "don't see color." In fact, we don't need to accuse any individual of being a racist to acknowledge that racism is to blame for the damage done to many urban Black communities across the country. To see color-blind racism in its true form, we need to ignore the rhetoric used to justify institutional practices and focus instead on the consequences of their implementation. *Who keeps getting the short end of the stick?*

For decades, outsiders were indifferent as corner hardware stores and shoe repair shops and corner markets disappeared from poor Black neighborhoods in small cities across the county. Whiter, richer neighborhoods lost small-scale retail, too. The difference is that wealthier neighborhoods were able to retain some nice options and—more importantly—keep *unsavory* retail at arm's length. Why? Retail inequality. Retail inequality is the result of purportedly "color-blind" practices that stripped urban Black neighborhoods of the collective wealth necessary to support "good retail" in a transformed retail environment. It is marked by an excess of "bad retail" options—the kinds of places that disproportionately exploit the poor (e.g., pawn shops, payday lenders, blood plasma centers) and cater to vice (i.e., selling alcohol, nicotine, and lottery tickets). And for decades, neighborhood complaints about the festering rise of retail inequality were dismissed as an unfortunate but inescapable function of the marketplace. "Supply and demand don't see color," outsiders would say. It seemed the problem of retail inequality was only capable of evoking a collective, apolitical shrug.

Then came the "food desert" concept. Economists started referring to the lack of grocery stores in these areas as a "market failure" (Bitler and Haider 2011), while activists used more politically loaded terms, like supermarket "redlining" (Eisenhaur 2001; D'Rozario and Williams 2005) and, more recently, "food apartheid" (Reese 2019). Whatever you call it, the lack of high-quality food in these areas—and the health problems we thought this caused—became a problem worth solving. Calls for the return of grocery stores had a sort of moral authority. "Healthy food" got the attention of scholars, the media, policy advocates, and politicians. All we needed was evidence.

A Subfield Is Born

By academic standards, the pace and proliferation of food desert research since the start of the new millennium has been impressive. Between 1966 and 1989, only seven peer-reviewed articles—vetted by other experts in the field—studied the relationship between geographic access to healthy food and health outcomes (Beaulac et al. 2009). The term *food desert* did not appear in a title of a peer-reviewed academic article until 2002.[5]

That year was an important milestone for food desert research. It saw the first published assessment of the impact of a retail intervention: the opening of a new supermarket in Leeds, England. Testing whether a new store can change diets is hard for public health researchers. Supermarkets can cost hundreds of thousands of dollars to build. However, when the new store announced its intention to open in a food desert, a team of scholars designed a study around it. This is called a "natural experiment": researchers did not install a store, but wrapped a study around its opening.[6] Residents were surveyed about their diets before and after the store was built, and the results were positive. Fruit and vegetable consumption increased among the poorest residents in the area (Wrigley et al. 2002). Food desert interventions seemed to be off to a strong start.

The same year, a series of scholarly articles appeared and tied a significant increase in fruit and vegetable consumption among Black residents in census tracts with more rather than fewer grocery stores. It wasn't a natural experiment like the Leeds intervention, but the study, which aimed to investigate the risk factors associated with atherosclerosis, leveraged data on over ten thousand participants (Morland et al. 2002). Their robust conclusion was that more grocers meant better neighborhood health.

Consensus was emerging in fits and starts. A second natural experiment around a new supermarket in Glasgow, Scotland, was inconclusive, while ongoing research from the atherosclerosis project found that people living near supermarkets were less likely to be obese, especially compared to those living closer to convenience stores (Morland et al. 2006). Another study showed that those who traveled more than 1.8 miles to a grocery store had higher body mass index (BMI) scores than those who lived closer to their food sources (Inagami et al. 2006).

By 2007, the field had started to mature. A sort of critical mass had been reached, with enough scholarly studies published to warrant systematic "review studies." These meta-analyses compare and contrast findings across a variety of different datasets, methodologies, and even scholarly fields. This is a significant step for any new subfield, as some areas of inquiry never produce enough scholarship to justify or support a holistic overview. One such review of twenty published articles on the "built environment and obesity" identified a few modest but significant findings supporting the food desert concept (Papas et al. 2007). For their part, national think tanks started producing comprehensive reports on the role that distance-to-store plays in Americans' health outcomes. For example, in 2007 the Robert Wood Johnson Foundation commissioned the Prevention Institute to publish a report summarizing *The Links between Neighborhood Food Environment and Childhood Nutrition* (Mikkelsen and Chehimi 2007).

By 2009, the US government began institutionalizing the food desert concept in its data collecting and reporting operations. First, the US Department of Agriculture (USDA) produced an official definition. Urban food deserts were now communities with a poverty rate of 20 percent or greater, a median family income below 80 percent of the surrounding area, and at least five hundred residents living more than a mile from a large grocery store.[7] The USDA also produced an online mapping tool that enabled people to plug in their address to see if they lived in a food desert. Media references to this food "atlas" spread quickly.

By 2010, policy advocates from two other think tanks, PolicyLink and The Food Trust, co-authored a forty-four-page report entitled, *The Grocery Gap: Who Has Access to Healthy Food and Why It Matters* (Treuhaft and Karpyn 2010). Consensus within academic, governmental, and policy circles was converging on a shared understanding of the causes of—and solutions to—urban health disparities.

Policy Momentum

It took very little time for publications about food deserts to translate into public support for governmental programs to fix them. In 2004, the first ever state level program to recruit grocery stores to do business in underserved areas, the Pennsylvania Fresh Food Financing Initiative, was founded. Soon, other public-private partnerships, like the New York Healthy Food Healthy Communities Fund and the New Orleans Fresh Food Retailer Initiative, appeared (Harries et al. 2014). And in 2010, based on recommendations by the Task Force on Childhood Obesity, the Obama administration elevated the theory that distance from supermarkets (and proximity to fast food) "plays a significant role in poor dietary decisions" into federal policy by creating the Healthy Food Financing Initiative (White House Task Force on Childhood Obesity 2010: 49). Its first budget included $400 million "to promote interventions that expand access to nutritious foods" (2010: 53). The following year, the US Department of Health and Human Services' Office of Community Services disbursed $16 million to support twenty-five food-related initiatives nationwide (US Department of Health and Human Services 2011).

Political momentum grew, and with each new initiative, the idea would become further cemented into public consciousness: all we had to do to improve health was fund grocery stores in poor areas, make healthier food more available, and educate people about their options. The academic consensus, on the other hand, was beginning to drift in the other direction.

Questions Emerge in the Academic Community

Ironically, just as the White House Task Force report was released in 2010, academic support for the idea that food deserts were the cause of poor health began to crumble. An evaluation of sixteen articles that focused on whether the presence of restaurants, convenience stores, or grocery stores was related to local obesity rates found that "there were as many or more studies that reported no evidence of association with obesity outcomes as there were that reported statistically significant associations" (Feng et al. 2010: 180).

One important point was that scholars simply did not understand the mechanics of how people in food deserts managed the distance between themselves and their shopping destinations. For example, one study in North Philadelphia found that only 45 percent of recipients of Special Supplemental Nutrition Program for Women, Infants, and Children (WIC) benefits had their own transportation, yet 75 percent of them traveled to the store by car (Hillier et al. 2011). This meant a significant number were not taking public transportation. Perhaps they were either borrowing vehicles or getting rides, we simply did not know. Another study found that shoppers regularly bypassed their closest option. In the Seattle area, for instance, where the average resident lived 1.18 miles from a supermarket, they shopped at stores an average 2.53 miles from their homes (Drewnowski et al. 2012).

As studies stacked up, the relationship between distance and diet became murkier, too. Meta-analysis survey studies (which reviewed multiple publications with different methods and samples) concluded that the relationship between distance and food was tenuous at best: in terms of causation, the authors wrote, there was only "moderate evidence in support of the causal hypothesis that neighborhood food environments influence dietary health" (Caspi et al. 2012: 1181). Bedrock assumptions, such as the idea that food desert residents shop primarily at nearby convenience stores, started to crumble. Researchers that mapped food desert residents' shopping routes in Detroit found that they "overwhelmingly" bypassed these small retailers to get to supermarkets farther away—traveling on average 3.6 miles (LeDoux and Vojnovic 2013: 9).

To try to better capture food consumption practices, academics took up some innovative approaches.[8] Conducting pre- and post-test surveys when a supermarket comes to town is not the only way to track changes in eating patterns. One research team tracked the food consumption of people as they moved residences—either increasing or decreasing their distance to healthy retail options. They found that changes in relative distance to nutritious food had little effect on diet: "Neighborhood supermarket and grocery store availability were generally unrelated to diet quality and adherence to fruit and vegetable recommendations" (Boone-Heinonen et al. 2011: 1165). Taking a similar approach, a 2012 study drew on data from thirteen thousand children and adolescents who took the California Health Interview Survey to conclude there was "no evidence to support the hypotheses that improved access to supermarkets, or that less exposure to fast-food restaurants or convenience stores within walking distance improve diet quality or reduce BMI" (An and Sturm 2012: 131).

The grocery store solution—which seemed so obvious—was now being closely scrutinized within scholarly circles: "Providing supermarkets in isolation of other efforts may not change consumer behavior or improve health" (Gordon-Larsen, Boone-Heinonen, and Popkin 2012: 196). More research only produced more questions.

Sowing Doubt

The media and the public had not yet caught on, but "think tanks" were beginning to notice. The Food Trust and PolicyLink, two organizations dedicated to improving access to healthy foods, were staunch supporters of the White House initiative in 2010, stating that there was "strong and consistent evidence indicating a positive relationship between access to healthy food and eating behaviors" (Treuhaft and Karpyn 2010: 16). Yet, three years later, the think tanks' revised joint report took a softer tone as it acknowledged the recent publication of "a smaller body of studies with findings that question the strength" of the connection between grocery store proximity and dietary choices (Bell et al. 2013: 13).

If the objective was to get people to eat better, the most popular solution to the food desert problem—building new grocery stores—was not working. In fact, the often publicly funded and incentivized interventions were missing the mark right and left. By 2014, a supermarket built in Philadelphia was known to have failed to produce the hoped-for dietary changes (Cummins, Flint, and Matthews 2014), just like ones in Pittsburgh

(Dubowitz et al. 2015a) and the Bronx (Elbel et al. 2015). Despite the newer, closer grocery store option in the Bronx, its residents not only kept traveling the same distance to shop at their old grocery store, but also kept eating the exact same way they did when they still lived in a food desert.

"Supermarket Entry Has Little Effect on Healthy Eating"

The grocery approach's failure was a wakeup call for many in academic and policy circles. Some researchers argued that we needed to rethink the concept altogether, publishing articles with titles like "Moving Beyond 'Food Deserts': Reorienting United States Policies to Reduce Disparities in Diet Quality" (Block and Subramanian 2015). Supermarkets had been framed as the key to improving nutritional intake; but now, researchers showed that more than half of food desert residents bypassed their closest grocery stores (Dubowitz et al. 2015b). And those who shopped in supermarkets ate just as poorly as those who got their food from convenience stores and fast-food outlets (Stern et al. 2016). A 2017 review of seven grocery store interventions in food deserts over the previous ten years found that *none* had significantly affected eating choices or health-related outcomes (Abeykoon, Engeler-Stringer, and Muhajarine 2017).

Producing dietary change is hard, and while grocery stores often have healthier and wider options than those available in bodegas and corner stores, they also sell a lot of unhealthy food. Researchers from the RAND Corporation published an article with the unequivocal title: "Where Do Residents of Food Deserts Buy Most of Their Junk Food? Supermarkets" (Vaughn et al. 2017). Studies began to acknowledge the complexity and nuance in people's grocery shopping practices. Given the entanglements and obligations of everyday life (both personal and financial), people have to travel; these journeys lead them to cross paths with all varieties of food options. Instead of focusing entirely on Euclidian distance from home address to grocery stores, researchers were demonstrating that most people plan their shopping around family, work, worship, and chores (DiSantis et al. 2016).

In November 2019, the concept of seeding food deserts with grocery stores to fix poor diets was definitively put to the test—and found lacking. Researchers partnered with the Nielsen Corporation (famous for its television ratings system) to survey a nationally representative sample of sixty-one thousand households. The surveys included questions about their health, food preferences, and nutrition knowledge (Allcott et al. 2019). The report also analyzed cash register receipts from thirty-five thousand different food retailers (representing about 40 percent of all food sold in the United States). By matching how people ate, where they lived, where stores were located, and what the stores sold, the study would track the relationship between distance and diet over a period of twelve years. The resulting paper was the most comprehensive economic study of food desert purchasing patterns ever conducted, and it was published in the most prestigious journal in the field of economics. Sadly, its results pointed out all the ways we got the food desert concept wrong.

First, people in food deserts do not rely on convenience stores for groceries: "even households living in ZIP codes with no supermarkets still buy 85% of their groceries from supermarkets" (Allcott et al. 2019: 1796). Just because food desert residents have to travel farther for food does not resign them to their closest options: "Households in food deserts spend only about 1% less of their grocery budgets at grocery stores, supercenters, and club stores than households that are not in food deserts" (1815).

Further, the authors concluded, putting a grocery store into a food desert wasn't a cure-all: "Supermarket entry has little effect on healthy eating" (1815). That is, when a new supermarket is built, it doesn't change what types of food people buy, just where they buy them. Improving geographic access only improved diet by a few percentage points. The study rejected the notion that a neighborhood's food environment caused poor health outcomes and argued that "policies aimed at eliminating food deserts likely generate little progress toward a goal of reducing nutritional inequality" (1840).

Unanswered Questions

At the beginning of my research, in 2014, I could see that the evidence on food deserts had taken a turn. Media accounts were sending mixed messages, but a number of high-profile stores built to meet pent-up demand were already going out of business. I tried to stay optimistic. I held out hope that longer distances to healthy food just *had* to affect what

Americans ate. The cause—grocery justice!—pulled at my heartstrings, and I wanted the straightforward solution to work. I urgently wanted to know *why* retail interventions did not seem to change diets and whether there was something I could learn from residents to come up with a better solution, like tapping into the abundance of locally grown food.

I became fascinated by how the food desert concept spread so far and so fast, capturing so much attention and so much government funding. Few academic findings break into the public consciousness with such speed and breadth. It was as if the idea had taken on a life of its own. How did a term originally meant to describe the poor areas around housing projects in Great Britain come to be used as a rallying cry in neighborhood meetings in Greenville, South Carolina?

To understand why people were suddenly so fixed on the grocery store solution despite growing skepticism that it accomplished its goal, I decided I needed to talk to people. I knew these neighborhoods well, but at this point I was still blinded by the "healthy food" solution. I desperately wanted to find the perfect kind of store that would change diets and meaningfully affect health outcomes (and health disparities). I figured the first step was to learn how residents navigate the food desert, how they interpret their available options, and why they make the food choices they do.

There are only a few books on food deserts that dig into the personal accounts of the people who live in them. From anthropology, we learn how a poor Black neighborhood on the edge of Washington, D.C., is grappling with the effects of racism, gentrification, and transnational food corporations (Reese 2019). From sociology, we learn how poor families cope with the unrealistic expectations of the home-cooked meal in the regions around Raleigh, North Carolina (Bowen, Brenton, and Elliot 2019). *Retail Inequality* adds to these accounts by putting the concept of food deserts into the context of a long-standing struggle over what is bought and sold in poor urban areas. Residents of these neighborhoods want better options, even if their food preparation and consumption practices are not so easy to change. By having real and honest conversations with people, I show how their eating habits are governed by a set of six everyday realities—some of which make the lives of people living in food deserts easier and some that make them far more difficult. *Retail Inequality* also includes the perspective of the people trying to improve the food options in these neighborhoods. The motivations of these "problem solvers" matter if we are going to propose solutions that neighborhood residents can realistically act upon.

Again, the transformation of retail in America began long before anyone had ever heard the term *food desert*. Urban decline nearly destroyed these neighborhoods, and urban renewal policies mostly made things worse. The battle over grocery stores today only makes sense in historical context: past policies made the real estate cheap in poor neighborhoods, setting the stage for the gentrification occurring today. Will new investment cater to the needs and tastes of longtime residents, or only to newcomers looking to make a return on their investment?

If putting supermarkets in food deserts doesn't entice people to eat better, we need to rethink why residents have been so adamant about this particular solution. They are fighting to be heard. Our job is to listen.

CASE STUDY: GREENVILLE, SOUTH CAROLINA

There are a number of reasons why I decided to study this topic and look for answers in Greenville. First, I live here. Directing my academic interests toward issues that people care about in the city where I live is important to me: I think of it as both a civic and a personal project. It is a civic project because it offers a service to my community on a topic that matters to them. By conducting a multiyear research project on the lack of grocery stores on this side of town, I hope to give something back to my neighbors.

It is also a personal project, because it matters to me: I love food. Always have. Growing up in Louisiana, I internalized the local grocery store's jingle. It still plays in my head: "Some people eat to live, but in New Orleans we live to eat." Later, in my mid-twenties, I joined the Peace Corps as a beekeeper on a farm in Paraguay. During those years, I grew vegetables and raised my own pigs and chickens—an experience that taught me to understand what "local food" could really mean.

Today, I live in a food desert—not that it really affects my diet. When I plug my address into the USDA's Food Access Research Atlas, I see my home just inside the edge of a yellow cloud hovering over my neighborhood— meaning it meets USDA standards for both "low income," "low access," and limited vehicle ownership. The site's database of store locations is not

perfect (Han et al. 2012), but it is correct when it comes to my neighborhood. Our closest full-size supermarket is 1.4 miles from my home and
situated on a busy road. Walking there would be difficult. However, my
family lives a privileged, white, middle-class life. My spouse and I share
a mortgage, and we each have our own car. Between our commutes and
shuttling our daughter to and from school, we drive by a combined three
full-size grocery stores on any given weekday. Routine chores, appointments, rehearsals, and lessons bring us past two more. Again, we live in a
food desert, but—for us—our circumstances shrink the map.

My personal connection to the people who live on the west side of
Greenville began in 2012, when the South Carolina State Department
of Transportation decided to tear down a decaying bridge that Southernside residents simply wanted restored. I contacted the neighborhood
association to see if there was anything I could do to help. A few months
later, with some students, I conducted a brief community-based research
project to document their opposition. Ultimately, we lost the battle, and
the bridge was removed the following summer. However, our small study
was included in a lawsuit filed with the Federal Highway Administration's
Office of Civil Rights. With that complaint in hand, local legislators saw a
new opening in negotiations to replace the bridge. Eventually, the Department of Transportation agreed to install a pedestrian bridge to reconnect
the two sides of the neighborhood (Mitchell 2019).

Through that project, which brought me into the neighborhood's meetings, protests, and cookouts, I learned that the bridge was not the neighborhood's only complaint. They felt left behind. While the rest of the city was
benefitting from the reemergence of retail and residential investment, their
side of town lacked even a grocery store. I was intrigued, especially at the
mention of grocery stores. As I asked around, I learned that this was also
an issue with an adjacent area, which called itself "West Greenville." Soon,
my connections introduced me around, and I began attending West Greenville's meetings, protests, and cookouts, too. Together, these two neighborhoods offered a large enough area and population to compare against the
findings of other food desert research being conducted around the country.

Southernside and West Greenville are representative food deserts—at
least, representative of the sorts of food deserts that get news coverage.
According to the USDA definition, food deserts are any community of
people without the means, financial and vehicular, to afford and access

healthy food. Rural food deserts can be particularly expansive and create incredible hardships for the people who live in them. The vast majority of political, media, and academic energy has, however, been directed toward another type of community: poor, urban, and largely Black. Communities like Southernside and West Greenville.

There are a number of reasons the discourse has focused on Black neighborhoods. To begin, food deserts are, by definition, areas with higher rates of poverty; according to the US Census Bureau, in 2018, 21 percent of Black people in the United States lived below the poverty level, compared to only 10 percent of whites. Black people are also more likely to experience poor diet-related health outcomes like diabetes, obesity, heart disease, and hypertension (Farmer 2005). In what is sometimes called the "Latino paradox" (Scribner 1996), foreign-born Hispanics and Latinos living in the United States have similar rates of poverty but slightly better health than their Black counterparts. Thus, even though the academic definition of food deserts is measured in economic class and health patterns, the emotional subplot for most Americans is one about race and inequality. In a country in which a shopping cart piled high with groceries is a symbol of our national identity, many people are struck by the lack of supermarkets in some areas. That they are so frequently Black neighborhoods does not go unnoticed.

When I began my research in 2014, Southernside and West Greenville looked a lot like neighborhoods featured in the most prominent academic research on food deserts (see Table 1): North Central Philadelphia (Cummins et al. 2014); Pittsburgh's "Hill District" (Dubowitz et al. 2015a, 2015b); "Carriage Town" in Flint, Michigan (Sadler, Gilliland, and Arku 2013); Detroit, Michigan (LeDoux and Vojnovic 2013); and the "Hollygrove" neighborhood of New Orleans (Kato 2013). All have significant Black populations, high rates of poverty, and low rates of vehicular access.

Despite its name, Southernside sits just north of West Greenville. It takes its name from the former Southern Railway Company (now Norfolk-Southern). Like West Greenville, it is classified as a "Special Emphasis Neighborhood" by the City of Greenville. Both are eligible for Community Development Block Grant funds from the US Department of Housing and Urban Development, which require that at least 51 percent of a neighborhood's households earn less than 80 percent of the median income of the rest of the city.

Table 1 Food Desert Areas Comparison

	West Greenville and Southernside	North Central Philadelphia[a]	"Hill District," Pittsburgh[b]	"Carriage Town," Flint, Michigan[c]	Detroit City, Michigan[d]	"Hollygrove," New Orleans[e]
Total Population	2,977	12,200	9,404	2,561	695,437	5,347
Race						
Black	72.4%	57.8%	76.9%	47.1%	81.0%	92.5%
Other	27.6%	42.2%	23.1%	52.9%	19.0%	7.5%
Education						
College Degree or Higher	11.3%	17.9%	13.5%	12.7%	13.2%	15.6%
Employment Status						
Unemployed	13.0%	7.6%	10.4%	12.6%	14.5%	9.3%
Income						
Median Household Income	$16,823	$19,015	$16,925	$20,208	$26,095	$20,276
Poverty						
Families Below Poverty Rate	43.3%	28.1%	39.1%	50.2%	34.8%	37.9%
Transportation						
Households without Vehicle	21.4%	61.2%	59.5%	22.8%	24.6%	22.9%

SOURCE: American Community Survey 5-year estimates (2014)

a. Cummins et al. 2014
b. Dubowitz et al. 2015a
c. Sadler, Gilliland, and Arku 2013
d. LeDoux and Vojnovic 2013
e. Kato 2013

The history of Greenville is also similar to that of other small southern cities adjusting to the decline of American manufacturing jobs. Once considered "The Textile Center of the World," Greenville no longer has mills humming along the banks of the Reedy River. Urban decline through the 1970s saw neighborhoods on the west side of the city neglected and left to blight. Urban renewal projects, like a proposed but never-built highway bypass, resulted in the removal of entire city blocks of dilapidated housing. This brought about a sharp decline in population in Southernside and West Greenville. By the time the redevelopment of the city center began in earnest in the 1980s and '90s, only a third of the population in these neighborhoods remained.

Greenville's rebirth started with the construction of a major hotel, a Hyatt, on one end of Main Street in 1982, and was bookended by the construction of The Peace Center, a performing arts venue, at the other end in 1991 (Huff 1995). Gentrification wasn't far behind. As in so many urban centers hollowed out by deindustrialization, residential renovation and construction in the poorer neighborhoods on the city's periphery started in the early 2000s, paused for a few years after the 2008 recession, and eventually picked up pace again. Neighborhoods that were historically segregated from the white side of town would soon be seen as attractive real estate opportunities for those wishing to enjoy the newfound amenities on Main Street. Rents and property prices have risen too high for many long-standing residents to stay, but they remain low enough to draw gentrifying families and businesses.

The greater metropolitan area that contains Greenville is similar, demographically, to other urban areas in the southeastern United States. It is about 30 percent Black, compared to roughly 13 percent for the nation as a whole. Although Hispanic and Latino populations are growing nationwide (17 percent of the population), in Greenville County they stand at about 9 percent. Inside the City of Greenville, Latinos were about 5.5 percent of the population in 2014, though just 3–4 percent on the west side of the city, where I was conducting research.

As I began talking to residents of Southernside and West Greenville, it was clear that longtime Black residents believed they had not benefited from citywide revitalization efforts in the same ways as other neighborhoods. The percentage of families below the poverty line on the west side of town was three times higher than the overall city rate. The median income there was two and half times lower. State-sponsored segregation may be over, but its legacy remains. Whites constituted two-thirds of the wider metropolitan area and three-fourths of the county, yet in 2014 these neglected neighborhoods were predominately and inarguably Black.

In terms of mobility and access to supermarkets, Southernside and West Greenville households faced much greater hardships. Greenville has a bus system, but most routes run on an hourly basis and most trips require a transfer at the central terminal. Assuming no wait times, no transfers, and perfectly timed pick-ups and drop-offs, a trip to the grocery store from this side of town *could* be done in less than two hours. It rarely was. Most people told me they traveled by their own car or got a ride when they needed to get groceries, and even that was difficult. In 2014, 21.4 percent of these neighborhood's households were without a vehicle compared to just 6.9 percent of households countywide. Two of the remaining supermarkets had closed in the five years before I began my research.

Living on the edge of a rebounding city, the people of Southernside and West Greenville wanted to benefit from revitalization, too. In terms of retail quality, they had logged some successes. They had pushed pawn shops outside the city limits and managed to prevent the arrival of some new businesses that had planned to serve alcohol. But the struggle required unyielding persistence on many fronts. Their concerns were both broad—crime, jobs, housing—and narrow—potholes, streetlights, sidewalks. For these issues, assistance was slow and public awareness was shallow. However, after 2010, when they started talking about the lack of a grocery store, ears began to perk up in unlikely places. Unlike many social problems, the food desert movement, here and throughout the country, enjoys support from a wide spectrum of activists and organizations. In my years of attending meetings and forums in and around Greenville, I learned that when "healthy food" is on the menu, people from all over town start coming to the table. Myself included.

A DIFFERENT APPROACH TO STUDYING RETAIL INEQUALITY

To understand the perspectives of people living in food deserts, I knew I would need to draw up a different set of questions. At the time, evidence was starting to show that inserting healthy food options in these neighborhoods was not changing the way people ate. Why not? What were we missing?

I start, in chapter 2, by outlining how the media framed the lack of grocery stores in some communities as the cause of residents' poor health—even after academic support for this idea started to fall apart. The clues that residents' shopping and eating behavior differed from their political slogans were there, had we looked. Very quickly, a number of high-profile business start-ups intended to fill the grocery gap went out of business. They had opened to great fanfare with journalists detailing the pent-up consumer demand, and as they closed, the media narrative held strong. Drawing upon over 389 news media accounts between 2011 and 2017, I show how several food desert misconceptions persisted amid business failures and the decline of academic support. I take a step back to analyze the conditions that made these media frames so attractive: the obesity crisis, easier and cheaper mapping technology, and the growth of food-related social movements. Media frames play an important role in shaping public policy, and their focus on a geographic argument helps explain why the same types of interventions kept getting proposed despite their consistent record of failing to produce dietary change.

After that, in chapter 3, I begin my report of what I learned from people who lived in Southernside and West Greenville. If media accounts were still repeating outdated ideas about why people like them ate healthy or unhealthy foods, even as retail interventions failed, well, what was the real story? If it was not to eat differently, why did they want a grocery store so badly? By talking to people in their homes, at their kitchen tables, I saw that, like my own, most of their consumption patterns were governed by the resources and constraints of their everyday lives. Their circumstances, from their food environment to access to transportation to economic resources, made shopping easier for some and more difficult for others. As I listened to people tell me what it was like to watch their retail options slowly decay, I documented their frustrations. I learned how those struggling to feed their families straddled the retail and donated food markets, seeing their menus largely dictated by others. I learned how small gaps in public transportation could make getting around town unfeasible for many, however short or long the distances traveled.

Chapter 4 explains how I finally came to recognize that the pleas for a grocery store were never really about wanting to eat differently. Those who could afford to buy groceries had already crafted innovative—and often overlooked—ways of getting to the store. Past research has shown that most people—including those who don't have cars—bypass their closest options. In Southernside and West Greenville, residents were not passive victims of circumstance: they constructed their own informal ride network by leveraging their social capital. Clearly, choosing whole foods that require home preparation was a separate proposition from being able to get to the store. My respondents' ultimate purchasing decisions factored in three additional everyday realities that I wasn't hearing in public policy discussions: social capital, household dynamics, and Americans' durable "taste for convenience." Through their social network, they found a way to get to the market. Yet decisions about what to buy or whether to cook depended on their household dynamics. Residents living alone and small households that felt obligated to provide a separate meal of "kid food" to their children often found that home cooking had become largely untenable. Without enough people in the house with the same tastes eating at the same time, pre-prepared foods could be the more logical and even economically sound choice. Of course, changes in household size have been in motion for decades, and they are just one part of the evolving food landscape that includes all of America, not just food deserts. Innovations in food processing technology, too, have tapped into innate cravings and found ways to suspend our natural aversions to overeating. These interactions between material food access and our physical bodies have produced a durable taste for convenience foods (pre- and par-cooked) that public health interventions will be hard pressed to dislodge.

In chapter 5, I set aside the decision-making process of food desert residents to enter into the wider issue of retail inequality. If you listen closely, you'll hear that the public and private voices of food desert residents sound very different. During private interviews, few residents expressed any real interest in dramatically changing their diets. They wanted closer and better retail options because it would save them time and transportation costs. But if a new store moved nearby, they had no intention of using those savings to buy more expensive, healthier items that took longer to prepare at home. Their diets and shopping choices, like those of all Americans, were wrapped up in their work and family obligations—few of which were going to change if a new store came to town. Despite all of this, in neighborhood meetings and public forums, the issue of "healthy food" came up over and over again. To explain why, I analyze the history of fights over retail in Black communities. Here we begin to understand that local retail is a signifier of a neighborhood's worth. Supermarkets and businesses that work with the community signal vibrancy and investment. They are "good retail." Purveyors of liquor and lottery tickets signal neglect and vice. They are "bad retail." Political leaders and local organizers used the language of food deserts as an inroad to addressing long-term grievances about their retail environment. When they reframed bad retail in the language of food and health, they were able to catch the attention of allies who rarely listened in the past.

Those allies are the focus of chapter 6, in which I consider outsiders' motivations for and ideas about intervening in food deserts. Some see themselves as food desert activists, trying to increase access to healthy food. Others are what I call "unwitting bystanders," included in media accounts and policy discussions as being well suited to fix the food desert problem, though they do not take that as their mission or objective. Together, I refer to these two groups as the "problem solvers": people identified (by themselves or others) as the key actors for improving diets in food deserts. Understanding their point of view is necessary if we are to decide which of them can change the way people eat and which can reduce retail inequality (the latter being easier to achieve than the former). Their efforts fall into five main categories: buying directly from farmers, nutritional education, urban agriculture, improving donated food options, and retail interventions. I return to the everyday realities shaping residents' shopping and eating patterns outlined in chapters 3 and 4, then use those to help assess the likelihood that any of the problem solvers' ideas will succeed. Unfortunately, few are likely to make a dent in dietary practices, but it's not for lack of trying. The problem solvers were not exclusively motivated by profit or publicity. Most were just trying to earn a living and make a few small improvements to the world at the same time. However, the world has a lot of problems, and it is not reasonable to expect any one initiative can solve them all.

In chapter 7, I conclude with a summary of how we got to where we are and what to do moving forward. Retail inequality in poor, Black neighborhoods in small cities across the country has been decades in the making.

Increasing "good retail" in these neighborhoods is the right and just thing to do, even though dietary nutritional change—getting people to eat more fresh fruits, vegetables, and whole foods—is hard. Possibly too hard. If we reconceptualize the food desert debate as being about *more than food*, we can still make things right. The fight is for the future. How can we offer retail that caters to these communities' needs rather than to real estate speculators with dollar signs in their eyes? How can we meet food desert residents where they are and—*if* they want to change their diets—offer a realistic path forward that accounts for their everyday realities.

The way people eat is stitched into the fabric of their lives; knotted tightly at the intersections of their families and commitments. Expecting wholescale changes to eating practices without altering people's material circumstances is merely wishful thinking. But this does not mean we have to give up on designing new fixes. I propose a few modest and practical approaches—incremental changes that will take a long time but might reduce retail inequality *and* improve health outcomes. We need information and perspective if we're going to have a fighting chance.

2 A Concept Catches Fire

The language of health and food got outsiders like me to pay attention to areas without grocery stores. We—the scholars, the media, the policy advocates, and the politicians—assumed that those living in food deserts wanted help to change their diets. But that wasn't it. The problem was so much bigger than food. They wanted justice. After decades of divestment and general neglect, they wanted their neighborhoods to have the "good retail" found in other parts of their cities, rather than the assortment of payday lenders, liquor stores, and pawn shops typically scattered in theirs. That we only agreed to help when we heard "healthy food" shows just how much we misunderstood what they were trying to tell us.

Looking back, media accounts of food deserts from the time seem so enthusiastic and *sure*. They repeatedly asserted there was pent-up demand for more nutritional food inside food deserts. They assumed that decreasing distance and costs would unleash residents' dietary ambitions. Rereading them, it seems all we had to do was look at the map and set down shiny new grocery stores to improve their health. But the types of food available to people in these neighborhoods was only part of the problem, and a complete dietary overhaul was never their request. We did not listen to them closely enough, and we did not heed the signals when it became apparent that the "solution" didn't fit the problem.

When I began my research in Southernside and West Greenville in 2014, the local newspaper had run a few articles about food deserts, grocery stores closing, and the "Unseen Greenville" that was being ignored while the rest of the city was being "revitalized." Speaking the words *food desert* got the attention of city officials in a way that decades of complaints about "bad retail" hadn't. Talking about grocery stores struck a chord with anyone interested in health or food, and it seemed so simple to address this one measure of inequality (and assume the effects would trickle down from new stores to better diets to better health to longer lives). People across the city were drawn to the issue, and it gained traction as a tool of political power.

As social scientific concepts go, the food desert idea had a good ride. It took only fifteen years for the coinage to move from its first mention in a British task force report (Cummins and Macintyre 2002) to a White House Task Force report on Childhood Obesity and three more years to rack up millions of views via a "guerilla gardener's" TED talk.[1] In the mid-2000s, as researchers began to investigate the phenomenon, it almost became settled science that the absence of grocery stores was the main driver of Americans' poor eating and health outcomes. Few ideas make it so far so fast.

By 2010, ripples of doubt had already begun to spread through the academic community, but it was too late. The media narrative had been set. From 2011 through 2017, newspaper writers, television anchors, and radio broadcasters continually referred to favorable research findings from the early 2000s. Even after the retail experiments designed to fix food deserts failed to change health and habits or even achieve profitability, a set of assumptions, solutions, and misconceptions kept getting repeated over and over again.

Why? What made it so hard for the public to rethink the relationship between food access and food choices? Why couldn't we hear what food desert residents were trying to tell us: the problem wasn't about food, it was about retail inequality and its historical root causes. These neighborhoods had no say in public sector policies that impoverished their neighborhoods or private sector transformations that made it more profitable for "good retail" to set up shop elsewhere. While the justifications for these decisions were cloaked in "color-blind" language (Bonilla-Silva 2014), they had devastating effects for the Black neighborhoods that were left behind. Why couldn't we see the food desert problem for what it was: a subset of the larger problem of retail inequality?

Before we chart a path forward, we first need to mark the spot when the academic community and the media framing of the issue parted ways.

WHY ACADEMICS CHANGED THEIR MINDS

As a reminder, initial academic support for the food desert concept was swift and certain. The first "natural experiment" that measured the effect of building a new supermarket unveiled evidence that distance plays a role in dietary choices (Wrigley et al. 2002). Over the next eight years, study after study affirmed that people who lived closer to healthier options were more likely to be healthier than those who lived far from them (Morland et al. 2002). We also learned that body mass index (BMI) scores were higher among people who lived farther from grocery stores (Inagami et al. 2006) and closer to convenience stores (Morland et al. 2006). High profile think tanks (Robert Wood Johnson Foundation, The Food Trust) commissioned and published comprehensive reports that buttressed the idea that grocery geography was the answer. These documents were heavily cited by the White House during its effort to establish the federal Healthy Food Financing Initiative.

At the same moment, with projects planned and funds budgeted, the academic support for the food desert concept began to dry up. The evidence linking poverty with obesity remains solid to this day. Still, proximity to healthy food makes little difference in our dietary choices and health outcomes. In 2012, a study of thirteen thousand children and adolescents in California found "no evidence to support the hypotheses that improved access to supermarkets, or that less exposure to fast-food restaurants or convenience stores within walking distance, improve diet quality or reduce BMI" (An and Sturm 2012: 131). In 2017, a systematic review of seven grocery store interventions in food deserts over the previous ten years found that none improved eating patterns (Abeykoon, Engeler-Stringer, and Muhajarine 2017). And in 2019, a nationally representative sample of sixty-one thousand households cross-analyzed with a database of purchase receipts from thirty-five thousand food retailers showed that "supermarket entry has little effect on healthy eating" (Allcott et al. 2019: 1815).[2]

This is where scholars stand today. They acknowledge the correlation between poverty, lack of grocery stores, and poor health outcomes, *and* they disagree that distance is the *cause* of poor eating and ill health. In other words, academics believe we need to rethink our prior assumptions about distance and food.

MEDIA FRAMES MATTER

Frames are simply a means of interpreting reality (Goffman 1974). They allow us to organize information and make sense of observations. Media frames distill (and sometimes distort) complex phenomena so that readers, viewers, and listeners can capture an idea of what is happening from afar. Relaying all the possible data would overwhelm their audience, so media accounts are framed in ways that put the focus on particular aspects and ignore others. The "health" and "food" frames were not the only options when discussing the lack of grocery stores in some areas. Instead, journalists and their editors could have chosen to dig into the historical root causes of bad retail, the consequences of urban decline for today's generation, or the emotional impact of being denied equal participation in our consumer economy. Those lines of inquiry are all equally plausible. But the media directed its focus elsewhere. And those choices matter. They determine which actions to describe, events to attend, and people to interview. Media frames are not representative of public opinion, but they can steer the conversation.

Measuring the impact of media frames on public policy is not an exact science, though it is fairly straightforward in this case. The media frame that "living in a food desert is bad for one's health" helped build and maintain political momentum for the Healthy Food Financing Initiative. When the federal program began disbursing millions of dollars to subsidize grocery stores and food markets, countless stories followed about other communities trying to address their own lack of quality food options and get healthier. Even the United States Department of Agriculture (USDA) Economic Research Service's "Food Desert Locator," an online mapping tool created in 2011 to respond to public interest, shows how media frames and policy can become self-reinforcing. The tool's launch spurred media accounts that, in turn, perpetuated the notion that distance and geography were the keys to understanding local health disparities. That led to the creation of new organizations and initiatives designed to get better food to neighborhoods without grocery stores to help the people there eat better. Media frames operate within this recursive cycle.

Past research has documented how faulty media frames can have immediate policy consequences. One clear example occurred during the aftermath of Hurricane Katrina in 2005. In the days after the storm made landfall, media accounts exaggerated reports of widespread looting and violence (Tierney, Bevc, and Kuligowski 2006; Berger 2009). I remember the images well. I am from New Orleans but was living in North Carolina at the time. I watched the slow-rolling catastrophe on television and ached over the endless cable news footage of groups identified as gangs roaming empty streets. My parents had evacuated, but I worried about the house I grew up in. What I—and the rest of America—didn't realize at the time was that this media framing of "dangerous" people on the ground distorted what was really happening. When Black residents held a loaf of bread above the floodwaters, the headlines read "looting." When it was white residents, the same survival tactic was called "finding" (Ralli 2005).

The false media frame of "rampant lawlessness" in the days and weeks after Katrina, especially in poor, Black neighborhoods, had real-life consequences. Unlike previous hurricane relief efforts, the rescue efforts in New Orleans would be punitive. They focused less on humanitarian operations and cooperating networks of charitable, religious, and nonprofit organizations and more on imposing "law and order" through police and military responses. The city police department created a "looter patrol." The governor went on television to promise to protect private property. And a lieutenant general from the US Army took charge of a newly created task force to handle recovery efforts. "Those in charge of the response placed law and order above the lives of hurricane survivors," one study concluded (Tierney, Bevc, and Kuligowski 2006: 75). In short, the media framing of those who weathered the storm as *criminals* rather than as *victims* led to a new form of "militarized disaster relief as social policy" (Berger 2009:502).[3]

FOOD DESERT FRAMES

During the years shortly before and after the passage of the Healthy Food Financing Initiative, media focus on the role that geography plays in how people eat came from a wide range of sources. Leading the way were famous journalists and authors who kept tabs and even influenced food trends and opinions during that period. Michael Pollan, in particular, caught the attention of the wider public with his work analyzing the determinants of diet. His high-profile books, including *The Omnivore's Dilemma* (2007) and *In Defense of Food* (2009), carefully and simply laid out the numerous traps our food system sets for us.

One of Pollan's more popular theories at the time was that the layout of grocery stores is designed to trick us into eating things we shouldn't. As an example, he cites the placement of milk toward the rear of the store. Pollan draws on scholarly studies to argue that supermarkets intentionally place staple products like dairy so as to force customers to walk past the more profitable and highly processed products in the center of the store. In a 2010 video entitled "Supermarket Secrets" (NourishLife 2010), Pollan gives us a scaled-down geographic theory of food placement and consumption:

> The height of items in the supermarket at eye level [are] the most profitable. . . . Lower profit items that might be better for you are at the bottom. . . . In general, the supermarket is laid out so whole foods are on the perimeter . . . and in the middle is the most profitable, highly processed, junk food. . . . So, one way to navigate the food market, if you are concerned about your health and trying to avoid eating a lot of junk, is try to shop along the edges and try not to go into the middle.

The underlying logic he presents is that distance and placement—even at the micro level—can steer consumer choices. Apparently, a few feet can make all the difference.

Michael Ruhlman, author of over twenty books on food and restaurants, echoes this type of spatial analysis but adds another variable: cost. In his 2017 best-selling book, *Grocery: The Buying and Selling of America*, he writes: "People tend to eat what's easiest and cheapest to find, and in food deserts that typically means fast food and food that can be purchased in a drugstore or a convenience store. I'm not sure that we need long-term, randomized, double-blind studies on the effect of eating food from these places, because the trials have played out naturally throughout the country in food deserts" (20). Ruhlman's claims about humans and food are clear and unambiguous: price and proximity trump all. He draws a straight line from the lack of grocery stores to poor health outcomes. From his perspective, the food desert debate is over, and now is the time for action—if we wait, it will be impossible for people to resist the convenient and cheap items under their noses. As for the solution, his answer is clear: healthier options. Put them in place, reduce the travel and purchase costs, and we will see dietary changes for the better. Build them and they will come.

And what if they don't? Across the country, healthy retail interventions were failing, in a big way. It was the first visible crack in the foundation of the food desert concept. It should have been the first clue that our goals (healthier eating) did not necessarily align with what people in food deserts really wanted (retail equality). The stores' openings enjoyed ample media coverage: nightly news and front-page images of politicians and community leaders cutting ribbons heralded their arrival. These stores were intentional efforts to insert healthy food into commercial markets abandoned by grocery stores, and many were opened with the help of public and private grants and extensive community support. Why didn't they change the way neighborhoods shopped and ate? Why couldn't they become viable businesses? And why didn't the media catch on?

I first noticed this pattern of high-profile launch, low-profile failure in Greenville. A nonprofit organization started a mobile farmers market to sell food in Southernside, but it failed to attract enough customers and eventually stopped coming. The same group then opened a market meant to increase the supply of fresh groceries in West Greenville, but it shut its doors within a year. I will describe these operations in more detail in chapter 6, but for now I'm concerned with what we might call a translation problem: How come these disappointments did not make a dent in the way the media were framing the issue at the time? Consumer demand did not support these efforts to increase consumption of healthy food. Did this have an effect on how the media covered the food desert concept? Unfortunately, no.

Media interest in food deserts began in earnest around 2010. The journalistic accounts I gathered come from electronic, print, and newswire sources as well as broadcast transcripts from radio and television. These sources sometimes attempt to translate contemporary research for a lay audience, but more often relay the wants, needs, and aspirations of people interviewed. I am not the first to adopt this kind of approach. I take my inspiration from the book *Taking the Heat: Women Chefs and Gender Inequality in the Professional Kitchen*. In it, sociologists Deborah Harris and Patti Giuffre (2015) analyzed articles about men and women chefs in two newspapers (the *New York Times* and the *San Francisco Chronicle*) as well as two food magazines (*Food & Wine* and *Gourmet*) over a period of years. From this review they were able to capture how the media framed women who cook for a living, and the real-life consequences of those frames within the restaurant industry.[4]

My goal was to soak up enough accounts to make sure all media voices were heard without drowning in the torrent of every social media platform. Some of these sources are hidden behind subscription paywalls, so I used a proprietary database—FACTIVA (owned by the Dow Jones corporation)—which offers access to tens of thousands of media services in the United States. I set my search parameters to begin in 2011 and run through the end of 2017, roughly the moment when academic scholarship on food deserts began to take a critical turn through to the ending point of intense public interest. The year 2011 also holds significance because in that year the federal government began disbursing tens of millions of dollars "to bring grocery stores and other healthy food retailers to underserved urban and rural communities across America" via the Healthy Food Financing Initiative (US Department of Health and Human Services 2016). I began my review with a simple question in mind: Given the growing skepticism among academics about whether decreased distance to healthy food led to better health outcomes, as well as the frequency of failed retail interventions, how did the media treat the food desert concept? Which solutions did journalists cover the most? Which misconceptions did reporters most often repeat?

An open-ended FACTIVA search for any news item from the start of 2011 through the end of 2017 that mentions the term "food desert" yielded 7,368 results. Many of these addressed food deserts only tangentially or in passing. To ensure that food deserts were the primary focus of these media accounts—I restricted my search to only items with the terms *food desert* or *food deserts* and either *grocery store* or *supermarket* or *health* in the title or lead paragraph. These parameters eliminated hundreds of other articles from the sample that focused extensively—but not exclusively—on food deserts.

The results generated by my search query included print sources that ranged from the *New York Times* ("An Oasis of Groceries" November 23, 2013) to the *Richmond Times-Dispatch* ("Goochland Farmers Help Residents of 'Food Deserts'" December 18, 2011). I also included Internet sources, like the *Kansas City Business Journal Online* ("City Considers Solution to Beacon Hill 'Food Desert'" January 14, 2013); radio transcripts from sources like National Public Radio; and newswire accounts (for example, the Associated Press).[5]

In total, my search yielded a more manageable data set of 389 media accounts from 2011 through 2017 that specifically addressed the food desert issue. The entire list with corresponding dates, titles, and sources can be found in the appendix. Half of the collection (196 of 389 accounts), the *business media sample*, focuses on the economic side of fixing food deserts. These stories most often address the economic importance of grocery stores and typically relay familiar claims about food desert residents' pent-up demand to purchase healthier food. These outlets' coverage *should have* given a great deal of attention to the failures of grocery store interventions, but did not. To show how, I will piece together four "before and after" accounts of stores that closed, highlighting what little impact these business closures had on the core theory that had media and the public rallying around food deserts.

The other half of the data set—*the health media sample* (193 of 389 accounts)—engages more fully with causal arguments regarding health. These accounts address the health implications of food deserts directly. These outlets' coverage *should have* given a great deal of attention to growing doubts about the role that distance to store plays in regard to people's diets and ultimately their health.

The business and health media samples focus on different facets of food deserts, yet they share some common themes. After summarizing my findings from each sample, I'll detail a few general findings of the entire data set; in particular, I'll identify the most commonly mentioned solutions and most persistent misperceptions about food deserts.

The biggest takeaway is that the most common health and business media frames repeatedly misdiagnose residents' core complaint: the food desert fight is not only about food; it is about fairness and justice. During my private interviews with neighborhood residents (whom I introduce in chapter 3), I learned that they wanted better and nicer stores *even if* their everyday realities preclude their frequenting them. In Greenville, they liked the *idea* of a mobile farmers market selling vegetables on their side of town, even if they didn't have the resources or the right circumstances to buy its products. They didn't want to change their diets, they just wanted public and private reinvestment in their communities. They wanted businesses to work with them as partners and as equals. In the past, no one seemed to care when they complained about lousy convenience stores and vacant strip malls. But in this moment, calls for healthy food attracted attention.

Business Media Sample

Food retail is a business. Accordingly, roughly half of my data set follows a "business news" template and chronicles groundbreaking and ribbon-cutting ceremonies. These rituals of commerce typically feature local politicians orating about how new stores mean new jobs. For example, in a *Triangle Business Journal Online* report ("Save-A-Lot store opening in April to replenish 'food desert' in south Raleigh," March 10, 2015) the focus was on a new store's twenty-five jobs and $2.7 million investment into the community. This sample also included sad tales of disappointment when these stores shut down. Those accounts were, perhaps, journalists' best opportunity to question the concept or consider the larger issue of retail inequality, yet few seemed to notice the canary in the coal mine.

FAILED GROCERY STORE EXPERIMENTS

During the past ten years, a number of American grocery store solutions and related retail interventions proved economically unsustainable; many promised ones never even materialized (Brinkley et al. 2019). Sadly, these accounts follow a familiar script. When the curtain opens, optimism abounds. Owners and onlookers predict that customers desperate for closer, cheaper, healthier options will flock to these stores and fix their diets. Food desert no more! The second act is more somber. Stores failed, and the blame was laid on all kinds of contextual factors. Yet even these retrospectives allowed the idea that price and proximity trump nutritional preferences to endure. Failed interventions were explained in ways that left the core idea unblemished. Reading article after article of why these stores failed to attract enough customers, it became clear that the people these journalists quoted had made up their minds before the experiment even began.

Sterling Farms: Marrero, Louisiana

Researching failed business ventures is a morbid affair. When I came across the first press reports in the data set about the Sterling Farms Grocery store in Marrero, Louisiana, I felt a twinge of guilt about using its demise to further my argument. The case stirred up old memories. To this day, I still read my hometown newspaper from time to time. I remember reading about Sterling Farms when it opened in 2013. When the name cropped up in my media database, I felt like a detective opening an old case file.

The project was spearheaded by Hollywood actor and native New Orleanian Wendell Pierce. In a 2013 article, Peirce's desire to help his community is heartwarming: "The lack of access to fresh produce sends people to other poor choices, which is fast food or processed foods. . . . We watched over the past couple of years at our convenience stores that when you give people the choice, as corny as it sounds, the impulse buy become[s] an apple or banana instead of a candy bar" ("'Treme's' Wendell Pierce Opens First Sterling Farms Grocery Store," *Times-Picayune*, March 22, 2013). There are two assumptions embedded in Pierce's statement. First, that there is plenty of demand; it is the lack of supply that "sends" residents elsewhere. Second, proximity (to the store, to the product) induces nutritional behavior: people eat what is in front of them. The store would close just a year later.

Media coverage of Sterling Farms' closure did not challenge either of Pierce's assumptions. The reporters and their sources uniformly placed the blame on poor strategy and nearby competition:

> "It was poorly executed, in my opinion," said David Livingston, a supermarket consultant in Wisconsin who visited the Sterling Farms store last year. "Somebody didn't really know what they were doing when they put that store together.". . . Some attributed the failure of the store to the presence of other viable grocery stores in the immediate vicinity. A Walmart Supercenter and a Budget Saver, both of which provide fresh produce, operate approximately one mile away ("Sterling Farms Grocery, Co-Owned by Wendell Pierce, Closes after Just One Year," *Times-Picayune*, April 20, 2014).

Nowhere is it mentioned that the competition had been in their locations, offering the same fresh produce, well before Sterling Farms arrived, or that their very existence shows that there was no additional economic demand for different options if "you give people the choice." The logic doesn't track, but the principal ideas underlying the food desert concept are unchallenged.

Maywood Market: Maywood, Illinois

Most interventions assume unmet demand in food deserts, with some predicting that newfound supply will increase consumers' appetite for fresh produce and wholesome foods. Another popular media frame depicts grocery stores as economic engines that will draw new people and business to the neighborhood, spurring further revitalization. On Chicago's outskirts, municipal leaders saw Maywood Market as a way to both increase food access and improve the local economy:

> "You look at the lack of fresh fruits, fresh vegetables within the community itself, this is something more than just a financial decision . . ." said Jason Erving, village manager. The village invested millions of dollars improving infrastructure along 5th Avenue. Now they expect the grocery store to be an anchor that will help attract other businesses. Residents say they're excited to have somewhere close by to get fresh meat and produce. "My grandma . . . she's going to be there all the time. She stays down the street," said Michael Johnson, Maywood resident (ABC7 Chicago, 2010).[6]

Here we see hints of the core complaint about retail inequality: the symbolic value of healthier options is greater than the sum of their nutritional benefits. Still, though, it's wrapped in the flawed assumption that grandmothers would readily change their shopping and cooking habits. Maywood Market wouldn't prove to be an anchor for business, but a sinking ship. It lasted just six months. "Intangibles" like neighborhood consumption patterns subtly introduced doubt about the simple cause-and-effect story of food desert interventions:

> The owners' experience underscores the promise and the problems that can arise when such stores open in so-called food deserts—often low-income communities where residents have trouble finding fresh foods. Their success or failure often hinges on a sobering array of intangibles that include income levels, eating habits and the proximity of fast-food restaurants, experts say ("Maywood Market Exemplifies Grocery Stores' Struggles in Food Deserts," *Chicago Tribune*, September 5, 2011).

Both in tone ("so-called food deserts") and in substance (its inclusion of scholarly experts), Maywood Market's obituary gestures toward a flaw in the dominant approach to fixing food deserts. The mention of "eating habits" also nods at the possibility of non-geographic influences on tastes. Still, the article retreats to the well-worn trope that shopping habits are predominately rational: the shorter distance to fast food is one of the driving forces behind food consumption in poor neighborhoods.

Key Food: Newark, New Jersey

Local leaders and politicians are aware of the economic challenges facing food desert solutions and acknowledge that they need help to get started. They explain how start-up subsidies will eventually "pay for themselves" by improving public health. In Newark, New Jersey, local officials used public funds to lure the Key Food grocery chain to the South Ward in 2013. Corey Booker, then the city's mayor, lauded the public-private partnership:

> "This is a mission of mine to end food deserts in Newark," Booker said today, before stocking up on some items for himself. In his basket: apples, baby carrots, cherry tomatoes, pre-cut pineapple and yams. City leaders say the 13,000-square-foot store's offerings of fresh produce, meats and dairy as well as a full deli counter and seafood section will give residents healthier options

than what's available at nearby bodegas or fast food chains. ("Cory Booker Touts Newark's Newest Supermarket, Says City's Food Desert Is Shrinking," NJ.com, February 19, 2013)

Subsidies, though, can't keep stores open forever. This particular Key Food failed a year later. Its closure could have started a conversation, but again, the lack of demand was blamed on high prices and external and unforeseen events (in this case, high rent, construction slowdowns, and delays in accepting WIC food stamps).

> "I went there a few times but it was a little bit expensive. And it really didn't have a lot of things that I buy in there so I didn't go in there anymore," said Angela Ogunbiyi. "It's sad because it has been years for a supermarket to even come to this area," said Newark resident Monica Jenkins. With no grocery store here, residents in this neighborhood will be forced to travel farther to find healthy food options—a phenomenon called a food desert ("Key Food Closes in Newark, Leaving Residents in 'Food Desert,'" *NJTV News*, February 11, 2014).

By the end of the article on the Key Food closure, we learn that the problem was another example of poor execution. Presumably, if prices go down and selection is widened, the next attempt will be able to tap into pent-up demand. It concludes: "And city officials hope to replace Key Food with another supermarket."

Fresh & Easy Neighborhood Market: San Francisco, California

Grand openings in food deserts draw out politicians and bureaucratic officials to celebrate and highlight the government's efforts to help neglected neighborhoods. When the Fresh & Easy Neighborhood Market opened in a largely Black community in San Francisco, all the food desert talking points were on display. In a 2011 article, we learn that driving miles to a supermarket cannot reasonably be a consumer's first choice and that fast food is too easy and accessible to resist. We also see the recursive cycle between media frames and the discourse of government officials:

> "You're a food desert no more," declared Herb Schultz, the western regional director for the U.S. Department of Health and Human Services. Community leaders had tried in vain for years to attract a full-service grocery store to the historically African American neighborhood in the city's southeast

corner. The major grocery chains have all balked, local leaders said, leaving just smaller markets whose shelves often heavily lean toward processed foods. . . . Residents would have to drive miles to a store, making it easier to turn to nearby high-fat, high-sodium fast food. ("Fresh & Easy Opens in S.F. Bayview-Hunters Point," *SFGate.com*, August 25, 2011).

Leaders assumed that, with the installation of the new store, neighbors would change what they ate and where they bought it. When it closed two years later, local politicians focused their blame on factors unique to this store:

> District 10 Supervisor Malia Cohen, who represents the Bayview, said that Fresh & Easy did little to support its Third Street store, and was unresponsive to efforts to work with the community. . . . She said city officials "made countless offers to meet with the general manager of the store to discuss neighborhood marketing campaigns in order to ensure it would remain successful." Supervisor Cohen said that the decision would force many Bayview residents to buy their groceries in other neighborhoods ("S.F. Supervisor Blasts Fresh & Easy for Closing Bayview Market, *San Francisco Business Times*, September 10, 2013).

Rather than analyze the closure as a typical business failure (i.e., "the food business is a tough one"), local officials held firm: the people wanted healthier products to buy, and the market would have succeeded if not for poor marketing. Again, I find that core disconnect: neighborhood residents want stores that coordinate their business strategies with them, that work for and with the community. Investors, activists, and officials remained deaf to their calls for retail equality.

Health Media Sample

In the "health media" half of the database, 64.7 percent of accounts stuck to the media frame that increasing the distance between one's residence and the nearest grocery store leads to poor health. The rest of the sample was more nuanced, with 17.6 percent implying a correlation between distance and health outcomes and 10.8 percent presenting a "both sides" analysis of arguments for and against. Only 6.2 percent reported views directly critical of the food desert concept.

LIVING IN A FOOD DESERT CAUSES POOR HEALTH (64.7%)

In this category, access is almost always discussed in geographic terms.[7] These accounts claim food deserts cause poor outcomes either by quoting "people on the street" or citing unnamed "studies." For example, in a *Charleston Gazette* op-ed ("Living in the Spring Hill Food Desert," May 8, 2015) the author begins by defining the term: "A food desert is specifically an area of relative exclusion where people experience physical and socio-economic barriers to accessing healthy foods." This definition largely aligns with past USDA definitions and is another example of how governmental discourse and media frames are mutually reinforcing. The causal claims come later: "The physical distance from fresh foods determines eating behaviors and palates that prefer highly processed, salty, fatty food. The distance is also a true indicator for a higher BMI (Body Mass Index)." The argument is clear and confident, without providing any citations to back up its bold claims.

Similarly, in an article from the *Orange County Register* ("Fresh Fare: Since It Hit the Road Last Year, the Mobile Fresh Bus Has More Than Doubled Its Stops," June 7, 2015) about an old city bus refurbished to sell vegetables, the director of the sponsoring organization is quoted about the impact of inaccessibility: "Everyone knows about the issues of not having access to healthy foods—health problems, developmental issues in children—so we decided to do something about it. . . . We're influencing people's eating habits." Again, in these accounts, the idea that distance determined diet (a media frame) was presented as conventional wisdom. In reality, contradictory evidence was hiding in plain sight. But statements like "everyone knows" renders that complexity invisible.

The same confidence marks an editorial ("Alleviate Food Deserts by Planting Crops," June 5, 2015) that appeared in the *Santa Fe New Mexican*: "In food deserts, residents have limited access to a sole, full-service grocery store, leading to a higher incidence of hunger and stress, as well as to obesity and diabetes. When people lack a real grocery store, they're more likely to rely on junk food." It starts off fine—yes, people live in areas that lack one-stop-shopping for all their grocery needs. But "leading to" is a causal claim, made without any citations that might back it up. In fact, just to reiterate, academic consensus had already begun to seriously question the link between distance and diet.

LIVING IN A FOOD DESERT CORRELATES WITH POOR HEALTH (17.6%)

Other articles frame the connection between distance and diet in softer terms. These correlational pieces describe the food desert phenomenon in one paragraph, then mention high rates of obesity, diabetes, heart disease, or hypertension in another. These articles note a co-occurrence but are careful not to make a clear causal connection. As an example, a *USA Today* article titled "Programs Cropping Up to Address 'Food Deserts,'" (July 13, 2011), introduces readers to an innovative urban farm and mobile market run by an organization called The Arcadia Center for Sustainable Food & Agriculture in Virginia. The first paragraph identifies their target market: "neighborhoods where residents' food choices are limited to corner stores, dollar stores and fast-food restaurants." Then the article defines food deserts, describes how many there are across the country, and offers a brief history of the term. Four hundred words later, we learn the purpose of the organization: "What motivates efforts such as Arcadia is the push for sustainable agriculture and awareness about obesity." The article never claims that living in a food desert causes obesity or even increases the odds of obesity. Instead, the two issues—food deserts and obesity awareness—bookend the piece. Correlational links like these appeared in roughly one out of six accounts in the health media sample.

LIVING IN A FOOD DESERT DOES AND DOES NOT CAUSE POOR HEALTH—"BOTH SIDES" (10.8%)

A handful of accounts referenced recent academic studies that disputed the proximity thesis. However, rather than take a firm stand either way, they framed the issue as an open debate. For example, an article in the *Oregonian*, "Oregon's Obesity Crisis: Seeking Solutions in the Design of Cities and Suburbs" (October 12, 2011), began by quoting a firm believer in the proximity thesis. This local public health department official said, "What we do know is that folks who have healthy choices available to them are more likely to make healthy choices." Later, the article cites a then-recent study contradicting that claim, "Research on the impact of the built environment is mixed. A large study on 'food deserts,' published July 11, found that a nearby supermarket or grocery made no difference in the amount of fruits and vegetables people ate or the overall quality of their diets."[8] This type of debate-between-experts article more accurately represented the state of the research at the time, but was clearly outnumbered.

LIVING IN A FOOD DESERT DOES NOT CAUSE
POOR HEALTH (6.2%)

A tiny minority of media accounts adopted a contrarian frame: openly disputing the idea that living far from a grocery store was the cause of poor health. These stories more accurately captured the evolution of academic thinking on the food desert concept. In the *Tampa Bay Times* ("Food Desert Finds Relief," September 28, 2014), we hear from a researcher at a Washington, D.C., think tank who casts doubt on the idea that a new Walmart will change the way people eat: "Opening the store will expand healthy food options in the neighborhood but won't guarantee shoppers change what they put in their stomachs, as one report has shown. "People's food choices are not solely governed by their proximity to supermarkets," said Gregory Mills, a senior fellow at the Urban Institute." Another skeptical media account appeared in the *New York Times*: "Giving the Poor Easy Access to Healthy Food Doesn't Mean They'll Buy It" (May 9, 2015). This author is concise: "It seems intuitive that a lack of nearby healthy food can contribute to a poor diet. But merely adding a grocery store to a poor neighborhood, it appears, doesn't make a very big difference." This article captures the skeptical side of the food desert debate well but is in the minority in this sample.

Full Media Data Set: Proposed Solutions

Media frames matter because they increase the visibility of proposed policies and solutions. By assuming food deserts are loaded with unmet demand to consume healthy food, media accounts framed a number of other food-related ventures as possible ways to improve the way people eat. Discussions of solutions appeared throughout the entire sample (see Table 2), which includes both the business and health media samples. The installation of new retail options was the most commonly discussed fix (appearing in 42.9% of the sample). These accounts focused on the benefits of new brick-and-mortar stores, both expected arrivals and wishful solicitations.

Table 2 Most Commonly Proposed Solutions to Food Desert Problem
in Media Accounts

All articles (*N* = 389)	
SOLUTION: Open new stores (*N* = 167)	42.9%
SOLUTION: Modify or improve existing retail options (*N* = 92)	23.6%
SOLUTION: Increase community gardening and urban farming (*N* = 64)	16.4%
SOLUTION: Support farmers markets (*N* = 88)	22.6%

Almost a quarter of all media stories (23.6%) reported on innovative ways to renovate or modify existing retail options. These focused on efforts to change the way that people shop, including innovative grocery delivery services: "N.Y.C.-Newcomer Meal Service Freshly Expands to 28 States," (*New York Business Journal Online*, April 25, 2016); modifying smaller venues, "Corner Markets Enlisted in Healthy Foods Initiative" (*Dayton Daily News*, June 24, 2016); and incentivizing shoppers to buy healthier options at the point of purchase, "Retailers Encouraged to Make Healthy Food Be More Than a Mirage," (*St. Louis Post-Dispatch*, December 10, 2015).

Alternatives to the retail store model of fixing food deserts are described in many articles, too. Initiatives to grow food within the community, either through community gardens or nearby urban farms appear in 16.4 percent of the sample, and direct-to-consumer sales by local farmers in 22.6 percent. The *Hartford Courant* lays out the potential benefits of a new community garden: "[Hartford's] North End is a food desert, meaning if someone wanted to purchase fresh fruits and vegetables they couldn't do that because they wouldn't be able to find [healthy food items] in the area, because the corner stores really just sell junk food. Knox Parks provides members of the community who want to garden with the space, tools, seeds and expertise to do so. Knox Parks already provides 15 community gardens throughout the city" ("Community Gardens Get Funding Boost," January 27, 2012).

Locally grown food (whether provided by residents or nearby farmers) is an intuitive solution. "If stores won't sell it, grow it," is the general idea. Yet there are some deep-seated structural barriers to improving diets this way. In chapter 6, I will outline the challenges that face proposed ways to increase healthy food options in more detail. As a preview of that critical analysis, consider the limitations on community gardens and urban/local farms. They are not a year-round answer, because they are limited by the growing season. Storage and preservation are partial solutions, though they add costs related to equipment and storage. Second, small-scale production does not benefit from the economies of scale of industrial agriculture, thus increasing the price per item. Even homegrown vegetables, which are wonderfully tasty and satisfying, are no way to save money once you consider the costs of inputs like time and materials. Supermarket prices—including transportation costs—are still cheaper in the long run. Optimistic media accounts largely sidestep these realities as they tout the very real joys of community gardens.

What the prevailing health and business media frames miss is that people living in and around food deserts want nicer amenities in their neighborhoods (like community gardens) even though they don't necessarily plan on revising their diets around them. Yet the repeated framing of health as a goal of these solutions sidesteps residents' deeper desire: undoing retail inequality decades in the making. No one faults community leaders or local politicians for trying anything and everything. However, framing these initiatives as potential ways to improve public health sets these solutions up for failure.

Full Media Data Set: Persistent Misconceptions

MISCONCEPTION: RESIDENTS DEPEND ON C-STORES AND FAST FOOD (33.7%)

Media frames, by definition, condense and simplify complex situations. Unfortunately, this sometimes includes repeating myths rather than digging deeper to determine their veracity. The most common myth repeated in media accounts—implicitly and explicitly—is the notion that residents of food deserts rely on convenience stores (c-stores) and fast-food outlets as their primary food sources (see Table 3). The 33.7 percent of accounts that repeat this myth make assertions like "For some residents in Madison's Allied Drive neighborhood, buying groceries at a gas station or drug store is their most likely option" (*Wisconsin State Journal*, "Madison Grocer Has Plan to Serve 'Food Desert,'" June 4, 2012). In the

Table 3   Most Common Misperceptions about Food Deserts in Media Accounts

All articles (*N* = 389)	
Claim that residents eat primarily food from c-stores and fast food (*N* = 131)	33.7%
Conflate food deserts with food insecurity (*N* = 69)	17.7%
Conflate issue with other social movements (*N* = 113)	29.0%

Topeka Capital-Journal (February 2, 2014), the author juxtaposes a correct statement with an incorrect one: "Food deserts are a health concern because low-income people may not easily be able to drive to buy healthy foods and have to rely on nearby convenience stores and fast food restaurants." The accuracy of these claims is hard for readers to assess for many reasons, but conflating "convenience stores" and "fast-food restaurants" within the same story makes it much harder.

First, there is no research to support the idea that people in food deserts rely on c-stores as their main source of food. These stores sell little in the way of raw ingredients and make most of their sales on quick items and soft drinks. People in food deserts do eat a significant amount of junk food, but they buy it primarily from grocery stores (Vaughn et al. 2017). The grocery stores just aren't *close*. An analysis of Detroit food desert residents' food shopping travel patterns found that "very few trips are made to local convenience stores" (LeDoux and Vojnovic 2013: 9). A 2019 study conducted by economists found that "even households living in ZIP codes with no supermarkets still buy 85 percent of their groceries from supermarkets" (Allcott et al. 2019: 1796). In the same study, we learn that "households in food deserts spend only about 1 percent less of their grocery budgets at grocery stores, supercenters, and club stores than households that are not in food deserts" (Allcott et al. 2019: 1815).[9] The reason that people buy different foods at c-stores and supermarkets is obvious: c-stores are for snacks and last-minute items, grocery stores are for everything else.

To be fair, the "fast-food" claim is not a complete myth; it is true that food desert residents eat a lot of fast food. But that's true of *all Americans*. According to the National Center for Health Statistics, nearly a third of people in this country consume at least some fast food every day (Fryar et al.

2018). It is not fair to say that residents in areas without grocery stores rely on fast food more than other Americans do, and research is clear: living closer to fast-food restaurants does not cause people to frequent them more often (An and Sturm 2012). Nor is fast-food consumption driven by poverty. The same National Center for Health Statistics study on fast food actually confirms that wealthy people eat more fast food than do poor people.

The persistence of these myths is a byproduct of framing the food desert issue in terms of pent-up demand for healthier food. When I talked to people in food deserts, they weren't actually clamoring for healthier food but nicer retail venues (even new convenience stores and updated fast-food outlets were brought up as acceptable if not necessarily "good retail" that would improve the neighborhood). In chapter 5, I'll show how even gas stations can be seen as "good retail" if they work with the neighborhood, ask for feedback, and accommodate requests. Food desert residents want quick access to prepared foods and last-minute items just like everyone else. What they resent are businesses that assume their neighborhood only wants the cheapest offerings.

MISCONCEPTION: FOOD DESERTS EQUAL FOOD INSECURITY (17.7%)

The way media frames simplify multifaceted phenomena is apparent, too, in the way they conflate food deserts with other food-related social problems. Nearly a third (29%) of all accounts in my full media database confuse food deserts with other issues like food waste, agricultural pesticides, and food justice. These other problems have different causes and require different solutions. For example, food justice advocates are more interested in labor issues, capitalism, and the rights of indigenous populations to harvest their native lands. While attracting attention to these causes is important, solving them will not reduce food desert residents' frustrations.

Of these related problems, food insecurity is the one most often entangled in the food desert debate. In my media analysis, 17.7 percent of all accounts in the database treat "food desert" and "food insecurity" as interchangeable synonyms. Yes, both issues underscore how difficult it is for some to acquire food, but commingling the problems muddies the waters. It also hints at how we got it wrong when it comes to understanding the wishes and perspectives of the people we tried to help.

Over the past forty years, policy makers concerned about insufficient nutrition have shifted their focus from fighting "hunger" to alleviating "food insecurity." The reason is that life-threatening hunger and starvation have largely been eradicated in developed countries like ours. Yet, despite the abundance of food, many American families continue to wonder what and when they'll eat next. They rely at least partially upon social service agencies, food pantries, and emergency assistance, which is what makes their relationship to food "insecure" compared to people who can afford to buy food (and thus not think too hard about it) throughout the month or year.

The overlap comes for a small subset of food desert residents who *could* afford to buy food in stores, were it not for the cost of travel to and from those stores. This group frequently falls within the US Census category "near poor." Economically precarious, these families bring in annual incomes right around the poverty line (earning between 100% and 125% of the poverty threshold—in 2020, for a family of four, that amounted to annual earnings between $26,200 and $32,750). About 5 percent of the US population is "near poor." They live on the edge in ways that mean their home address really can determine whether or not they are food insecure.

For those who live well below the poverty line, travel costs are but one of many economic barriers to getting nutritious, predictable, and culturally appropriate calories. That is, food deserts and food insecurity have similar, but different root causes. Food insecurity is primarily caused by poverty. Food deserts can be traced to transformations in the grocery industry, the urban decline caused by deindustrialization in the 1970s and '80s, and the racialized consequences of "urban renewal" public planning programs.

Returning stores to poorer neighborhoods can reduce food insecurity and retail inequality. Yet, as we have seen already, we should not assume that access will guarantee residents' adoption of healthier diets. One *Business Wire* report, entitled "UnitedHealthcare Fights Food Insecurity with Donation to Second Harvest Food Bank of Northwest North Carolina" (June 10, 2015), is a great example of identifying health as an additional goal beyond achieving food security: "With more than 340 food deserts across 80 counties in the state, limited access to nutritious foods is a major issue statewide and particularly in the Triad. UnitedHealthcare has partnered with organizations like the Second Harvest Food Bank to reduce food insecurity across North Carolina and help people live healthier lives."

The author fails to acknowledge that food banks, food pantries, shelters, and soup kitchens can reduce food insecurity without improving diets (not unlike how a store can fill a void in a food desert without improving the way people eat). An empty stomach can be satiated with unhealthy food. Indeed, the bulk of donated food offerings are inexpensive, shelf-stable, canned, and dried foods. Few agencies turn away unhealthy donations or demand that their clients consume healthier foods. Occasionally, they can offer fresh food, but it is often "rescued" (i.e., nearly expired) food that requires expensive refrigeration space. It doesn't take many visits to food pantries to see that most of what they have on offer is inexpensive, quick to satisfy, easy to store, and in constant demand.[10] While they often cannot support a healthy diet (Simmet et al. 2017), charitable organizations know that these foods will get eaten. The same goes for many items eligible for purchase through the Supplemental Nutrition Assistance Programs (SNAP). Commonly referred to as "food stamps," it is the largest federal program to reduce food insecurity—and it is tied to the "food insecurity-obesity paradox" (Franklin et al. 2012). SNAP participants spend a higher proportion of their food budgets on unhealthy food (Taillie et al. 2018). Why? Healthy food is more expensive per calorie. Increasing access to healthy food can only improve diets *after* people reach a level of economic security that, for many, is out of reach.

By confusing the food desert problem with food insecurity, media accounts mix together two different social problems into a confusing kettle of causes and solutions. From this brew has emerged a powerful coalition of advocates for food desert interventions ranging from community gardens to full-size supermarkets. These social movements collided in an era eager for clear and simple solutions to a growing public health crisis. What they missed was that residents wanted access to healthy food for a different reason. It wasn't about wanting to buy more of it, it was about wanting business to grant them the option. It was about respect.

THE BIRTH OF IRRESISTIBLE CONCEPTS

The speedy emergence and continued durability of the idea that distance determines diet is remarkable. Policies to improve access to healthy and affordable food as a means to improve public health have received wide-spread support. So much so that, even when researchers began to question the idea and businesses built upon the concept failed, the media frame rarely waivered. The food desert concept and widely agreed upon solutions became irresistible to community advocates and impervious to contradictory evidence. Understanding how public accounts masked the core problem—retail inequality—is important, so we don't make the same mistake again.

Under the right circumstances, irresistible concepts can capture the public's imagination and embed themselves within the zeitgeist. How do we know this? Because it has happened before.

The Rise and Fall of "Broken Windows"

The food desert concept followed the same path as another idea that caught fire in the 1990s: "broken windows theory." In the 1980s, municipalities nationwide were abuzz about a new way to fight crime inspired by this academic theory. It would rise in popularity, cultivate an enduring following, and continue to find adherents among media outlets and policy makers long after the academic community largely debunked the core idea. It still has its champions today.

"Broken windows" was introduced in 1982 by a political scientist and a criminologist and offered a simple solution to a persistent social problem: crime. It proposes that evidence of disorder (like a broken window or graffiti) signals to outsiders that neighborhood residents are indifferent to illegal behavior. As a result, potential lawbreakers will assume they can act in these areas with impunity: their crimes will go unnoticed, or unpunished, or both (Wilson and Kelling 1982). Further, the theory posits that small acts of illegality lead to larger ones—tagging a garage door with a graffiti handle leads, for instance, to breaking into garages and stealing things. Thus, if there is a broken window, local government should fix it—quickly. Loitering, littering, and other seemingly minor disruptions cannot be tolerated, and police should impose penalties and restore order swiftly. Addressing broken windows, then, is a way to make it known that a neighborhood is the sort of place that's under constant surveillance and control.

That tying signs of disrepair in a neighborhood to an assumed unwill-ingness to keep things nice and tidy sounded an awful lot like blaming the victim—both of petty crimes and decades of political neglect—would not be sufficiently critiqued for some time. Meanwhile, like food deserts, bro-ken windows theory became immensely popular among policy makers and politicians. Policing circles were particularly eager to spread the idea across the country. By the mid-1990s, then mayor Rudy Giuliani and New York City police chief William Bratton would make broken widows a central tenet of their law enforcement philosophy. (Even today, broken windows theory endures in police and sheriffs' departments nationwide. During my research in Southernside and West Greenville, I heard it evoked repeatedly by law enforcement representatives at neighborhood meetings.)

The theory enjoyed substantial support in media accounts for years, and it was not until complaints of overzealous policing, police brutality, and racial disparities in "stop and frisk" encounters that it came under serious scrutiny ("The Truth behind Stop-and-Frisk," September 2, 2011). Even when critiques came, they were not aimed at whether the theory was sound nor the approach to solving the problem worked, but at the ways "zero-tolerance" policing was carried out. Put differently, like media coverage of failed grocery store experiments in food deserts, the criticism of broken windows theory was limited to execution, not the concept itself. Consequently, nearly four decades later, we know that broken windows theory is not an effective way to reduce crime. But people with power and influence still hold it to be true.

The first major scholarly challenge to broken windows theory came in 1999. Two researchers compiled a research team in Chicago to drive down every street in nearly two hundred neighborhoods (Sampson and Rauden-bush 1999). They collected over twenty thousand city-block-long observa-tions of two types of minor deviance by driving down each street at five miles per hour while videotaping from both sides of the car. They then ana-lyzed the film and mapped every single instance of physical disorder (think litter, graffiti, abandoned cars, and, well, broken windows) and social dis-order (public drinking, solicitation, fighting, selling drugs, etc.). Accord-ing to broken windows theory, these minor things should be tied to higher incidences of more serious crimes, like assault and homicide. They weren't. When Sampson and Raudenbush examined the crime data for the same city blocks, they *did not find* that the presence of social and physical disorder was accompanied by more dangerous crimes in the same locations.

That study has been cited in more than twenty-five hundred academic books and articles since it was published. Sampson and Raudenbush's debunking of broken windows theory has had a major impact on the direction of the disciplines of criminology and sociology. But it has yet to change urban policing policy: police chiefs and mayors are still promoting broken windows theory as a logical way to support a specific style of punitive policing and community control concentrated in areas of poverty and residential segregation.

DESPERATE TIMES MAKE FOR RECEPTIVE AUDIENCES

The media framing of food deserts as a health issue coincided with the rise of the "obesity epidemic," much like broken windows policing gained traction at the same time US crime rates peaked (actually, as it would happen, slightly after the peak of US violent crime rates). In both cases, the public and policy makers were eager for solutions, and early results were promising. New York embraced broken windows theory, and crime dropped. The first assessment of a food desert intervention also yielded positive results (Wrigley et al. 2002). In hindsight, we know that these initial findings did not tell the whole story. Crime drops turned out to be an as-yet unexplained national phenomenon independent of new policing strategies (as reported by Harcourt [2005], for instance, crime dropped in Los Angeles, too, even though it had not adopted broken windows policing), and that first supermarket intervention turned out to be an outlier amid a string of failures.

To this day, we still do not fully understand why crime dropped as much as it did. And we don't totally know why dietary choices and nutrition patterns failed to change either. In both cases, though, the initial *perception* of success helped cement a political and even popular consensus. When later research contradicted earlier findings, it had little effect: many minds had already been made up.

THE POWER OF MAPS

Broken windows and food deserts are also great examples of the way new mapping technologies can impact the dissemination of academic and policy ideas to the wider public. Cartography has existed in some form or another for thousands of years. Criminologists began mapping crime rates across Europe in the 1830s (Weisburd et al. 2009) and public health researchers used maps to pinpoint the cause of a cholera outbreak in the 1850s (Gilbert 1958; Johnson 2006). With the rise of computing technology and proliferation of data sources, geographic representations of social problems have become powerful, seemingly omnipresent tools for solving social problems.

The power of maps to persuade the public reached a tipping point in the 1990s when Geographic Information Systems (GIS) software became more powerful, easier to use, and less expensive. That's the moment when New York police departments integrated broken windows theory into their well-known CompStat mapping and response program.[11] Two decades later, the USDA released its dynamic online map of food environments around the country. In my sample of media accounts, the USDA Food Desert Locator (later renamed the Food Access Research Atlas) was frequently cited as a convenient tool for anyone with internet access to see whether they lived in a food desert. Countless national and local articles helped cement the media framing of health outcomes as having geographic determinants. Decades earlier, it would have taken years to produce and distribute such an atlas. It would have been out of date by the time it was published.

For all their ability to start conversations, maps are poorly suited to identifying the causal mechanisms of social phenomena. In other words, maps are good at outlining geographic hotspots (of crime and poor health, among many other possibilities), but they're bad at explaining why those hotspots are where they are. Thus, maps are better suited at drawing out correlation than causation—a point easily missed by those eager for action.

SOCIAL PROBLEMS MAKE STRANGE BEDFELLOWS

As shown in the media accounts about food deserts since 2011, the media framing of the issue often conflated it with numerous other food-related issues (food insecurity chief among them). The broad support for dealing with the parallel issues of food deserts and food insecurity made it easier for people living in food deserts to recruit supporters. In their book, *Foodies*, sociologists Josée Johnston and Shyon Baumann argue that food-related social movements provide ways for participants to exercise the democratic ideals of justice and equality *and* distinguish their gastronomical tastes from others' (2015). For example, adherents to the slow, local, non-GMO, sustainable, and organic food movements may not live in impoverished areas devoid of healthy retail options, but fighting for supermarkets in food deserts is one way they can exhibit their political beliefs. For members of this largely white, middle-class social movement, fighting for fresher food can feel—and taste—good. Addressing the root cause of retail inequality, on the other hand, forces foodies to engage in difficult conversations about our country's history of discriminatory housing and transportation policies, white flight to the suburbs, and the residential segregation of Black people into areas without jobs or opportunity. In short, by focusing on "healthy food" rather than retail inequality, the food desert movement was able to avoid talking about tougher problems like poverty and "color-blind" racism.

Similarly, even if broken windows theory did not cause crime rates to drop in New York City, many residents—particularly those whose civil liberties were *not* being violated—supported efforts to remove litter and loitering from eyeshot. As a result, white and middle-class constituents applauded police efforts to reduce panhandling, turnstile jumping, and graffiti, regardless of whether these minor forms of physical and social disorder were not tied to incidences of more serious types of crimes (like assault and homicide). Even flawed ideas can gain popular and political support when people are more interested in the means than the ends.

When it comes to addressing food deserts, the solutions are outcomes lots of different people want: shiny new grocery stores full of high-quality food, mobile farmers markets, and support for local food producers. They allow social justice–minded foodies to see themselves as part of the solution. They just don't seem to address the root causes of American inequality.

CONCLUSION

As I began my research into the Southernside and West Greenville neighborhoods in 2014, I was struck by the attention residents were able to get when they evoked key words and phrases about grocery stores, health, and food. Their other requests (job training, youth programs) and complaints (loitering, bad retail) received only limited responses from cops and government officials who insisted, time and time again, "We are doing all we can." Pleading for a supermarket got a full-throated response. City officials bought up an abandoned strip mall and tried to lure commercial developers to build a store there; an outside consultant was hired to conduct an economic market analysis of the area; and nonprofits started proposing new ideas. Uttering the term *food desert* commanded attention.

After bursting onto the scene in the early 1990s, the concept has shown remarkable resilience in the face of evidence of its invalidity. Neither high-profile store closures nor a growing body of academic literature could change the framing of the issue in popular media accounts. By 2010, it garnered enough political support to earn budgeting allocations at the state and federal levels. Twenty years may seem like a long time, but considering that most social science concepts never gain purchase outside academia, its rise was impressive.

At ribbon-cutting ceremonies across the country, movie stars and mayors brimmed with optimism. Grand openings were community celebrations. That we could turn our nation's declining health around by simply putting grocery stores in food deserts seemed like a true success story. After all, residents were not asking for money, they were asking for the opportunity to spend their own.

Tired of being neglected, neighborhood members argued that they deserved nice retail options, too. Had the media, policy makers, and politicians listened closer, they might have understood what these residents were really complaining about, but they didn't. Those who recruited stores to go back into the urban core pinned their hopes on pent-up demand for healthy food. Now was the time to show everyone that the old stores never should have left. To feed themselves and their families, all these residents needed was a chance. Installing grocery stores was a straightforward solution with moral certainty.

That the grocery store interventions did not work is not necessarily the fault of public health scholars or community activists. Instead, the blame lies primarily in the economics of the industry and the everyday realities of people in communities still recovering from urban decline. From a business perspective, small, urban grocery stores can't survive in a new economy of food in which scale is king. This trend is bigger than groceries; the big box-store model has driven out independent hardware stores, bookstores, and department stores, too. Neighborhood residents would love the luxury of spending more at smaller stores nearby, but their lack of consumer buying power is not a random occurrence, either. And they know it. Their family budgets are a product of historically racist policies that denied their great-grandparents the same chance to build intergenerational wealth that was offered to white householders who fled to the suburbs.

Failed experiments to bring grocery stores back are interesting in that they had little impact on the popularity and durability of the food desert concept behind them. Media accounts critiqued their failed execution, not the theory behind their feasibility. The utilitarian logic that grocery shoppers use distance as their primary variable went unchallenged. Distance determined diet, and no amount of evidence could break the media frame for good.

Within the academic community, the tide has shifted. Food desert scholars are rethinking past assumptions. The proximity thesis may not even be wrong, just far more complex than a direct causal relationship would imply. Slow rolling waves of human behavior cannot be stopped overnight. The ecological array of factors that manifest in the form of public and even personal health cannot be reduced to a single solution.

This newfound skepticism would take some time to break into popular discourse. From 2011 to 2017, the media and governmental agencies fed off of each other's talking points. The irony of the popularity of the food desert concept during this window is that for once researchers were able to exercise rare influence when disseminating an idea—which they promptly lost once the public grabbed hold of it. Academics simply lost control of the narrative.

That scholars and journalists couldn't correct public perception after initially grabbing attention speaks to something about our nation's psyche. That is, this is not the first—nor will it be the last—irresistible social scientific concept. It is not the first or the last to take on a life of its own, either. I highlight the parallels between the rise of these two theories, food deserts and broken windows, because even though they address vastly different social problems they were similarly able to be embedded into policy and public opinion. Each was aimed at dealing with problems for which the public urgently wanted answers. New mapping technologies enabled policy makers to locate and communicate problem hotspots. And the solutions they proposed enjoyed widespread support from a public less concerned with the soundness of the theory and more concerned with their ability to enact policies conducive to white and middle-class tastes. What makes these concepts irresistible to this constituency (of which I am a member) is that they offer an easy way out: they address the symptoms of social problems, not their root causes, like racism and poverty.

There are other, more detailed reasons why food deserts have become a feature of our political landscape. To learn them, we need to listen to the voices of the people who live in areas with limited food retail options. Their stories about how, where, when, and why they consume what they consume will show why the current menu of public health retail interventions are so unsuitable for producing clear-cut nutritional behavioral change. In private, residents admitted that their eating habits were not likely to change if a new store arrived. Their habits were governed by an array of everyday entanglements and obligations—distance to the nearest grocery store was just one among many.

The fight over retail inequality is not necessarily a battle to buy new things. It is about demanding that outside investors offer all neighborhoods the same quality options. Whether or not residents can afford or will even make use of these options is another matter. Food desert residents go through the same logical decisions about when and where to shop, how to get there, and what and how much to buy as everybody else. They just operate within a different set of resources and constraints. Let's start with some of the most familiar of these everyday realities: residents' perceptions of their food environment, their economic resources, and their transportation options.

3 Food Desert Realities

PERCEPTION, MONEY, AND TRANSPORTATION

It wasn't until I started talking to people in Southernside and West Greenville about food that I learned how wrong I was. At the beginning of my research, I presumed to know what they wanted—grocery stores—and why—to change their diets. But that wasn't it. They wanted a grocery store, to be sure. But a new store wouldn't change the way they ate, it would just make it easier, cheaper, and quicker to buy the things they always buy.

At kitchen tables, on front porches, and in living rooms, I asked people about how they shopped and what they ate. I started these conversations with questions about three significant barriers to accessing healthy options, wondering whether food desert residents knew where to find them, how to afford them, or how to get to them (or, I hypothesized, some combination of these three factors). Beyond distance, these variables are the focus of most food desert research: perception of food environment, money, and transportation. Each can mean the difference between a nutritious diet and a poor one—if one is looking to change theirs. These intertwined factors represent the "everyday realities" of food desert residents.[1] Depending on circumstances, they can act as resources or constraints. For some, they open up new pathways; for others, they serve as roadblocks.

To understand why people in food deserts are unlikely to change their diets even if presented with new retail options, we need to account for these everyday realities. We need to understand their history and acknowledge their inertia in the face of change. People in these neighborhoods are not going to forget past retail abandonment, their incomes are not going to increase overnight, and new transportation options are not going to appear anytime soon. This is the predicament. If we want to help people change their diets, interventions must meet them where they are. But they also need to address their core complaints. Neglected by the public sector and abandoned by the private sector, people living in what are now known as food deserts have been speaking out about retail inequality for generations. Now it is our turn to listen.

THE SOUTHERNSIDE AND WEST GREENVILLE NEIGHBORHOODS

Learning about people's lives requires trust. I began working with the Southernside neighborhood in Greenville, South Carolina, in 2012, when I tried to help them keep the state Department of Transportation from tearing down a dilapidated bridge. Locals wanted the Hampton Avenue bridge, once their main connection to a sister community on the other side of a railyard, fixed. The state won that battle, and the bridge came down. But legal and political negotiations lingered for years. I kept up with the neighborhood association, attended its meetings, and provided research assistance on their behalf at any city or county meeting that addressed the issue of the bridge. Eight years later, a pedestrian bridge would finally be built. The neighborhood won the war.

Over those years, I learned about another issue persistently needling Southernside residents: the disappearance of grocery stores. When a small supermarket a mile away from the eastern edge of their community shut its doors in 2013—"'Baby BI-LO' on North Main Closing," *Upstate Business Journal* (Jackson 2013)—Southernside officially became a food desert. The next closest option, a Publix Super Market, was on the other side of downtown (nearly two miles from Southernside's farthest corner) and perceived as more expensive and up-scale. Meanwhile, their immediate food environment had hit rock bottom. The nearest grocery stores for bargain shoppers (other BI-LO stores and a Walmart Supercenter) were three and four miles away. On foot, with groceries, that meant at least a two-hour roundtrip walk. Buses were theoretically options, but locals saw them as inadequate.

Exasperated, the Southernside community resigned themselves to the new normal. As usual, they would find a way to make it work, but they asked anyone who would listen: Why do *we* always have to adjust? The city was experiencing a rebound in terms of business development and investment. Things were supposedly improving in downtown, yet the options for Southernside seemed to be getting worse.

Having finished a different book project and spent two years getting to know the community, I began my research on food deserts in 2014. I had connections in Southernside, but I wanted to expand my study. So, with the help of some friends, I reached out to the neighborhood association in an adjacent area that called itself West Greenville. Its residents had experienced similar demographic and retail changes, including witnessing firsthand the collapse of the textile industry in the 1970s and '80s and the loss of population and housing stock that followed. They had weathered the Great Recession of the 2000s and, like Southernside, they were beginning to see signs of business returning. But something had changed. Where there had been merchandise and appliance stores, now they saw coffee shops and farm-to-table restaurants. Vacant buildings on the edge of the neighborhood were being reconfigured into artists' studios. The city created an ad campaign—much to the confusion of longtime residents—to market this "revitalized" strip as "The Village of West Greenville." Pockets of gentrification were transforming the neighborhood. The city was on the rebound. But for whom?

How I Got People to Open Up to Me

I made my pitch to interview residents at any meeting or gathering I could, focusing on finding people whose lives (and diets) would seemingly be most improved by the return of grocery stores to their neighborhoods. Thus, while my sample *generally* reflects the demographic composition of the neighborhoods at the time—largely poor, Black, with a high percentage of people without access to a car—it is not strictly, statistically representative of these Census tracts. Making matters more complicated, the neighborhood was changing rapidly. White residents who had largely avoided the area were now buying property and starting businesses. Official population estimates, made variable by the influx, had trouble keeping up with the real numbers. So I tried to interview a variety of people living in different circumstances to learn how everyday realities help and hinder their ability to navigate the food retail environment.

Within a few years, I interviewed eighty-five residents across the two neighborhoods. I also interviewed fifteen people in food-related nonprofits or businesses in Greenville (more on them in chapter 6). Individual interviews lasted roughly an hour—more if you include the unrecorded South Carolina small talk that accompanied my arrival into a family's home and the gracious goodbyes that came after I clicked my voice recorder off. Indeed, most of the interviews with residents took place in their homes, with just a few in nearby quiet places. If two adults lived in the home, I tried to interview them together. These joint interviews took twice as long, but I found that pairs of people could help prompt each other, remembering what the neighborhood used to be like and recounting recent trips and purchases. Talking to people in the same household also illuminated how diets can differ, even under the same roof.

To interview clusters of neighboring households, I developed relationships with managers of public housing, Section 8 housing, and senior housing units. They pointed me in the direction of potential interviewees, and "snowball sampling" meant that interviewing one resident helped me gain access with their neighbor. The process helped me see how people who live the exact same distance to bus stops and grocery stores can take enormously different paths—both to the store and to making their meals work.

Some may think it would be hard to get strangers to open up to me, a middle-class white male professor at an expensive private university. I expect many will doubt my ability to get honest answers, especially from my Black interviewees living in hard economic circumstances. That skepticism is reasonable and one I encourage my own students to consider when they do research of their own. Still, topics like neighborhood memories and recent meals are easy conversation starters, and the interviews for this book felt more like conversations than scientific surveys. Questions about money—especially for those who relied on food pantries—were a little more sensitive, but having other neighborhood members vouch for me helped ease most of the tension. In return for their honesty, I promised to keep their identities confidential.

I am not naive enough to think everyone told me everything. Readers will have to decide for themselves if they find my data credible, but I stand by what I present. I am happy to let my interviewees' quotes speak for themselves.

People opened up more than even I expected. For example, at the end of each interview, I was able to methodically walk almost every interviewee through every meal they had eaten in the past five days. At first, I thought this goal was too lofty. But it turns out, people can remember a lot if you can give them time to situate their food choices in relation to what they did earlier that day (e.g., "When you got home after your doctor's appointment, what did you eat for lunch?"). One eighty-year-old woman was able to go back nine days. But this process took patience and nonjudgment. Some became embarrassed as they came to realize they indulged in unhealthy food multiple times a day. No one's diet is perfect, including mine, and so I always made a point of admitting my own dietary shortcomings.

With enough assurance that I was on their side, people offered me a brief tour of their lives and—in some cases—their kitchen cabinets. My elderly interviewees who lived alone seemed genuinely happy to have someone to talk to, especially on a topic of which they were an expert: themselves. The single parents appreciated a sympathetic ear when we talked about satisfying kids' picky palates. Still, trust was never a given: I had to earn it every time through honesty, respect, and a genuine interest in their worlds.

The People I Interviewed

I made a point of seeking out people who had the hardest time getting to and buying healthy food. Sadly, finding poor people with transportation challenges was easy. Of the people I interviewed, 41 percent did not have access to a car and 56 percent either were on a fixed income or received some type of public assistance.[2] Perhaps a better measure of my interviewee's economic precarity is the 32 percent who reported at least one instance of food insecurity in the prior three months. When I asked whether they had accepted donated food from a pantry, soup kitchen, or a free bag of groceries from extended family during that same time,

57 percent responded yes. That means fully a quarter of my sample—even if they technically had enough income to feed themselves— occasionally accepted donated food as a way to make room in their budgets for other bills and expenses. Living on the edge means never knowing when the next crisis will come, so it was best not to turn down free food that might come in handy later.

Despite recent demographic changes caused by gentrification, Southernside and West Greenville were still predominately Black neighborhoods when I started my interviews. Accordingly, Black residents constitute 85 percent of my sample. Greenville's growing Latino population is mostly in its western portions of the county, rather than the neighborhoods I studied. The remaining 15 percent of my interviews were with white, recent transplants to Southernside and West Greenville. Most of these were part of the recent wave of newcomers, with some moving in search of potential returns on their real estate investments and others genuinely hoping to become part of the community.

I interviewed mostly women (67%), because, although social norms are changing, they still do the vast majority of food-related work in American households (Oleschuk 2019).[3] For instance, according to the 2016 American Time Use Survey, women spend nearly double the time men do grocery shopping (fifty-five minutes per week compared to twenty-nine minutes) (Bureau of Labor Statistics 2016). Additionally, the number of households led by single mothers has tripled over the past half century; 23 percent of American children currently live with only their mother, compared to 4 percent of with only their father (US Census Bureau 2016). Until children grow old enough to prepare their own food, it is most often a woman making sure they are fed.

Half of the people I interviewed lived alone. That was important and intentional: when we read stories about food deserts, single people living alone are cast as the hardest hit. No one else can share the chores of shopping, cooking, and cleaning up. This is particularly challenging for the 15 percent of my interviewees I describe as *ultravulnerable* (over fifty-five, living alone, relying on a fixed retirement or public benefit income, without a car).

Although my full sample ranges from age twenty-two to eighty-seven, the median age was fifty-nine. As people age, the physical challenges to grocery shopping increase. A two-mile roundtrip walk, for example, may sound reasonable for someone in their twenties, but is less so for older folks. Even small issues with mobility and health can make minor physical challenges (lugging grocery bags, waiting for buses in bad weather) into formidable obstacles. Additionally, the struggles facing elderly residents in food deserts warrant attention on ethical and moral grounds, regardless of whether improving access will change their diets.

I also included people who are not part of the popular narrative on food deserts. I interviewed people who owned their own cars, shopped for eclectic items in more expensive stores, and could forego closer options for non-dietary reasons—such as whether a store treated its workers well. People who live in food deserts but have disposable incomes and personal transportation are not part of the national conversation, but they should be: They can show how having money and owning a vehicle do not necessarily ensure a better diet.

Media accounts of the people who live in food deserts frequently frame them as desperately and constantly seeking the closest, cheapest options, as relying exclusively on the meals they can glean from convenience stores and fast food outlets. This framing is wrong.

As residents told me about their lives, I saw that they were neither one-dimensional nor utilitarian eaters. Sometimes they bypassed nearby stores and intentionally shopped at locations farther away. Other times they gave away food to their neighbors—even when they were barely surviving financially themselves. Whatever their everyday practices, their motivations did not always sit neatly in boxes labeled "cost" or "benefit." The logic of their habits made sense once you understood their circumstances. All you had to do was ask. And if you listened long enough, you'd hear how the absence of grocery stores is really only the beginning of the story.

THE EVERYDAY REALITIES OF PEOPLE
WHO LIVE IN FOOD DESERTS

The way people acquire and consume goods and services is shaped by their existing circumstances. They cannot buy what they cannot see, purchase what they cannot afford, or shop where they cannot travel. In a food desert, these everyday realities boil down to their perception of their food environment, their economic resources, and their transportation options.

I begin with *perception* because it was the backdrop for all their shopping choices. We might, for instance, deduce that people who chose to travel miles outside the bounds of their neighborhood to do their shopping were dissatisfied with the options closer to home. Those included peripheral retail stores that, to varying degrees, sold groceries. The USDA's online Food Access Research Atlas (formerly known as the Food Desert Locator) ignores these operations because they are not full-size grocery stores. Around Southernside and West Greenville, these options mostly consisted of convenience and dollar stores. Compared to supermarkets, the quality, variety, and affordability of their healthy options were severely lacking. However, perception is subjective. What did the people who lived there think?

Factors like money and transportation play an even larger role in the conversation around food deserts. Economic resources can increase the array of available options, and transportation can increase a shopper's range. Consider that, for the truly poor, proximity to retail food options means little if they cannot afford anything in those shops and restaurants. And no matter how feasible bus routes look on paper, increasing their number and frequency does little for anyone with mobility constraints. But economic and transportation resources are not static. Add a spot of bad weather and the trip to the bus stop can seem farther than it looks. Add an unforeseen utility bill to the equation and a planned shop can fall apart: sometimes when it rains it pours.

In the next chapter, I'll add three more factors to this list: social capital, household dynamics, and Americans' "taste for convenience." In the end, understanding people's acquisition and consumption habits requires an accounting of all six sets of these everyday realities. Just as building a library—or offering free transportation to them—is unlikely to increase reading among people without the time or energy to do so, dropping a grocery store into a food desert is unlikely to change diets without attending to the context of eaters' lives. This is why we misdiagnosed the food desert problem: we failed to see the "deserts" from the point of view of the people who live there.

Perceptions of the Local Food Environment: Past to Present

I began each interview by asking people about their first memory of the neighborhood. Whether they were born and raised in their neighborhood or arrived as adults, I wanted to know what my respondents thought of this place and what direction it was headed. Some of their stories were painful, like the ones about the chaos that followed the fatal shooting of a police officer in West Greenville in the 1990s. Others were sentimental, like descriptions of the awe accompanying a child's first memory of a supermarket.

For people who grew up in Southernside or West Greenville, the most common memory I heard was about the historic Kash and Karry grocery. From the 1950s through the '70s, Kash and Karry stood on Southernside's eastern edge. Its fifty thousand square feet, twenty-five check-out stations, and 225 employees made the store a beacon of progress (Willis 2003: 117). Its wooden floors were legendary. Kash and Karry wasn't always the first memory people cited, but it was mentioned by every longtime resident when I asked about food retailers of days past. Cora, a sixty-six-year-old Black woman, spoke of it reverently.

> It was big. . . . I remember the squeaky hardwood floors and I remember that you can get day work there. The men could. If they lived in the community. Because the management knew the families because we were always going there. And it was within walking distance and our parents could send us with the right amount of change, and one of the things that my mother appreciated about it you knew what you were going to pay. . . . She would count out the change of what she would need, and usually she would have a big buggy full of stuff . . . and by the time she got to the cash register she knew within a few pennies of how much she had gotten.

A store with squeaky floors that offered men temporary work might not seem like the stuff of sentimental reverie. But it wasn't the quality of Kash and Karry's food or décor that led residents to remember it as "good retail," it was the level of trust and goodwill it had earned in the neighborhood. The scope of its services made the store a community hub. Derrick, a Black septuagenarian, lived just a few hundred yards from the store. All these decades later, he recalled: "It occupied a whole block. . . . It was huge, and at one time it was almost like a bank, because customers could buy groceries and pay light bills: water bill, electric, all the bills . . . gas bills."

At forty-four, Lloyd was the youngest interviewee to remember shopping at Kash and Karry. His generation was the dividing line: those older knew what it was like before the retail exodus, and those younger could only speculate. Lloyd saw the closure of the first Kash and Karry store as a historical turning point: "It was maybe the earliest, earliest form of Walmart, everything under the sun. They had the little drug store, they had groceries, everything. . . . It was a big store; it was a huge store for that time. It was a place where you could get everything that you needed within a short distance. My earliest memory in the neighborhood was Kash and Karry, and then Kash and Karry disappeared and everything changed." *Everything changed.* For residents who remembered the old Kash and Karry, their fond memories made the current reality of their grocery options sting.[4]

The older residents also talked about the neighborhood as much livelier and more densely populated fifty years ago. They were right—according to Census data, Southernside and West Greenville once housed three times as many residents. The decline began when the manufacturing jobs (mostly textile) began to disappear and the public and private sector decided to invest in suburban housing and infrastructure. White families were the first to go. Divestment led to blight, and the housing stock (already poor quality and built in a floodplain) was demolished. I'll provide a fuller accounting in chapter 5, but the takeaway is that most of the people who could afford to leave, left. So did the stores. What remained was residential segregation, concentrated poverty, and unsavory retail on the Black side of town.

I heard about days when corner stores and "mom and pop" operations dotted the neighborhood. So many had come and gone in half a century. At first, I tried to compile a list of the places my interviewees remembered—Mr. Kurry's store, Norriss's, Sijon's, Miss Siss's—but as the number increased, the task of identifying their former locations by oral description became too difficult. So, to measure the scope of former grocery retail in the area, I printed a three-foot-by-three-foot map to which residents at neighborhood meetings and community gatherings could affix stickers and identify locations. I asked them to name any stores they remembered as a child and occasionally prompted them with names

I had heard during my interviews. A student assistant helped me log the names and general locations of each business. After three events, we had exhausted the list and confirmed the location of thirty-one separate stores that once existed across multiple locations.

Our research on the historic retail options shows just how much the food landscape has changed. These older stores, everyone acknowledged, had limited offerings (mostly canned goods and staples), but they meant more than what was on their shelves. They were family owned and operated. They supported—and were supported by—the local Black community. They were "good retail." Elderly interviewees shared childhood stories about being sent to the store to fetch a few items and being offered credit when times were tight. All these stores are gone now. On the east side of Greenville, small stores were replaced by larger ones with more modern amenities. Here in Southernside and West Greenville, they're still waiting for the retail revival.

Younger interviewees and newcomers to the neighborhoods were less nostalgic. They had no memories of past food retail, and thus did not mourn its departure. Instead, they expressed mild annoyance that three full-size grocery stores in the wider area had closed in the past ten years, all "BI-LO Supermarkets" owned by Southeastern Grocers. None was identified, like the historic Kash and Karry remembered so fondly by longtime Black residents, as "our store." For newcomers, the current retail landscape was what it was. If you wanted to go to a supermarket with all the bells and whistles (deli, bakery, pharmacy), you had to drive. To them, things were getting slightly worse, but had never been much better.

Their irritation came from comparing their options to those available to people in other parts of the city. Everyone acknowledged that nearby food retail was lacking. The closest option to the Southernside neighborhood today is a Dollar General location about three-quarters of a mile from the neighborhood's easternmost edge. To get there on foot, you'd have to cross the heavily trafficked six-lane Pete Hollis Boulevard, cars whizzing by at forty miles per hour. The dollar store was newly constructed, so the interior does not offend, but the options are limited and few of my interviewees reported doing regular grocery shopping there. Only 16 percent used it to by shelf-stable goods, dairy products, or frozen meals. An additional 7 percent frequented other dollar stores, though only for purchasing snacks and soft drinks, and 77 percent said they visited dollar stores but only to purchase paper products and cleaning supplies. Of those who did buy food in dollar stores, the vast majority got there by car (whether by getting a ride or driving themselves). Only a few interviewees actually walked to the nearest dollar store in order to purchase groceries more substantial than just chips and sweets.

The closest option in the West Greenville neighborhood, on the other hand, was a real sore spot with everyone. Named Kash & Karry, the convenience store was nothing like the historic, similarly named grocery store.[5] This convenience store, by the time of my study, marked the southernmost gateway to West Greenville, but had changed owners and locations multiple times. Now it was the unwelcome welcome sign for the neighborhood, a symbol of neglect almost as salient as the pride associated with the historic Kash and Karry grocery store. When I visited the current Kash & Karry, I saw freezers and coolers jumbled with disheveled, disorganized goods. TV dinners and frozen family fish packs (a dozen filets of tilapia with no expiration date) were side by side, and scattered produce, worse for the wear, had no prices. Residents told me the convenience store was a place to get beer, cigarettes, and lottery tickets—its food options were only for last-minute needs and true desperation. Just 5 percent of interviewees relied on the store consistently for food. Nearly everyone referred to it with disdain. It was "bad retail."

When I asked Thomas, a fifty-eight-year-old Black resident, about his first experience with the Kash & Karry, his face soured. "The store wasn't clean, that store wasn't clean. When I walked up to it I was like 'this will be my last time.'" He was a recovering alcoholic, put off by the open drinking and loitering near the entrance. Another Black neighborhood member, sixty-five-year-old Dorothy, spoke of her resentment at its prices. Everyone I talked to understood why convenience store prices are higher than those found in supermarkets (you pay for the convenience), but almost all saw this store's markups as particularly exploitative. Dorothy told me of her exasperation: "I saw too little small pieces of fish and I can't remember what the price was but it was ridiculous, and I threw it back in there. That killed me because I love fish. It was ridiculous."

Even residents without cars found ways to avoid the Kash & Karry. Bessie was an ultravulnerable seventy-four-year-old Black woman who could no longer drive because of her eyesight. In what follows, she discussed how even she saw this place as the store of last resort:

KEN: Have you ever been to that Kash & Karry?

BESSIE: I try to stay away, but I have to go sometimes.

KEN: When was the last time you went?

BESSIE: Maybe a week ago.

KEN: Okay. What did you get?

BESSIE: I go and get sodas, and you know, things like that. I don't get much up there . . .

KEN: Okay.

BESSIE: . . . 'cause they overcharge.

KEN: Okay. Any food? Do you ever get food there?

BESSIE: Yeah, my son got some cornmeal last Saturday.

KEN: Uh huh.

BESSIE: He paid two dollars for a little bag—a small bag.

KEN: Yeah.

BESSIE: And I could've put down forty more cents and got a five-pound bag [at a supermarket].

When I asked about the most immediate food options in private interviews, respondents were annoyed and disappointed, but never expressed rage or anger. If anything, they were resigned to making do. Still, they knew that not everyone in the city was surrounded by dollar stores and convenience stores. Two years after I began my interviews, the supermarket chain Harris Teeter (an upscale brand owned by national chain Kroger) announced that two new stores would be built on the other side of the city. Although only two and three miles away, those neighborhoods had quadruple the median household income of Southernside and West Greenville. My interviewees traveled through those areas during their daily chores and errands and seeing what was on offer in other parts of the city rubbed salt in their wounds. It was always apparent that their neighborhoods' retail options were not up to par.

Reading the local newspapers, Greenville was improving on a number of fronts. But each announced improvement—according to my interviewees—seemed to cater to different neighborhoods and different interests.[6] Such perceptions matter. Excessive loitering and heavy traffic can make nearby destinations undesirable. Memories of better options past can make the current selection pale in comparison. Even if the precise details were hazy, the points against their current food options slowly added up into discontent.

Black neighborhoods in the American South have faced overtly discriminatory tactics in the past—denied access to all sorts of retail amenities. Today, things are better, but the people I spoke to still saw their neighborhoods as left behind, no matter how many white newcomers were buying, building, and renovating property. They were not surprised by the lack of elite retail in their neighborhood, but they believed they deserved better than places like the current Kash & Karry.

Jaded, but with a shard of hope still glinting, residents never failed to ask during our interview if I had any secret information about a store coming to their side of town. I tried to explain that I was only a sociologist and had no special industry or even public planning knowledge, still I got some variation on the question: "So, do you think we'll get one?" My answer was always pessimistic. My respondents were never surprised.

I was as open and honest as possible when they asked why I doubted a store was coming any time soon. With the exception of areas that are densely populated and those with high median incomes, US city centers have mostly lost their full-sized grocery stores. The industry prefers to build bigger stores on cheaper land, where being able to sell higher volume makes up for the lower prices per item. Aside from massive metropolitan areas, the low-margin, high-volume, box-store model has stripped the small corner stores of yesteryear from American cities and towns.[7] With practice, I got my explanation down to about a minute. Even so, their attention wavered. It wasn't because the economics of it are complicated—they aren't. It was because my answer reminded them that there was nothing either one of us could do about it.

After a few dozen interviews, I started to understand their disappointment better. To them, the grocery store exodus wasn't a business school case study; it was their life. My analytic explanation of supermarket real

estate acquisition practices never made anyone feel better. Their perceptions were shaped by both the past and the present. Before, nearby options
were better; now, nice stores are on the *other* side of town.

Economic Resources: Navigating the Retail and Donated Food Markets

The most pressing barrier to accessing healthy food is cost. Unhealthy
food is cheaper. If measuring price-per-calorie, energy dense foods with
added sugar and added fats are the most cost effective (Drenowski and
Darmon 2005). Thus, if you can make it to a supermarket, healthy eating
is an option, but it's not the cheapest option.

Getting to the store also has costs. Vehicles require fuel and maintenance; cabs and buses have set fares and rates. These costs can increase
with distance, making convenience stores a potentially more attractive
option, though the money saved by going to the smaller, closer venues does
not always offset the higher prices contained within them (McDermott
and Stephens 2010). As always, it is expensive to be poor.

Of course, expense can also come in the form of time. Getting to and
from the store takes up time. There are opportunity costs associated
with it. What is the value of two hours spent taking the bus? The answer
depends on what a given person could be doing instead of waiting by the
curb. For those with means, it may be worth it to spend more money to
save time. For those who have more time than money, spending time can
be a way to save cash. When both are scarce, well, that's a big problem.

For those living in dire poverty, retail food is not always an option,
no matter where it is located. The poverty line in the United States was
originally based on the premise that the cost of food necessary to feed a
family—depending on family size—should constitute one-third of one's
monthly budget. The figure is recalculated each year, adjusting for inflation using the Consumer Price Index. While it is not a perfect measure,
the federal poverty threshold gives a general sense of how much one
needs to purchase a bare minimum of goods and services.[8] When I began
my research, 40 percent of the Southernside and West Greenville families lived at or below the poverty line. This figure explains why stores are
unlikely to locate there (poor consumer buying power), and how their

absence increases the travel costs for those who need less expensive food the most.

None of my interviewees reported suffering bouts of absolute hunger. Almost all who lived below the poverty line bought some retail food for some portion of their monthly diet. While not technically starving, a third of my interviews met the general definition of food insecurity: they lacked "assured access at all times to enough food for a healthy life (Carlson, Andrews, and Bickel 1999: 511S).[9] To keep from going hungry at some point during the month, they had to rely on donated food sources, like food pantries. They were grateful they could find a way to get enough food, yet they could not predict what it would be or where it would come from. From their interviews I wanted to learn, where do they go and what do they get? And what of the *ultravulnerables*? Older residents who lived alone, on fixed incomes, without transportation. How did they navigate the economic constraints in their path?

The quality and proximity of the retail food market had little impact on the food choices of my poorest interviewees. It was made plain when I interviewed Lucas. Blind in one eye, the fifty-six-year-old Black man could easily pass for someone in his early seventies. His life was difficult. His living room was sparse. His furniture consisted of a low coffee table and two white plastic lawn chairs. The cracked chair in which I sat repeatedly pinched my shirt, and I shifted uncomfortably the whole time. Lucas had lived in this apartment for over five years. His accommodations were neither new nor temporary.

Lucas relied on a monthly income cobbled together from the Supplemental Security Income (SSI) he earned on account of his disability and $55 a month in food stamps. He had no car, and either walked or used his bike to get around. A few years ago, he was able to ride his bike to a small supermarket that was only 1.2 miles away. That store (known locally as the "Baby BI-LO") closed in 2013. His last trip to the dreaded Kash & Karry was weeks ago—his food stamps couldn't cover their high prices, so why spend the time or money to get there? Lucas's diet consisted, almost entirely, of donated food.

Southernside and West Greenville boast a broad network of donated food options. A number of local churches run food pantries open to both congregants and neighbors. Some are organized and offer prepacked boxes of food that people can get at weekly intervals, while others are more informal, offering food to walk-ins when requested. When Lucas "ate out," as he called it, he did so at one of the "soup kitchens" in the immediate area. These provided free prepared food ranging from sit-down meals to take-away bag lunches. Lucas told me he had visited four out of the five nearby soup kitchens in the past two months (skipping only the one that catered primarily to residents of its homeless shelter).

Lucas extended his reach into the donated food market by tapping into a secondary trading market. He explained that food pantries depend upon donated food, and some offerings are less appealing than others. Bread and cookies, just on the edge of going stale, are prime examples. Interviewees who solicited food at pantries reported regularly giving away or trading items they didn't like or already had. In Lucas's case, he knew an elderly woman nearby who regularly gave away some of her pre-cooked frozen meals she received from Meals on Wheels: "Sometimes I eat Meals on Wheels. . . . I got this lady at [senior housing development], sometimes she'll give me the Meals on Wheels she can't eat. She can't eat pork. So I go up there and help out a little bit and she'll give me the Meals on Wheels. I'll do a little yard work and she'll give them to me." Meals on Wheels is a charitable organization that delivers food to homebound elderly in order to prevent hunger and isolation. Even though Lucas was not yet old enough to sign up for the program (minimum age, sixty), he still found a way to access its resources.

Lucas's case shows that food systems are more complex than just retail options. For those who know how to navigate the donated food market and trade and barter to extend their options, Southernside and West Greenville's networks can be enough to stave off hunger.[10] Lucas noted how he was able to pick and choose from what he was given (he gave away boxes of dried macaroni and cheese, for example). Of course, not all calories are created equally (I'll address the limits on food pantries to deliver healthy options in chapter 6). But there were options, even if they were not visible to those who focus on what can be bought or sold.

Terry got into the details as he described keeping himself fed. Like Lucas, he lived alone, did not have a car, and was dependent on SSI. Terry occasionally ate at fast-food restaurants (two to three times a month) and would shop at grocery stores once a month, either paying others to drive him to the store or walking almost a mile to and from the bus stop. He mostly bought breakfast items like eggs and sausages to cook at home. The smell of bacon grease hung heavy during our interview in his public housing apartment. Terry did not cook lunch or dinner, though he would assemble deli meats into a sandwich.

"If a person starves to death in Greenville, he *wants* to starve to death," Terry said wryly after listing his top five places to get free food. Like others experiencing food insecurity, there was a sense of resignation to his circumstances and pride in his resourcefulness. Terry had a deep understanding of the free food options nearby. To keep from running out of money by the end of the month, he visited soup kitchens and food pantries four to five times a week—even if he had to pay others to drive him to the pantries on their open-to-the-public days. He was savvy enough to inform me that the largest soup kitchen, "Project Host," was considering moving their location because its surrounding neighborhood was rapidly gentrifying (a fact I later confirmed with Project Host's director).

Terry was not the first person to tell me that there was an abundance of free food options in Southernside and West Greenville. A recent proposal to expand the services provided by the local Salvation Army was met with resistance from residents of wealthier, adjacent neighborhoods. They argued that the concentration of services to the homeless and the hungry in these areas served as a magnet to the indigent (Landrum 2017). At public forums on the topic, local residents often mentioned the "circuit" of church to shelter to pantry to soup kitchen that the needy would trek to meet their dietary needs throughout the week. It was not evoked to evidence their resourcefulness and persistence, but rather to underscore a sense that these people living in economic precarity were somehow complacent and coddled.

Most media accounts and scholarly discussions generally focus on the retail *or* donated food market. Terry, like many I met in Southernside and West Greenville, navigated both. He bought some foods that required only simple cooking or preparation and supplemented with food from pantries and soup kitchens. He was in an economically precarious position, but still able to exercise some agency over where and what he would eat on a daily basis.

Lucas and Terry's ingenuity are no cause for celebration, but they are worth noting. These men were being strategic about their food choices.[11]

Acknowledging their agency is a crucial part of understanding how they make choices. When it comes to food, the retail market is not available to all people all the time, no matter how close they live. People with financial constraints weigh retail and charitable options based on their circumstances on any given day.

For the *ultravulnerable*, donated food is a literal lifeline helping keep starvation at bay near the end of each month. When I interviewed Harriet, the audio recording was overwhelmed by an oscillating fan rattling noisily in the corner. It was hot, even by June-in-South-Carolina standards, in the fifty-five-year-old Black woman's apartment. Harriet had an air-conditioning unit balanced in her window but could not afford to run it. Like Terry, she suffered from hypertension. She also had diabetes and was weak from a recent heart surgery. Compounding her struggles, Harriet's husband was in jail. She had access to his truck, but she didn't have a driver's license. The truck sat idle.

Harriet was one of just five interviewees (out of eighty-five) who regularly shopped at the run-down Kash & Karry. It was only a few blocks from her home, and unlike those who saw it as a symbol of enduring neglect, the store, Harriet said, had a good meat selection. Once a month, one of her daughters would drive her to a discount grocery store, the Sav A Lot just over two miles from her home, and Harriet would get some fruits and vegetables. Though she cooked at home, her diet consisted mostly of pan-fried cuts of meat. The perishable items she got at Sav A Lot wouldn't last the entire month, and she couldn't afford to shop more often. So, to make it through the month until her next check arrived, her daughter would bring her a box of food from a nearby pantry. In total, Harriet pieced together her meals from three sources, dry and canned goods from the pantry, meats from the nearby convenience store, and other perishable items from a single monthly trip to the discount grocery.

What the cases of Lucas, Terry, and Harriet teach us is obviously that being poor makes it more difficult to access healthy food. Fresh fruits and vegetables are more expensive (per calorie) and hard to get to without a car. When you rely on getting rides from others, you can't make many trips, and that translates into long stretches of each month without fresh, unfrozen, perishable food. But with their economic constraints, would getting a full-sized, nearby grocery store actually help them to eat differently?

It would certainly decrease transportation costs for Terry, who paid $5 to get rides to the store once a month. He would be able to buy some breakfast items slightly cheaper, but because he didn't cook meals other than breakfast, he didn't actually need a wide variety of ingredients. For Harriet, it would mean less reliance on her daughter for rides, but the discount grocery store two miles away would remain the less expensive, albeit limited option (with less variety and fewer name brands). For Lucas, who was not a participant in the retail food market, it would likely have little effect. Given his circumstances, Lucas could live next door to a supermarket and its products would still be economically unavailable once he exhausted his $55 monthly food stamp budget. Even without grocery stores, there is still food in the food desert. Not all of it is healthy, but some of it can be acquired for free. And the need for donated food isn't going to go away if a new grocery store comes to this side of town.

These people's accounts should remind us of the resiliency of food desert residents—a quality often forgotten in research and news articles. Just because they had limited means does not mean they always sought the cheapest calories: Terry, Harriet, and Lucas all reported giving away at least some extra food to family or neighbors in the past month. Just because fruits and vegetables were harder to access does not mean their consumption was guaranteed if acquired: Terry and Harriet had, for instance, recently thrown away tomatoes that rotted before they could eat them all on their own. By identifying the actual practices of economically constrained food desert residents, we begin to paint a more complex and nuanced portrait of their food consumption patterns.

Transportation: The Last Mile Problem

Economic resources can shorten travel times, but listening to people talk about how, where, and when they shopped, I came to understand the concept of distance in a new light. Academic research on food deserts focuses on people's home addresses as their primary point of reference to their food environment. This assumes we travel from home to store and back. We need to change that way of thinking.

Even the most isolated of my interviewees still left the house occasionally. Whether to go to work or worship, to see friends or family, food desert residents are entangled in everyday obligations just like the rest of us (Widener et al. 2013). Using their homes as their universal starting point treats "distance to store" as a static feature of their lives. Instead, we should think of home addresses as waypoints.[12] Put differently, figuring out how people overcome transportation obstacles to grocery shopping requires acknowledging their *dynamic* geographic relationship with retail food options.

Interviewees with their own car, or easy access to someone else's, traveled far and wide to buy groceries. Even though there was a supermarket roughly 1.5 miles away from the central point between the two neighborhoods, people with vehicular access had, on average, driven 4.05 miles on their most recent trips. Those without cars took the bus or (more commonly) got rides that averaged 3.42 miles. Nearest didn't mean most frequented when it came to buying food: 71 percent of all interviewees bypassed their nearest supermarket option to shop at one farther away. Of the 35 percent of interviewees without cars, only 21 percent took the bus; 91 percent of the car-less got rides at some point during the month, and 14 percent walked or biked to the store. (That these figures do not total 100 percent reveals that some interviewees blended their transportation options).

These findings are consistent with other food desert research conducted in Pittsburgh that found that food desert residents traveled an average of 2.7 miles to shop for groceries, on average a mile farther than the store closest to their house (Dubowitz et al. 2015b). Research conducted in Philadelphia focused on people who relied on Women and Infant Children (WIC) food coupons and found similar results: women there bypassed their nearest option, traveling an average of .65 of a mile farther than they would to shop at the nearest chain supermarket. Additionally, it concluded that for study participants, the "one-mile radius around one's residence held no meaning for food shopping" (Hillier et al. 2011: 725).

Public transportation is often lauded as a "difference maker" when it comes to accessing healthy food. Like many around the country, Greenville's system—Greenlink—operates on a hub model, with all transfers at a central location. Residents of West Greenville were lucky to be on a route that went directly to a Walmart Supercenter, located roughly three miles from most residences. Southernside residents had to transfer to get to the Walmart, making the journey about two miles longer. Given that

42 percent of all interviewees reported shopping at that Walmart in the past two months, the bus system should have been a good resource for the neighborhoods. However, talking to those who used the bus to shop for groceries, I started to learn why only a fifth of those without cars used it.[13]

Ernie, a sixty-eight-year-old Black man, was one of only two people who told me he actually enjoyed riding the bus. Occasionally, Ernie would pay the fare just "to go for a ride." He lived only .3 miles from his nearest stop, had the schedule memorized, and took at least two shopping trips a month (and got rides in cars at other times). He did not have his own vehicle, but from an outsider's perspective was in a perfect situation to use public transportation and overcome the obstacles presented by living in a food desert. However, when I asked him to describe his last journey, he listed a number of problems that come with using the bus.

From Ernie's home address, the 2.6-mile, one-way trip to the Walmart is ten minutes by car. By bus, it takes fifty minutes: ten minutes to walk to the nearest bus stop, ten minutes to wait (it usually ran late), twenty minutes to ride, and ten minutes to walk from bus stop to store. Luckily, he did not have to transfer, but since the bus ran on an hourly basis, Ernie often had to wait two cycles for his return trip home. He added that the wait didn't bother him—he was retired, and he preferred to take his time rather than rush to catch the very next bus.

I pressed for reasons why Ernie, who frequented the city buses, had such a low opinion of the system. Yes, the trip took longer than a car ride, but it seemed less arduous because he had a direct route and lived a short walk away from a bus stop. Before responding, he sighed, gazed off to the side for a moment, and said, "Public transportation down here is horrible." Ernie had lived in West Greenville for fifteen years but was originally from New York. So his disappointment was partly comparative. But his complaints about the bus system were backed up by other interviewees. A 2017 investigative report generated by a nonprofit located in Greenville, The Piedmont Health Foundation (2017), confirmed that the system was woefully underfunded, with city and county funds contributing only $3.76 per service area resident. (By way of comparison, other small southern cities receive much greater revenue support per capita: In Mobile, Alabama, for example, the city and county budget $28.46 per capita to run its bus system, and in Chattanooga, Tennessee, public transportation is funded at $30.69 per resident). With its paltry funding, Greenville's bus system wasn't improving any time soon.

Ernie ticked off a list of the challenges to grocery shopping by bus. First, the stop nearest his house was not covered. If it was raining, he stayed home. The stop near the Walmart had a small shelter, but it was located on the opposite end of the store's expansive parking lot—a quarter mile from the entrance and up a thirty-foot incline: "You've got to come down a steep hill, and then you are walking to Walmart, and by the time you come out of there with your groceries, I'm not going to walk back up that hill, so I walk all the way around." Years earlier, my interviewees remembered, the bus entered the Walmart parking lot and dropped riders off at its front doors. Changing the route created a serious problem for riders with any type of mobility problem. Ernie had suffered a heart attack years before. As a result, walking up a steep incline with his purchases was not an option. Instead, he walked a half mile to use a different bus stop. A longer trek, but less strenuous.

Longtime Southernside resident Tina confirmed Ernie's account. Like him, she also qualified as ultravulnerable. A fifty-seven-year-old Black woman with mobility issues of her own (knee pain), Tina lamented the placement of the bus stop: "They messed up Walmart. [In the past] you could catch a bus and go to Walmart, no problem. . . . [Now] you've got to climb that hill to get there. I don't like that, I wish they would turn it back around and let it get back down in there, because you've got a lot of people who can't walk up that hill." Even when residents could get to and from the bus, they were limited by the amount of goods they could comfortably carry. Most interviewees who took the bus reported being only able to carry three to four bags of groceries—not always enough to last through the month.

Around the country, public transportation systems often offer "paratransit" services to those with certified mobility problems. These typically include smaller buses or vans that can extend the reach of the system to the rider's front curb. Still, paratransit systems like the one in Greenville accommodate some mobility issues but with limitations on the number of bags all riders can bring aboard. Ethel, a seventy-eight-year-old white woman, explained that the bag limit forced her to use paratransit for only the first leg of her round-trip grocery run. First, she would call (at least one day in advance) to make an appointment for paratransit pickup. Then, for the way home after a big shop, she would call a cab. It cost her $3 to get to the store, and $10 to get back home.

The bus riders I interviewed were facing a smaller scale version of what business supply chain managers call "the last mile problem." In business, sometimes it is easier to ship goods across an ocean than it is to deliver it the last mile to a store's shelf. Utility companies face similar struggles; central lines can efficiently deliver services to centralized nodes, but getting them connected all the way to individual houses is much more difficult. Public transportation is primarily designed to get people from bus stop to bus stop. For those with serious mobility issues, that last little distance—home to the stop, store to the stop—is insurmountable. Curbside service can help some riders, but it is expensive to maintain.

I had initially assumed that the big struggle with bus transit would be the frequency of rides and the limitations of the system's routes. Instead, it was the small things that could—literally—trip up the folks I talked with. Bus stop topography, insufficient rain shelters, and bag limitations are not factored into most research on food deserts, but they can grind to a halt many systems that move people.

This is a problem for car owners with physical limitations, too. Camille, a sixty-five-year-old Black woman, had a vehicle and shopped at grocery stores up to five miles away. She occasionally drove her neighbors and friends to the store. Camille was a retired teacher with a modest pension, but she was relatively fortunate: she lived within her means, owned her own home, and was able to pay all her bills each month. The kink in her supply chain was getting her groceries from car to cupboard. Her last mile problem(s) were the five steps on her back porch. To haul her groceries inside, she had to rely on a homeless man who regularly walked through the neighborhood and would do odd jobs and lawn work for her.

After hearing this strategy, I pressed Camille for more details. How could she rely on this man to do this for her? He did not have a phone. She did not even know where he lived. She explained her strategy to me: upon her return from the store, she would bring in the most perishable items and put them away herself, leaving the rest on the porch. Knowing that the man typically stopped by her house once a day, Camille would then wait for him to bring the rest of her bags from the back porch to her threshold: "Usually what I would do, when I go to the store and I have a heavy bag, I just get my meat out and bring it in [to put in the refrigerator]. And I wait until the guy comes and [he'll] get my heavier stuff in. . . . I don't carry things too much, because I have to concentrate on walking." Despite the precariousness of this arrangement, Camille made it work. And though her strategy was rare—more often interviewees with mobility problems relied on relatives or friends—it shows that car ownership does not solve all food access problems and that people who live alone have particular challenges (see chapter 4).

Cars, of course, can be unreliable. Of the interviewees who lived in a household with a car, 11 percent were still unable to drive to the store. Either the person no longer had a license or the vehicle was experiencing mechanical problems, was used by someone else to commute to work (but not shop), or was recently repossessed. There could be arguments and tough choices to make about who gets to use the car or whether to use it to shop.

Amanda, a twenty-seven-year-old white woman, shared a vehicle with her husband. However, even when she had the car, she regularly shopped with her mother and sister. As a stay-at-home mother of two kids under two years old, she initially found shopping alone to be too physically and emotionally demanding. Over time, as her oldest became a toddler, she was able to manage on her own. But, by then, she had become accustomed to getting rides with her mother or sister. "So, like, for the first eight months of his life, I couldn't handle going grocery shopping by myself. And, so then, maybe for that four months, maybe I could have, but I just don't think of it. When I think, 'Oh, I need groceries' I call my mom and say, 'You want to go grocery shopping? When are you going? What do you want to do?'" Amanda's husband worked full-time (forty hours a week at $10 per hour), earning just enough to keep the family afloat. Having a car wasn't enough to make grocery shopping possible—especially after she had given birth twice in twenty months. It was Amanda's social network that kept the cupboards stocked.

Some of my most surprising discoveries during my interviews with food desert residents were the intricate and complex ways that people cultivated ride networks. People frequently gave and got rides to the store; 91 percent of my interviewees without cars had gotten rides to the store in the past month. They found their own ways to fill the gaps left by uneven car ownership and inadequate public transit. Of interviewees who had cars, 54 percent had recently given grocery store rides to others in the past three months. And even those who had cars still sometimes got rides. A quarter of my interviewees with vehicular access reported still getting rides to the store from time to time even though on paper it would seem they wouldn't need one. Social capital played a huge role in grocery shopping strategies for these food desert residents, as we will see in the next chapter.

CONCLUSION

Like all retail shopping practices, food desert residents' ways of buying food are shaped by their perception of their retail environment, their personal economic resources, and their private and public transportation options. Depending on their circumstances, each of these can operate as either a resource or a constraint. But even when they served as resources for my interviewees, no single factor was enough to make healthy food accessible. Rather, each served as a necessary—but not sufficient—condition for acquiring nutritious food.

I began with perception, because that is where my interviewees decisions to travel out of their neighborhoods began. They deemed the nearest options on the edges of their neighborhood unsuitable. Why? For long-time residents, the current offerings did not measure up to the past. They remembered a time when things were better, when the neighborhood had more people and nicer stores. The amenities of the historic Kash and Karry may not compare to today's superstores, but it was a legitimate, full-size supermarket located right in their neighborhood. It was considered a good form of retail not just because of what it sold, but because it was a community partner. Today, there's nothing even remotely similar.

Newcomers to the neighborhood perceived the food environment to be a poor comparison to other options elsewhere in the city. Their discontent was most often focused on the current Kash & Karry convenience store (no relation to the historic store), which they saw as exploitative, preying upon the vulnerabilities of those without transportation and the vices of those without hope. It was the poster child of retail inequality. Younger

residents and old-timers alike wanted better retail options—ones that signaled vibrancy, not decay.

In chapter 5, I will offer a more detailed historical overview of the
causes and consequences of urban decay, but for now it is safe to say
that the west side of Greenville is not unique. For a half a century, urban
pockets of cities all over the country have seen steady decreases in population and consumer buying power. Public and private divestment meant
funds going not to city cores, but to suburban infrastructure and to big
box-stores on the periphery. Like other forms of retail, supermarkets'
business model has changed to a high-volume, low-margin strategy that
undercuts small stores in residential areas.[14] Consequently, *many* people
in the country have limited options for buying healthy food at reasonable
prices. So how do they manage?

The economic constraints of food desert residents set up a cascade of
difficult choices. There are lots of times each month when cash-strapped
people like Lucas, Terry, and Harriet don't have the option to buy food.
Like them, more than half of my interviewees tapped into an extensive
donated food market by eating, sharing, and swapping free food from pantries, soup kitchens, friends, and neighbors. Much of this food was located
in the heart of the neighborhood, hidden in plain sight. It is important to
understand how the truly poor find calories, because their stories can tell
us which types of remedies can and cannot help them. Inserting a grocery
store near them would save them the costs of traveling to the store, but
if they cannot afford the price of the healthy options within it, the store
might as well be a hundred miles away.

The donated food market was not the exclusive territory of the truly
poor. One-third of my interviewees reported experiencing food insecurity
in the past two months, but 57 percent consumed at least some donated
food during the same time. That means roughly 25 percent of my interviewees consumed free food over two months, even though they were
technically not food insecure. Why? Because they were living on the edge
with just enough to get by. A free box of groceries now and then made
other bills easier to pay. Straddling the retail and donated food markets
on a week-to-week basis, allowed them to shift their resources to the most
pressing needs. For them, managing a monthly budget is like sailing in a
leaky boat: plug one hole and another appears.

On the flip side, those in more comfortable economic positions likely have cars and already bypass a number of stores during their everyday travels. Everyone who had a job drove past at least one store on their commute. Rich or poor, only 29 percent of interviewees shopped at their closest large-scale retail option. Everyone who participated in the retail food market chose stores for the same reasons as people who have access to supermarkets: availability of particular items, attractive sales, brand loyalty, familiarity, cleanliness, lighting, organization, and so on. Closer options may save food desert residents some time and a percentage of their transportation costs, but their reach is more extensive than commonly thought and distance is not the primary determinant of where they shop. They still wanted a grocery store to move back to the area, but admitted that if they got one, they would likely still shop where they currently do and buy the same types of products they already use. Their current shopping and consumption practices were tailored to their regular routine.

By examining the strategies of those with and without economic means, we identify a small fraction of people who would benefit the most from closer retail options: Those with just enough economic means to purchase the bulk of their retail items, but highly sensitive to any additional transportation costs required to get to them. For food desert residents in the middle—the "near poor"—distance is a very big deal. This 10 percent of the population in Southernside and West Greenville (5% nationwide) would see a world of difference if a new, nearby grocery store suddenly appeared.[15] Retail interventions could change their lives quickly and dramatically.

The national discussion around the role that transportation resources play within food deserts also needs to be rethought. First, the longitude and latitude of one's residence may not be the best way to determine their geographic relationship to their food environment. People move around. They go to church services, birthday parties, appointments. They travel to meet their everyday obligations—weaving in and around retail and donated food options. Ironically, the entire food desert debate has focused on the distance of supermarkets to where people sleep—the one period of the day when they neither eat nor shop.

The stories of people who use public and private transportation to shop for groceries show us that simply having a car or a nearby bus route isn't enough. While the corporations that sell to supermarkets grapple with the "last mile" problem of stocking store shelves, shoppers face the last mile problem of shopping at those stores. In many cases, getting *most-of-the-way* to the store is easier than getting *all-of-the-way* to the store. Poorly placed bus stops can make it difficult to get bags from bus to door or from trunk to cupboard. Whether it be difficulty traversing elevation changes, steps, or the strain of shopping with very young children, public and private transportation cannot always remedy personal supply-chain problems.

In this chapter, I focused on three factors frequently mentioned during the food desert debate. In the next chapter, I will expand the list to include three more that deserve more attention: social capital, household dynamics, and taste. I add these to the list of resources and constraints that affect grocery shopping because they reveal how consuming food is a social endeavor, even when done alone. The choices we make about what, when, and how to eat are heavily influenced by others. Whether it be coordinating a ride to the store or making a meal your mother fed you as a child, our food choices are widely shaped by those around us, both past and present. These last three factors prove the case: residents' complaints about the lack of grocery stores were not about wanting to consume different kinds of food. The people I interviewed liked what they currently ate. What they disliked was how their retail options made their lives inconvenient. They wanted newer, nicer options that reflected the value they saw in their own community.

4 Food Desert Realities

SOCIAL CAPITAL, HOUSEHOLD DYNAMICS, AND TASTE

Food deserts are filled with resourceful and innovative people. If necessity is the mother of invention, they have more than enough incentive to find new ways of getting the things they need. They are not resigned to their closest and cheapest retail options. The people I interviewed were upset by the lack of nearby grocery stores, but that did not keep them from getting to ones farther away. They wanted fresh and healthy food to be sold in their neighborhood even though many of them did not plan on buying or eating more of it. Many of them asked for healthier options "not for me, but others" without realizing their neighbors were saying the same thing.

Wanting better, closer retail and wanting to change the way they ate were two different issues to the people I talked with. Conflating the two is how we failed to understand their frustration about retail inequality in their neighborhoods. By making the food desert debate about better nutrition, we blamed health disparities on the lack of grocery stores rather than their deeper root causes: racism and poverty. The neglect of these communities by the public sector as well as the exodus of businesses seeking more profit elsewhere were justified in "color-blind" language, but we can see now that their impact fell largely along racial lines. They are the source of residents' resources and constraints today—the everyday realities that now shape their eating practices. You can't change their habits without addressing their circumstances.

In the last chapter I focused on people's perceptions of their food environment, their economic resources, and their transportation options. These factors help explain which stores they will consider visiting, what they can afford to buy in them, and how they will get there and back home again. But those are not the only resources and constraints I saw shaping the purchasing patterns of the primarily Black neighborhoods of West Greenville and Southernside, food deserts nestled within the city of Greenville, South Carolina. In this chapter I explore three additional factors—social capital, household dynamics, and Americans' "taste for convenience"—that can help explain why and how a new grocery store cannot change eating habits any time soon.

Exploring social capital and household dynamics helps illustrate the benefits of cooperation and the costs of isolation. Travel to access food was less difficult than I had expected—not easy, but not impossible (see chapter 3). My interviewees used their social capital to cultivate informal ride networks to shop for groceries if they wanted to, but household dynamics (how many people who had the same tastes were in the house at the same time) determined whether or not it was worth their time to cook them at home.

And looking to the American taste for convenience, both inside and outside food deserts, I show how the method of buying raw ingredients and unprocessed foods to cook at home is on the decline. I refer to this practice as "the traditional grocery store model" of food preparation, and I will explain why it is becoming increasingly untenable for Americans across socioeconomic, demographic, and geographic strata. To the extent that people shop in grocery stores, it is more often to buy foods that require only heating and minimal assembly, rather than raw ingredients. By bringing in research from beyond sociology, I show how our tastes have evolved in relation to our biology, our socialization practices, and our access to foods. Considering how food is processed and sold today, our current preferences are unlikely to reverse course quickly.

EVERYDAY REALITIES

Social capital, household dynamics, and an embodied taste for convenience are not typically used to explain routine food practices in areas without grocery stores, but they should be. Understanding these realities shows how the people I interviewed are experts at solving problems. My interviewees made decisions just like people who live outside food deserts, they just operated under a different set of circumstances. If they did not want to remake their most personal rituals—breakfast, lunch, and dinner—it was for the same reason most people decline to do so: because they have already settled on food habits and practices that work for them.

Social Capital

The value of knowing others—our social connections—is a long-standing topic among social scientists. Whether you're trying to get a job or get out of a jam, connections matter. Of the people I interviewed, 91 percent of the people without cars were able to get rides to go shopping. How? They used their social capital to cultivate an informal ride network to get them to and from the store.

Political scientist Robert Putnam is one of the most famous theorists of this *social capital*. Putnam argues that civic society cannot function without social capital, just as it cannot function without other forms of capital, including money. Our fate is bound with others' fates, and if our net social capital declines, daily life becomes isolated and lonely (Putnam 2000). Less poetically, perhaps, we can say that society is an inherently cooperative venture, and our willingness to help others depends on trusting that they will return the favor. Sociologist James Coleman sums it up as: "If A does something for B and trusts B to reciprocate in the future, this establishes an expectation in A and an obligation on the part of B" (Coleman 1988: S102). For people in food deserts without their own transportation, social capital is a vital asset. They need help. Some of their connections can provide it. Yet the ways they create, develop, and maintain these informal ride opportunities is relatively unexplored in the research on food deserts.[1]

Determining a given person's relative level of social capital involves, first, taking an inventory of the obligations owed to them by others.[2] Within families, asking for rides is easier; obligations to help an aunt or grandmother are built into the expectations of being a nephew or granddaughter (and are reinforced by social pressures from parents, siblings, etc.). Repayment in family networks need not be direct or immediate. The person who gets a ride doesn't necessarily owe something to the person giving it—perhaps another family member will reciprocate on a more relaxed schedule. When networks extend beyond kin, settling up may be more prompt. Drivers outside the family, in our example, might ask for a few dollars in gas money or help with a task. This is less convenient, but still worth it. As a passenger in the informal ride network, paying debts builds trust—an unofficial credit score or Yelp rating, so to speak. It increases social capital.

Some people's shopping needs require tailored solutions too complex for public transportation to provide. As detailed in chapter 3, people with mobility issues need help with the physical challenges before and after a trip to the store. People with unpredictable work schedules may find the bus schedule impractical. Again, this is where the ride network comes in. So long as riders tend the relationship, a member of this network can meet their idiosyncratic needs. If food desert residents without cars use their social capital wisely, these connections can serve as investments that yield dividends like any other. In some cases, the resulting personal transportation system is more robust and reliable than any bus system.

My goal in this section is to show how residents of Southernside and West Greenville used their social capital to acquire food in either the retail or donated food market, or sometimes both. From their interviews, I learned that their informal ride network did not just happen. It required consistent and concerted effort. This is because "food related relationships" are different (Morton et al. 2005: 97). The stakes are higher: we need food to survive.

CULTIVATING INFORMAL RIDE NETWORKS

At first glance, Ella would seemingly have little social capital. When we met, this seventy-nine-year-old Black woman had only been in Southernside for about six months. She liked her neighbors, but—originally from the Midwest—she found them a bit provincial in what they ate and how they shopped. As I defined in chapter 3, she was what I call *ultravulnerable* (over fifty-five, living alone, relying on a fixed retirement or public benefit income, without a car). Ella had to build her ride network from scratch—looking for potential drivers as soon as she moved into her new apartment. Within weeks, she was getting rides from other members at her new church, as well as one of its custodians.

Ella credited her ability to get rides with her willingness to adjust to other people's schedules: "I tried to make my grocery shopping conducive to their days, so it works out fine for me." First, she would create a list of everything she needed for the next few weeks. Then she would organize it into different types of products. If one of her contacts was going to a dollar store, she would use that opportunity to get non-food items, "That is when I get all my taxables . . . my foil, my saran wrap, my baggies, all of that."[3] She also knew that she could spend more time in the store when driven by some people rather than take the bus ("I like to just wander around."). However, if need be, she could speed up her shopping to accommodate her drivers ("It is easy for me to run in and get what I need"). Because her social capital "exists in the *relations* among persons" (emphasis in the original) (Coleman 1988: 100–101), Ella was careful not to overdraw her account; she knew she would likely need each driver's help again.

Money also helped Ella get rides. Developing an informal ride network sometimes requires relying on connections outside your immediate circle. The weaker the connection, the greater the cost. Ella reported paying varying amounts, $5 for short rides, up to $15 for longer trips. She let each driver dictate how she would reimburse for their time and trouble: "I say, 'We can do two things, we can go to lunch or I can give you gas money, what do you want?'" Of my interviewees who got rides, roughly half paid their driver (with "fares" ranging from $3 to $20). Amounts varied by closeness of the connection (relatives charged less, friends-of-friends charged more) as well as the type of ride. Most drivers waited or shopped at the same time. A few would drop off and pick up later. In all cases, riders felt the informal ride network cheaper than cabs, especially considering the extra services these drivers provided.

CALCULATING THE COST OF INCONVENIENCE TO OTHERS

Ella's payment strategy worked, but it could become expensive. For riders unable to cover the full cost of inconvenience to others, keeping their ride network viable was a delicate balance. Claudette, a sixty-three-year-old Black woman, knew this well. She grew up in Southernside, moved away as an adult, and had recently returned to be the caretaker for her three great-nieces. Because of some mobility problems and the difficulty of wrangling small children on the bus, she needed to be driven to the store. She had family in the area, so her rides mostly stemmed from that network. She paid a family member $6 and a friend of the family $10. But Claudette wished she could afford to pay more. "I feel like I am imposing," she lamented.

When one of her connections eventually cut her off, Claudette learned the limits of that imposition. "One person, he don't answer the phone anymore. I guess I wore him out," she laughed. "But he took me maybe seven or eight months straight." From this experience, she stopped expecting same-day pickup: "They will try to work me in, but they are doing other things in their lives." She also sped up her shopping, even though this was hard for her: "Just running around trying to rush and get this and that, and telling the kids to be quiet and let me concentrate." To keep her social capital intact, she had to pay in a combination of cash and gratitude, using her flexible schedule and shopping speed to make up the difference.

The burden of these emotional costs can be heavy. I interviewed Daisy on the front porch of the home in which she had grown up. A sixty-nine-year-old Black woman, Daisy had moved back into her childhood home after divorcing. She shared the home with one of her adult sons, but he was unemployed. She had lived a hard life, and was wracked with aches, pains, and dental problems. Her Supplemental Security Income benefits and $14 in monthly SNAP funds ("food stamps") covered only half of her monthly bills.

Daisy was in a precarious economic and social position, and she needed rides to both the (retail) grocery store and the (donated) food pantry. Her sister lived only a few blocks away but worked during the day and could not pick her up at a moment's notice. So Daisy said she typically had to wait until the weekend for a ride. When her sister was unavailable, Daisy would resort to calling her ex-husband:

> Sometimes I get my ex-husband [to drive me], I hate to say it. I am trying to cut that back because we don't get along, so I am trying to get somebody else. . . . He would say, "I've got something to do; get somebody else to take you." So you see, he realizes that I don't have no transportation. And that is why I tell my sister and my brother, that I don't have no transportation, and then I have another brother who lives . . . so far away I can't get him, so he might have to wait until his day off. And I'll say, "okay," but sometimes, my

sister, she will say, "Well, I will do it the next day or Thursday or Friday or something like that." And I'll say, "Okay I'll wait."

Daisy's predicament was compounded by her lack of economic and social capital. She needed to save all her money for food, making her totally dependent on others. She felt guilty about not being able to return the favor with her drivers. This weighed on her. What is the cost of feeling like an imposition? Of having to spend time with an ex-spouse you dislike? These emotional costs are hard to quantify—but they are still real.

ACCESSING NEW VENUES AND OPTIONS

People with ample social capital could expand the scope and reach of their food options beyond even their informal ride networks. Their options opened up in amount, quality, and type, because their acquaintances and associations helped them "shrink the map" as they navigated life in a food desert.

Diane was one of the most connected women I interviewed in West Greenville. She was an active member of her church, helped run the local neighborhood association meetings at the community center, volunteered for the board of elections as a poll monitor, and was on the advisory board for a nonprofit agency that built affordable housing. Although she lived alone (widowed) and had retired from her full-time housekeeping job years ago, Diane happily rattled off a list of lunch dates she'd had with friends over the past month. The time and energy she spent in her community allowed her to forge trusting, reciprocal relationships. And through these relations, her "social capital [was] productive, making possible the achievement of certain ends that in its absence would not be possible" (Coleman 1988: S98).

Diane invested in others, and they returned the favor. Because of her work with the church, she developed a close friendship with another member. Over the years, the two frequently ate and shopped together. When this friend's car broke down, Diane gave her rides; a year later, when Diane's car was in the shop, her friend gave her rides. Another set of Diane's friends hired her to do the grocery shopping for their disabled son. His insurance reimbursed her expenses, and the trips for specialty items related to his disability brought her to stores beyond her regularly beaten path.

Diane's work with the church also led her to become one of the managers of its food pantry. She oversaw incoming deliveries and decided how and where the items would be shelved, refrigerated, or frozen.[4] She disbursed items on scheduled days, and regularly opened the pantry after hours for those with immediate needs (she had a key). And because the pantry often had soon-to-be-expired food, she and the other members of the church were able to take some home before it went to waste. I asked whether the food pantry was open to any church member. Diane said, "Any member of the church, and as we deem necessary, any member of the neighborhood, too. Because people in the neighborhood come. So yesterday I had a salad, and I got it from [the pantry]. And I made me a tossed salad. That was for lunch." Despite living in a food desert, Diane had built trust among her friends and within the church that opened up new food options, items, and sources.

Even so, Diane's access to food had a limited effect on her overall diet. Despite her ability to acquire fresh foods, she rarely cooked raw or unprocessed ingredients at home. She could easily make meals from scratch, but she chose to eat food prepared outside the home two to three times per week. To understand why, we need to look beyond availability. As I will show in the next section, once food desert residents cross the threshold of access (geographic and economic), they still need to calculate whether cooking at home is worth it. For many, the challenge is not getting the ingredients home, but justifying the effort required to cook them.

Household Dynamics

While social capital helped people get to the store, the dynamics within the household played a more important role when deciding what to buy when there. Even when people could afford the cost of transportation and items on their list, some aspects of their home lives made shopping for fresh and unprocessed ingredients impractical and inefficient.

By household dynamics, I mean the amount, roles, and relationships of people within a given residence. Size, as I will show, is important when deciding whether or not to buy ingredients in order to prepare them at home for a meal. When four people are living under one roof, preparing meals *can* save money. For those living alone, the economics are different.

Roles and relationships affect choices, too: If the four people are simply sharing housing to save money on rent, they may have little desire to coordinate food preparation. And even if they do, their work schedules and dietary needs may make cooperation infeasible. These constraints on home cooking are driven by long-term demographic changes that began long before food deserts entered into the public lexicon.

HOUSEHOLD SIZE

American households are getting smaller, and this is altering the equation of home food preparation. The larger the household, the more cooking makes sense—with multiple people to feed, buying prepared food (even fast food) can get expensive quickly, and economies of scale can make scratch-cooking cheaper. There are savings to be made when the labor of cooking (buying, measuring, chopping, cooking, cleaning) can be divided within the household, and buying larger quantities can reduce serving prices. The smaller the household, the less efficient home cooking becomes. Thus, considering nationwide changes in household size over the past fifty years, it is not surprising that 2010 was the first year on record when people spent more on food prepared by others than they did at the grocery store (USDA Economic Research Service 2018).

Which is to say, large households are no longer the norm in the United States. They haven't been for forty years (see Figure 1). In 1960, the average number of people living together was 3.3. Now it is roughly 2.5. Demographically, that is significant. Over the same time span, the percentage of households with a single person has doubled, from 13 percent to 28 percent. Today, 1 in every seven adults lives alone, for a total of nearly thirty-four million single-person American households.

Among my interviewees who lived alone, eating food prepared by others was the more attractive option. Only 28 percent of this group adhered to the traditional grocery store model (buying raw ingredients to cook at home). The rest predominately bought already cooked or premade food. Chris, a thirty-six-year-old white bartender, was a prime example. He lived roughly a mile away from where he worked, and traveled by moped rather than car. This saved him money, made for a quick commute, and enabled easy parking. On the flip side, it made going to the grocery store and buying large quantities more difficult. He would use his ample social

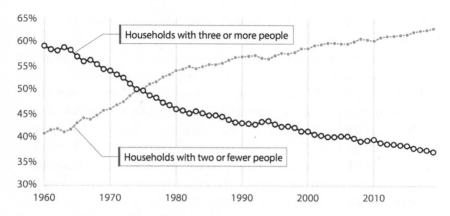

Figure 1. Smaller versus larger American households over time. SOURCE: US Census.

capital to access a substantial ride network when necessary—yet Chris rarely asked for rides.

That's because Chris rarely cooked. He bought all of his paper and cleaning products at a nearby dollar store. There he also purchased his milk and dried goods like cereal, pasta, and snack items. He seldom needed raw or unprocessed ingredients because his workplace granted him a free meal each shift. His job was also located near other food venues where he routinely purchased meals before and after work. At home, he ate a cold breakfast in the morning and made the occasional sandwich for lunch. To call that "cooking" is a stretch. It would be more accurate to say that he "assembled" his meals.

Perhaps the best illustration of how household size played into Chris's food acquisition and preparation strategy came when he had guests. Once a month or so, Chris would invite people over for a weekend barbecue. It was only then—when there were enough mouths to feed—that he would seek out a ride to the grocery store and cook a meal. And that created a new problem: leftovers. They were a challenge, he noted: "it just ends up going bad before I get to it."

For those living alone, purchasing and eating perishable items can be a race to the finish. It was a common theme in my interviews, to the extent that 72 percent of people in single-person households reported they did not cook at home on a regular basis. Instead, they mostly ate out or brought prepared food to be reheated or assembled at home. The exception? When they shared a meal with others.

Gayle, a sixty-one-year-old Black woman, also needed others to justify cooking. She lived alone, was a case worker at a nearby nonprofit, and had her own car (although periodic mechanical problems forced her to get rides from time to time). She told me, "I don't do a lot of cooking, as much as I used to because it is just me. I do cook a lot when I have people over and that is when I do a lot of cooking for entertaining." It was just that, after her husband passed away, Gayle found eating out became a more attractive option than cooking for one. It was a better return on her investments of time and money, and the advantages of buying ingredients and preparing them herself only made sense when she had others to feed.

Christie, a sixty-one-year-old white woman, had gone through a divorce that changed her views on cooking. "It is just me," she began as I asked her to describe her eating and cooking habits. "I bought some asparagus last week, and I ended up throwing it out. There are nights where I don't feel like cooking, and being single has an awful lot of freedom to it, and if you don't want to do it, you don't have to do it. And if I have an opportunity to go out, then I'll go out." Christie had her own car and made a modest living. Her job as a medical lab technician required her to travel around the county to collect specimens. She had the opportunity to stop at numerous supermarkets during her daily travels. However, as the dynamics of her household changed, so did her perspective on the traditional grocery store model.

The people who lived alone and did *not* have their own transportation found the barriers to eating fresh fruits and vegetables even higher. When getting to the store requires paying for rides (in money, in time, in emotional indebtedness), the incentive to reduce the number of trips increases. As trip frequency decreases, so does the likelihood that perishable items will stay fresh throughout the period between trips. Of interviewees without access to private transportation, 37 percent tried to do all their shopping in one or two trips per month; for those living alone without a vehicle, that percentage rose slightly to 42 percent. Fruits and vegetables could be frozen to extend their shelf lives, but "once-a-month shoppers" stated that any secondary trip was primarily for milk.

Smaller households see cooking differently. Without many mouths to feed, the rate of turnover between dishes slows. That's why Florence and Martin said they preferred to eat convenience foods over cooking—bringing home pre- or par-cooked meals or just eating out. Without the promise of variety, the appeal of home cooking waned. Thus, this Black couple in their mid-fifties changed their eating and cooking choices as their household got smaller.

First and foremost, Florence and Martin saw themselves as economical eaters. She worked, and he earned a small retirement pension. She clipped coupons, and he kept an eye out for deals on his favorite brand-name soda. They owned a modest home and lived well within their means. Between their two cars, they could easily access a supermarket. In fact, on Florence's commute to and from work, she passed three different full-sized grocery stores. For the couple, access and affordability were important, but not deciding factors in what to eat. Once their two daughters became adults and left the house, Florence explained that cooking big meals posed problems: monotony and waste. "I ain't a waster. I can take it and do something with it . . . but it is kind of harder now, since it is just me and him. I'm a big cooker, I used to cook, so I know how to prepare and cook it and freeze it, but it is kind of harder now that it is just me and Martin. . . . And I'm learning now to buy smaller quantities than what I used to. . . . I did learn that after I got older." According to Florence and Martin, cooking for four people had been a chore worth the effort. It saved money and time, and leftovers created even more savings. Now, as empty nesters, cooking came to mean something different. Their conclusion was partly utilitarian (food waste is costly) but also moral (food waste is wrong). Put together, it made the traditional grocery store model seem less efficient and less virtuous.

My interviews also documented the opposite effect: I learned that as households grew bigger, cooking began to make more sense. Sherry, a sixty-seven-year-old Black woman, lived in a multigenerational home. The grandmother did most of the cooking and made up the grocery lists, while her thirty-one-year-old granddaughter Trinity would grocery shop during work commutes or when transporting her children to school and events. At times, Sherry's household would swell to seven or eight people.

To save money, they bought "family packs" of meat that could be divided, frozen, and parceled out over time: "Most of the time, I get sometimes five and six and seven packages [of turkey necks], and they run about $2 [each]. . . . And I bring them home and wash them, and then

I put them in plastic bags and put how much we going to eat and put them in the freezer. And, so, about the most that I spend for the turkey necks sometimes would be about $20, and that's enough to feed us for at least two or three months." Buying in bulk is an easier option for bigger families like Sherry's, a cost-saving strategy that becomes less attractive as households shrink. But it wasn't just about the money. All of the examples in this section featured households with a vehicle and at least one member who worked. Access wasn't stopping such families from cooking raw and unprocessed ingredients.

COORDINATED TASTES AND NEEDS

Bigger households require bigger meals, but they can also go through them quickly enough to reduce the fear of monotony. Yet household size alone cannot explain the choice to cook at home or turn to convenience foods. To take advantage of economies of scale, for example, a household has to eat as a unit.[5]

That is, *living* together does not always mean *eating* together. Under the same roof there may be multiple sets of food preferences, work schedules, and special dietary needs. But to make the traditional grocery store model really work, the same dishes need to be consumed by everyone. The most common barrier to meal-sharing my interviewees cited was the need to accommodate children's palates. In Sherry's household, there were two different diets. The children sat and ate with adults at the same time and place, but they often had their own separate meal. Roughly a third of her family's purchases at warehouse stores like Sam's Club and Costco were for the children. As Sherry put it: "At Sam's you can get the little whoppers, for my grandbabies. So it is basically for kids. . . . It's not really for us. Because I have a house full of kids most of the time." Although eight people might be at Sherry's dinner table, half would eat "adult food" and half ate "kid food."

Over the past half-century, the divide between adult food and kid food has grown throughout the United States. It has not always been this way in the United States, nor is this a worldwide shift: Children in many cultures eat the same foods as their parents, albeit sometimes in pureed or softened form (Lawless 2018). The divergence seems to owe at least partly to advertising and marketing aimed at children. Public health researchers have found that "in the United States, more than 98 percent of the television food ads seen by children and 89 percent of those seen by adolescents are for products high in fat, sugar, and/or sodium" (Harris et al. 2009: 213). Children in the United States now know that items like chicken nuggets, canned pastas, and sugary cereals are for them and not grownups (Elliot 2011).

This poses an especially difficult problem for single parents. Whereas adult couples could cook for two, single parents often reported preparing entirely different foods for their children than for themselves. Forest, fifty-six, was late to fatherhood. The single Black father took pride in feeding his eight-year-old son as best he could. But a past shoulder injury made it impossible for Forest to seek out paid work and could make home cooking painful. He referred to himself as an "old country boy" who often had a craving for head cheese and souse (meat jellies made from typically discarded cuts), but knew his son did not share his tastes. So Forest reported eating out multiple times per week and relying primarily on processed and prepared meals for his son.

> [My son] would eat McDonald's already every day and stuff like that. . . . And sometimes my shoulder's bothering me I just don't feel like cooking or stuff like that . . . and I will work out a couple dollars and get him something to eat. . . . As long as he is eating. . . . And I keep a lot of those little Lunchables and stuff in the refrigerator . . . and these little dinners like right here and stuff like that. I got the fish sticks and stuff like that, so I just pop it in the oven, and he eats that and he is good to go.

Forest shopped at grocery stores often. He had a car and drove past a number of them during weekly trips to his physical therapist. But when he was at the store, this single dad was shopping for two different meal plans.

The divide wasn't always between parents and children, but between adults sharing the same space. This was the case for Lloyd, a Black man and longtime resident of Southernside. Earlier, we learned of the forty-four-year-old's childhood memories of the historic Kash and Karry grocery store that had long since closed. I had known Lloyd for years through the neighborhood association, but it took me ten months to schedule an interview with him. Lloyd's job at the time required constant travel, which made it difficult to find a time to meet. But a job change led to easier hours. We talked at his living room table one weeknight. During the interview, we were the only people in the apartment. He lived with his adult sister and her child, but they were visiting relatives at the moment. Their different schedules, dietary needs, and Lloyd's new job made cooperation around household food difficult.

Although Lloyd's apartment was in a food desert, he crossed paths with grocery stores on his way to and from work. He also had a car, but preferred taking the bus because he saw the one mile walk to the transfer station as a way to get some exercise. Still, despite his access to healthier options, he ate at fast food and family style restaurants at least once a day, sometimes twice on weekdays. When I asked him the last time he cooked a meal in the house, he said it had been almost a month.

Lloyd shared his apartment with two other people, but his sister shopped for food separately and they rarely ate together. He worked days, and she worked nights. His sister cooked for herself and made separate meals for her six-year-old child. Even an otherwise easy-to-share item like milk was separated—Lloyd's sister and his niece were lactose intolerant. Their three, distinctive diets strained fridge space in ways that were rarely a problem except in the largest families (a number of my interviewees in large households indicated that they had removed plastic shelving in the freezer to create more bulk storage room, for example). In Lloyd's household, the cramping was caused by a lack of coordination.

In addition to not wanting to cook for just himself, Lloyd explained that he valued his time off. Being able to spend evenings at home was a newfound luxury. He used his commute time for exercise and preferred not to spend the night prepping and cleaning. Indeed, cooking from scratch takes time, and time is a depleted resource for working adults. Scholars have long documented the effects of being "overworked" (Schor 1992) and living in a "time bind" (Hochschild 1997); more recently, studies have shown the negative effects of nontraditional work hours and unpredictable schedules (Gerstel and Clawson 2018). When looking for ways to "make time," eating out can be an attractive option.

Another barrier for Lloyd was his workplace. In his past job, he would bring leftovers to eat on the road or stop at grocery stores to pick up fruit and snacks along the way. His new job did not allow workers to stay on the premises during their lunch break (there was no lounge or break room). Returning home was not an option because of the travel time, and neither was sitting on a park bench (his building was located on a busy commercial strip). If Lloyd wanted to eat lunch, his only option was to bide his time at one of a handful of nearby fast-food restaurants.

This arrangement did not particularly bother Lloyd. He liked eating out every day. Walking home from the transfer station, he almost always picked up something for dinner to save time on cooking and cleaning when he got home. And on the few occasions he did cook—mostly on weekends—he made meals for one, explicitly avoiding leftovers: "I make sure whatever I cook, I can eat right then. I don't make huge amounts of food. I don't make spaghetti for five. I just cook just enough for me. And when I am finished, I'm finished. I can wash everything up and it is pretty much done." Finishing the whole meal was important: Lloyd couldn't eat leftovers at work and had little space to store them in the refrigerator at home. He summarized: "A lot of times I eat out. . . . That solves the food issue of how much I have to have at the house."

A Taste for Convenience

After interviewing residents of food deserts for nearly two years, I came to see that people's food choices are more complex than any calculation of price and proximity. By that point in my research, I was only beginning to understand that retail inequality was behind their attention-grabbing pleas for a grocery store. Yet I was fairly sure what they were *not* about: changing their diets.

Admitting that dietary change is not food desert residents' primary objective poses political problems for those who want to help them get a grocery store. Talking points like "Fighting for health!" claim the moral high ground. But for all its effectiveness, this strategy is flawed. It frames the current tastes and preferences of those for whom we claim we are "fighting" as a "problem." One that only we—the scholars, the media, the policy advocates, and the politicians who think we know best—can fix. By casting food desert residents as "perfect victims," we set them up to fail.

Turns out, that's our problem, not theirs. My past research on domestic violence taught me that the perfect victim is a myth (Kolb 2014). Victims behave in all sorts of irrational and unexpected ways. They lash out in rage. They skip court hearings. They forget to act stoic and contemplative.

Why? *Because they have been abused.* They have suffered an injustice. And from this experience they have developed survival mechanisms that can be confusing to the people trying to help them. Food desert residents shouldn't have to be perfect victims any more than people affected by intimate partner violence should be. If, politically, we don't want to admit that they might actually like the food they currently eat, that is our problem, not theirs.

In this and the previous chapter, I have so far analyzed five different factors that played a clear role in my interviewees' diets. The first three—perception, money, and transportation—are clearly necessary conditions for healthy food acquisition; but necessary conditions do not offer sufficient explanations for why people eat the way they do. The next two—individuals' social capital and household dynamics—deserve greater attention in the food desert debate. The sixth and final item on the list—their taste—is both the easiest and hardest to analyze. Everyone has an opinion about why people prefer different foods. In this section, I try to summarize and synthesize the most popular theories into an explanation tailored to the context of the American food environment today. Why have we developed such a durable and embodied taste for convenience foods?

That *all* Americans have shifted their eating habits should force us to reconsider many taken-for-granted assumptions in the food desert debate. Yes, some convenience foods can be healthy. And many home-cooked meals are unhealthy. But the premise of the food desert concept was that it was inaccessibility of fresh vegetables, lean meats, and whole foods—all of which require home preparation—that was causing poor health outcomes. Yet, if all Americans are turning toward convenience foods, lack of access can't be solely responsible for the high rates of diabetes, obesity, and hypertension in food deserts. Focusing on distance to stores ignores the fact that wealthier people in areas with nice retail options eat fast food, too (more so, in fact, than poor people). Those with economic resources can also consume healthier, more expensive versions of prepared foods. But most importantly, people in food deserts cannot offset their taste for convenience with the physical and emotional benefits of quality health care, housing, education, and recreation. Poor Black neighborhoods in cities across the country don't have those advantages. Their health suffers as a result. When you combine that with the daily stressors of discrimination in public life, it becomes clear how we got the food desert concept wrong: It's not about the grocery stores, it's about racism, poverty, and the legacy of divestment.

The traditional grocery store model (buying raw or unprocessed ingredients and preparing them at home) was not very popular among my interviewees. Less than half (46%) cooked at all in the traditional sense of the term. And of those who did cook, roughly a third (36%) still ate out at least twice a week. Keep in mind, they *shopped at grocery stores.* Of those who did not cook at home, 91 percent had still visited a mid- or full-size supermarket in the past month. The majority of their "convenient" meals came from the grocery store.[6] And this data is generally consistent with national trends. In 2008, only 56 percent of Americans cooked at home, and since the 1960s, "The overall amount of time spent in food preparation has decreased, as fewer people cook per day and those who cook spend less time on cooking" (Smith, Ng, and Popkin 2013: 5).[7]

By "convenience" foods, I mean dishes prepared by others and available upon demand (from a restaurant, take-out, fast-food venue, delivery service, etc.) or in packaged form requiring minimal assembly and preparation (say, making sandwiches, heating instant soups, or microwaving frozen dinners). Beyond breakfast foods and the occasional cut of meat, interviewees who ate mostly convenience foods only used their stoves, ovens, or microwaves to heat pre- or par-cooked food.

Over hours and hours of listening to their stories about how and why they ate the foods they did, I came to understand that my interviewees' taste for convenience was not a reflection of resignation or surrender. They *preferred* easy foods. And for good reasons. One, convenience foods enabled quick consumption and clean up. Two, they offered more flexibility in regard to when and where they could be eaten. Three, they did not require much—if any—coordination with others. To my interviewees, convenience foods meant more variety from day to day, less refrigerated storage requirements, and less likelihood of waste. But, most importantly, they honestly liked these foods. They were filling, flavorful, and familiar.

EXPLAINING TASTE: BIOLOGY, SOCIALIZATION, AND ACCESS

Sociologists have long grappled with questions regarding taste. How do we acquire it? Why does it vary from place to place, from people to people?

But we are not the only ones to ask these questions. In this extended section, I draw from a number of different academic disciplines for additional perspectives on taste. I begin with biology and outline how our basic cravings and aversions can explain some—but not all—of our eating practices. Then I jump over to the assumption that all tastes are inherited from one's family: this line of thinking argues that we are socialized to eat according to subcultural conventions that we then pass on to future generations. And third, I consider the impact of access—the more recent entrant into the debate on taste. Arguments from this perspective hinge on availability and imply that we can't resist tastes we are increasingly exposed to, nor maintain our tastes for things of which we have been deprived.

Alone, any one of these three categories (biology, socialization, and access) offers only an incomplete explanation of what we are drawn to eat, taught to eat, and offered to eat. Taken together, these three drivers of taste offer a more nuanced and complex explanation. By highlighting the ways they interact, I show how recent changes in the food retail industry and our household dynamics in the United States have produced a durable taste for convenience, and not just in food deserts. The traditional grocery store model is in decline. It has been for decades. These changes may be exacerbated in food deserts and among poor people, but they are taking place all across America.

Biology

To explain our growing taste for convenience, I'll start with the most basic: the body. Human taste receptors relay sensations to our brain that reward our consumption of some foods and penalize others. We have cravings. We also have aversions. Of course, these sensations are mediated by socialization and access, but we must start somewhere. And biology is only the beginning.

Human evolution has ingrained "a preference for sweet and salty tastes (tastes that could predict the presence of nutrients) . . . and a predisposition to learn to prefer energy-dense foods (which would be adaptive in contexts where food is scarce)" (Katz and Sadacca 2011: 1118). Put simply, we have hardwired responses to salt, sugar, and fat that have helped us evolve to who we are today, even if they can lead us to eat in unhealthy ways in our current circumstances.

We have also evolved natural aversions. These include: "a tendency to reject bitter and sour tastes (which could be toxic)" as well as "a neophobic rejection of novel foods and flavors (which might be dangerous)" (Katz and Sadacca 2011: 1118). As a species, our dislike toward bitterness and sourness and our disinclination to try new foods and flavors have helped us avoid contaminated or potentially poisonous items. In some cases, the mere thought of eating them can trigger "emotional expressions, behaviors, and physiological responses such as nausea" (Rozin, Haidt, and Fincher 2009: 1179–80). Infants pucker when you put a lemon slice to their lips not because they have been socialized to do so, but because they are born with an automatic response to the citric acid in it. Innate responses do not explain all of our likes and dislikes, but they are part of the equation.

Unlike other species, humans have found a way to manipulate foods in order to exploit our cravings and manage our aversions. In the modern era, this can be seen in the ways that food processors amplify our enjoyment of particular foods. As Michael Moss, author of the book, *Salt, Sugar, Fat: How the Food Giants Hooked Us*, describes it, our bodies want salt, but not too much. Talking to food scientists, he learned that more sugar solicits a positive response, but too much and we turn away. Via Magnetic Resonance Imagery (MRI), food scientists can watch as they administer the perfect middle point—the "bliss point"—until a consumable item lights up the brain's electrical circuitry and "floods [people] with feelings of pleasure." (Moss 2014: 274). We have natural mechanisms to prevent overeating when we have had too much "bliss," but food processors have learned how to cut the brake lines.

These changes to processed food can produce preferences across generations. Mothers can pass tastes on to their children. In one experiment, women who drank carrot juice during pregnancy (prenatal) and while still breastfeeding (postnatal) were more likely to transfer that taste to their children. Once born, their children accepted and enjoyed carrot flavored cereal more than children who were not previously exposed to it (Mennella, Jagnow, and Beauchamp 2001). What does this mean? "Early sensory experience during gestation and lactation can provide a 'flavor bridge,' facilitating the acceptance of foods consumed by the mother" (Anzman, Rollins, and Birch 2011: 1118). What mothers consume can also change the gene expressions of their children. This finding is the basis of the field of epigenetics, or the "mechanisms that lead to long-term changes in gene expression through chemical modification to or alterations in the packaging of DNA" (Gluckman and Hanson 2009: S63).

The implication of epigenetic research on tastes is that what we eat today can change the ways that we and our offspring respond to food in the future. Obese mothers, for example, can increase the propensity of their children to be obese by altering the way their children's genes express themselves in response to their environment. The type and amount of food given to infants serve as "developmental cues" that can "create sensitivity to later conditions, impacting on behavior (appetite, food choice and possibly activity levels) and on metabolic partitioning" (Gluckman and Hanson 2009: S68). Our bodies have evolved to do this in order to best respond to the world they are about to enter. To prepare for a world of scarcity and starvation, for example, infants' bodies can become "thriftier" in order to store as much fat as possible. Ironically, in modern societies, the genes of infants who are overfed respond to their "hypernutritive" environment similarly—by storing as much fat as possible. Either way, obesity rates can be explained primarily by how much people eat now, but also by the type and quantity of food their mothers ate and fed to them when they were fetuses and newborns.

Cravings and aversions can of course be mediated through socialization, but it can be expensive. Although young children are initially averse to the bitter and sour components of many calorie-light, nutrient rich foods, their parents can help them develop a taste for those foods through extensive exposure (Beauchamp and Mannella 2009). This means repeated trials at feeding time and pushing through multiple rejections (just imagine yourself enticing a toddler to eat their kale, five nights in a row). This process is costly—it can mean preparing foods to make them more palatable and wasting a lot of food in the process. Healthy foods are more expensive per calorie than cheaper options loaded with salt, sugar, and fat. In a study of low-income mothers' grocery shopping habits, fear of wasting food (and money) caused mothers living in poverty to give in to their children's innate cravings. They knew their children would eat salty, sweet, and fatty foods, so they made the practical choice to avoid "experimenting with new items or reintroducing foods that their children initially turned down"

(Daniel 2016: 39). Once you combine parents' economic constraints with their toddlers' innate preferences, it becomes easier to grasp the difficulty of raising children with healthier tastes.

So biology offers some reasons that Americans have developed a durable taste for convenience. First, biology helps us understand why some processed foods are so attractive: they accentuate our cravings, sidestep our aversions, and mask signals when we have had enough. Second, biology helps us understand how we can inherit tastes from our parents: exposure to some flavors shortly before and after birth can create our first preferences in childhood. And third, biology helps us understand why tastes change so slowly: our food environment early in life can produce epigenetic changes that last a lifetime. Put together, these three facts offer a starting point for explaining how taste, once acquired, can take generations to change.

Biology can only take us so far, however. Through repetition and acculturation, we can learn to suspend our cravings and aversions. Additionally, a change in economic circumstances can make experimenting with new foods and flavors less risky, even though our biology remains the same. So, as we seek more answers to understand our taste for convenience, we arrive where we started: biology is only the beginning, not the end.

Socialization

Cultural influences on our tastes are real. In the United States, people prefer different foods in different parts of the country. Across the globe, these distinctions sharpen. Considering all of humanity has the same basic capacities for taste, biology has clearly left some questions unanswered. To fill this void, sociologists offer an alternative explanation: socialization.

According to this concept, parents and caregivers train their children—explicitly and implicitly—how to adhere to the norms, rules, and values of their given culture and subculture. As children grow, they learn more and different lessons from their friends and peers. Over time, other agents of socialization, including educational and religious institutions, enter into the conversation. Socialization via face-to-face contact is augmented by other forms of influence. Through media, for instance, people observe and learn from the actions of others, which ultimately shapes their understanding of what objects and behaviors mean. These meanings are also embedded in ceremonies and rituals, keeping them alive over time.

Sociologists are not alone in outlining how society encourages individuals to conform to external expectations. According to psychoanalysts, without socialization, we would be left to our most basic impulses and desires. In Freud's terms, internalizing societal "tastes and standards . . . dispositions and traditions" (1949/1989: 96), puts a check on our "id," or the component of our personality "directed exclusively to obtaining pleasure" (86). Thus, the process of socialization parallels the development of the "super-ego." When applied to taste, the super-ego is said to help control our compulsions. Even if we really want an extra slice of cake, we can develop the restraint necessary to push it away. Consequently, our bodies may come with basic cravings and aversions, but socialization tells us what to do with them. Or, as sociologist Shamus Khan (2015) puts it, "Desire might be biologically driven, but it moves on tracks laid forth by human culture."

Socialization teaches us how to label and interpret the sensations that foods produce. This enables us to acquire tastes and the motivation to do so. For example, loved ones can be disappointed if we do not enjoy the food they have cooked for us. Our inability to find pleasure in these meals can mean failing to please others—people who are important to us. Put another way, eating comes with its own set of "feeling rules," or basic guideposts on what sensations others expect us to experience. This process is called emotion management. If we sense a discrepancy between our feelings and others' expectations, we can manage our emotion accordingly (Hochschild 1983). In the case of food, we can think through our sensations to search for *elements* we like. If not its texture, we can try to find something pleasing in a dish's smell. In some cases, we may need to fight against our natural aversions to adhere to cultural conventions, like when we are guests in someone else's home. In short, we can learn to like what we initially do not. The raw physiological response is just the first step. Culture provides the context and significance to our sensations, enabling us to give them "a name, a history, a meaning, and a consequence of a certain sort" (Hochschild 1990: 120).[8]

Managing our senses requires more than just telling ourselves how we should feel; true cultural membership entails a taste that feels natural and not faked. Even biological responses we presume to be automatic, like feeling "high" after consuming drugs, require work to interpret and manage. In his classic study of how marijuana users "learn" how to experience smoking the drug, Howard Becker found that first-timers sometimes struggled with identifying and understanding these new sensations: "The taste for such experience is a socially acquired one, not different in kind from acquired tastes for oysters or dry martinis. The user feels dizzy, thirsty; his scalp tingles; he misjudges time and distances; and so on. Are these things pleasurable? He isn't sure" (1953: 239). The lesson here is that acquiring a taste for something is not a solitary process. We learn the criteria for what is good and what is not from others and then seek their verification to see if we have responded appropriately.

Once acquired through socialization, tastes are stored deep. This is the basis of the concept of "habitus" as articulated by sociologist Pierre Bourdieu (1984). He argued that people are socialized into different sets of tastes, skills, and knowledge depending upon the socioeconomic strata they occupy. These preferences—habituated through lifelong practice—become embodied, more corporeal than cognitive. Sitting down to eat each evening becomes another class in which parents teach their children how and what to consume, so that "each time the lesson is laid down once again, the skills are embedded deeper and deeper into who they are" (Khan 2011: 92). In the case of "foodies" (Johnston and Baumann 2015), knowing the right farmer from which to buy the right produce during the right season is a skill and ability that requires practice and repetition—to the point of becoming taken for granted.[9]

There is one shortcoming with the concept of socialization when it comes to explaining taste, however. It is easy to see how children inherit their parents' tastes, but how do we explain shifting tastes *between* generations? Eating practices in America have clearly changed. Many of my older interviewees reported having different food preferences than their parents had. They liked some similar flavors and types of dishes, but in pre- or par-cooked form. In other words, they were socialized into one set of kitchen practices, yet grew up to prefer another. This poses an interesting theoretical question: How can people raised on home-cooked meals grow up to be adults who rarely cook?

According to Bourdieu, the answer lies in changes to their material circumstances. That is, taste does not flow from the inside out, but from the outside in. Those without economic means will develop a "taste of necessity" or a taste "for what they are anyway condemned to" (1984: 178). From this perspective, taste is "a forced choice, produced by conditions of existence which rule out all alternatives as mere daydreams" (Bourdieu 1984: 178). Clearly the habitus of food desert residents has changed in response to their "conditions of existence," but how?

To explain, I will focus on how the changing conditions within the home interact with the wider food environment, namely greater relative access to unhealthy and processed foods. These shifting conditions cannot produce changes overnight; our food preferences move slowly because they are bound to our primary cravings, aversions, and cultural moorings. But the new social arrangements and material world we have created for ourselves has been pulling us toward a taste for convenience for decades.

Access

America is undergoing a fundamental shift in how people eat; a change that is bigger than just food deserts. In 2010, for the first time in history, Americans spent more money on food prepared outside the home than on food prepared inside the home (Elitzak and Okrent 2018). Additionally, the National Center for Health Statistics recently found that "36.6% of adults consumed fast food on a given day" (Fryar et al. 2018). These figures roughly match the behaviors of my interviewees, 41 percent of whom reported eating food from some type of restaurant (sit-down, take-out, or drive-through) at least twice in the past week.

How did "convenience" become so paramount? Our circumstances changed. As previously mentioned, household sizes have decreased, and parents now feel more pressure to serve their children "kids' food" (Elliot 2011). Much of this type of food is already in "convenient" form or cooked as a different dish. These factors, combined with the fact that our "free time" has diminished considerably (Hochschild 1997; Schor 1992), have made the traditional grocery store model less efficient for many individuals and families. Remember, the economy of scale of cooperative meal preparation and consumption hinges on the presence of multiple people with the same tastes. Without several mouths to feed (the same dish), cooking raw or unprocessed ingredients becomes less time and cost effective.

The food environment also changed. As detailed already, in the 1960s the grocery store industry began to shift to a business model based on "scale"; this entailed low-margin transactions at a high volume in large stores restocked with bulk deliveries (Deener 2017). The site demands of these operations required relocation to bigger-box stores on the periphery of cities. For their customers, as transportation time and costs to travel to groceries stores increased, so did the attractiveness of "one-stop shopping." Food processing has also changed the landscape of options available in these stores. Food scientists have refined their ability to target our most basic biological cravings with pre- and par-cooked convenience foods (Moss 2013; Lawless 2018).

These innovations have meant increased exposure to foods that can manipulate our taste receptors combined with a deprivation from nearby "slower" foods. These social trends have consequences. Americans' preference for "convenience" did not occur in a vacuum.

According to social theorists, the idea that values are produced by "conditions of existence" (Bourdieu 1984) is what is classically called a "materialist" approach. Not all scholars agree, but this approach is particularly well-suited to explaining how changes in resources (for better or worse) can change cultural values over time. It shows us how the values we cite to explain our behaviors are a *response* to the conditions in which we live.[10]

Among sociologists, this materialist approach is most often used to explain how shifts in economic conditions can change people's values toward work and family life. William Julius Wilson used this perspective to explain how the depletion of urban manufacturing jobs in the 1970s and '80s produced hopelessness and despair, or what some politicians and pundits refer to as a "culture of poverty." However, instead of claiming poverty is caused by "laziness," a materialist approach takes the opposite view. From this perspective, "cultural values emerge from specific circumstances and life chances and reflect an individual's position in the class structure" (Wilson 1987: 158). In this sense, people's values are created and shaped by "changes in the economic and social situations" (159) in which they live.

A materialist approach is also able to explain how values can change across generations. If one generation grows up in a healthy economy, but the next does not, the principles of the past can become less persuasive to the children of today. In one study of the consequences of American urban decay, sociologist Elijah Anderson found that "When gainful employment and its rewards are not forthcoming, [younger generations] easily conclude that the moral lessons of the [older generation] concerning the work ethic, punctuality, and honesty do not fit their own circumstances" (1990: 72). In regard to the importance of cooking, many of my older interviewees reported growing up in a world in which "eating in" was a cherished childhood memory. But nostalgia was not enough to keep the tradition alive amid all the challenges to home food preparation in their adult lives.

The materialist view allows us to see that food desert residents are *innovative* and resourceful. They must slalom the shifting constraints in their path, not all of which involve price and proximity. For example, recent research on food preferences of the urban poor found that, if given the possibility, they prefer corporate brands, even though they are more expensive. That's because consuming name-brand food is one of the few ways marginalized people can feel like they are part of the cultural mainstream (Baumann, Szabo, and Johnston 2019). Similarly, research on fast food workers found that they ate what was on offer at work partly because of their employee discount and partly because their work and school schedules left little other time to eat (Woodhall-Melnik and Matheson 2017). Materialists do not have to blame the poor for buying name brands and eating fast food, instead we can acknowledge their resilience in the face of daunting circumstances.

It would be nice if instantly making healthy food more accessible could impact on our taste for convenience, but the pace of change will likely be measured in generations. Recall that I've referred to this as a "durable" taste for convenience.

Consider initiatives to alleviate the educational gap in areas of concentrated poverty. In one study of Black children in very poor neighborhoods, researchers found that "exposure to concentrated disadvantage [has] detrimental and long-lasting consequences for black children's cognitive ability, rivaling in magnitude the effects of missing 1 year of schooling" (Sampson, Sharkey, and Raudenbush 2008). When a government program intervened and moved them to better neighborhoods, the negative effects still lingered: "the strongest effects appear several years after" (852). This means it took students transplanted to better neighborhoods years to catch up with the kids who were born there. This lagged effect helps explain why retail interventions in food deserts have so far failed to change eating habits. Our taste for convenience has become embedded and embodied. It is not going away anytime soon. Change takes time. A long time.

CONCLUSION

When I started my research in 2014, I wanted to believe that a closer grocery store could lead people to eat healthier food. I thought that was what the debate over food deserts was all about. And I was wrong. Although dietary change was possible, the people I interviewed saw an overhaul as impractical and—more importantly—undesirable. When I pressed on whether a new store would change the way they ate, the vast majority said that it would not. If a new store arrived, they would switch if it sold the same products at similar prices. That way they could save time and money. Hypothetically, these savings could free up their budget to buy more expensive, healthier products and free up their schedules to prepare them at home. But that is not what they wanted. They liked what they were currently buying and eating. They were pragmatic, and their current diets were their best solution given their preferences and circumstances.

While most media accounts of food deserts depict residents as passive victims to their food environments—pitiable prey to the cheapest and closest options—I heard a different story from my interviewees. Among those who were participants in the retail food market, getting to the grocery store was difficult, but not impossible. Because the public transportation system was so inadequate, they developed alternative paths. They put their social capital to work and cultivated informal ride networks to get themselves to and from the store. Those rides came at a cost, both economical and emotional, but they made it work: a testament to their innovation and resiliency. However, I also learned that getting to a store and wanting to buy healthier food from one are two different things.

Food desert residents, like most households in America, increasingly see the traditional grocery store model of home cooking as simply not worth it. Raw or unprocessed ingredients require time and coordination within the household to cook and prepare. Interview after interview, I kept waiting to document the familial, home-cooked meal that our culture values so highly. It is just too difficult to manage.[11] To make it worthwhile, a household needs enough people at the table, at the same time, with the same tastes. Those odds are too steep for people living alone, people feeding themselves one thing and their kids another, and people who live under the same roof but have different dietary needs.

The decline in home cooking was not paired with a decline in supermarket usage. With the exception of the truly poor, who relied almost exclusively on donated food, my interviewees still bought food in supermarkets. But if they were not planning to cook raw ingredients from scratch, what exactly were they buying? Convenience.

In the second half of this chapter, I explained why inserting full-size grocery stores in food deserts has not yet changed eating habits. This is because food desert residents, and roughly the one-third of Americans who consume fast food on a daily basis (Fryar et al. 2018), have developed a durable taste for convenience foods. That taste has several underpinnings: basic biology, for one, has programmed species-wide preferences for foods marked by salt, sugar, and fat. They are calorie-dense and likely safe, while bitter and unfamiliar foods can signal potential danger and require habituation to become preferences.

Even though cravings are hardwired, they are also malleable. They can be moderated through socialization. We can learn to avoid certain foods, and we can work to acquire tastes for others. Some processed foods, for example, can manipulate our brains into ignoring signals that we are full, and exposure to flavors in utero can create tastes that remain after birth.

So all humans have the same basic sensory framework, yet cuisines evolve and vary across time, place, and culture. These food cultures remain distinct through the process of socialization. Every generation passes down cultural lessons about how and what "people like us" eat. The content of those lessons, and their changes over time, led me to discuss the effects of material access—how changing "conditions of existence" change food values.

We live in a food environment of our own making. Processed foods manipulate our biological reward centers and deplete our food environment of the healthiest options. These changes have consequences, one of which is a taste for convenience that feels so natural, so embodied, that its origin goes unquestioned. But it is worth asking where it came from.

Once I understood that what the fight for grocery stores was not about (wanting to eat differently), I could see it for what it really was (retail inequality). Missing supermarkets were a proxy for a bigger complaint about what could be bought and sold in their neighborhoods. Coming to this conclusion enabled me to watch the public debate about food deserts with new eyes.

During my research, I spent more than five years attending neighborhood meetings, town halls, and citywide events related to food access and the "revitalization" of the west side of Greenville. That public pleas for a grocery store sounded different from private accounts of my interviewees' actual eating habits became almost embarrassingly clear once I thought about it alongside the history of retail inequality and racial segregation, rooted in not-so-distant incidences of outright discrimination, the concentrated poverty attesting to past abandonment by the public and private sector. Today, when it comes to food retail, residents fight this battle by subjecting retailers to the "healthy food" test—not because they necessarily want to eat it, but because this test lays bare a business's true intentions: *Do you want to make the community a better place, or do you just want to make money?* Watching this fight play out in public for years, I—once a true believer in the possibility of food desert interventions—was surprised to learn that being seen as "good retail" did not necessarily require selling healthy food. Businesses earned good will when they worked with the neighborhood residents, told them the truth, listened to their requests, and treated them as partners. It wasn't about healthy food; it was about fairness.

After interviewing food desert residents in their homes about how they found a way to buy and consume food, I came to respect their problem-solving strategies. The logic of their food consumption practices was governed by their everyday realities. The residents of Southernside and West Greenville wanted a new grocery store. A nice store. One that would make it quicker and cheaper for them to check off the items on their list. But they had no real intention to reallocate those savings in time and money to healthier items that were more expensive and took more time to prepare. What they wanted was better retail, an investment in their community.

In private, during their interviews, the vast majority of my interviewees did not see their food environment as the main driver of their eating practices. Their routine obligations (doctor's appointments, family visits, church services) carried them across the path of grocery stores multiple times per month. They wanted to eat better, and many had diet-related health problems. Still, few intended on making wholesale dietary changes anytime soon. Their lives were complex, and the entrance of a new store was just one of a number of things that would have to change. They certainly did not plan to start cooking exclusively from scratch—the one dietary practice that only grocery stores can enable.[1] They needed a better

118

bargaining chip—a more attention-grabbing one that tugged at the heart-strings of potential allies—to change the bigger problem of retail inequality.

It took me years before I felt confident enough to write this: the healthy food frame is largely a political tactic used by community leaders in food deserts to get the attention of outsiders. At first, I assumed this disconnect between what I was hearing in private interviews versus what I observed during public meetings was my misunderstanding. Maybe I, as a white man, had missed what my mostly Black interviewees were trying to say. I had been doing research in these neighborhoods for years by this point, yet it would be silly to believe that familiarity could erase the tensions sur-rounding race and gentrification that simmer in Greenville, South Caro-lina. Maybe I was asking the wrong questions. I had asked about their health during our interviews, expecting—but not getting—fuller accounts of what these residents had told reporters and city officials. Or maybe they were not telling me the truth?

So, to make sure, one last time, I made a plan. When someone I inter-viewed spoke out in a meeting or forum, I followed up privately. If their public comments seemed inconsistent with what they told me privately, I asked about it. After doing this a few times, I finally saw through the talking points to the core complaint.

What I learned—and what most outsiders fail to recognize—was that their pleas for a grocery store are only the latest iteration of a long-standing grievance about what can (and cannot) be bought in their neighborhoods. When the manufacturing sector started to collapse and cities in the United States started to decline in the 1960s and '70s, a decision was made by local, state, and federal governments: abandon the urban center. The public and private sector divested from neighborhoods like Southernside and West Greenville, redirecting those resources to the city periphery. Suburban development drained whatever tax base these Black neighborhoods had left, and large-scale retail on the outskirts devoured the remaining mom-and-pop stores. The language of these decisions may have used color-blind terms, but their consequences were plain to see: racially segregated and concentrated poverty. This void of investment created a vacuum that was filled by "bad retail" like liquor stores and pawn shops. Today, people in food deserts make the best of these inherited circumstances, but their inge-nuity should not erase the historical legacy of this institutionalized neglect.

In the past, few powerful people took these neighborhoods and their grievances seriously. When local leaders started translating their lack of good retail into the language of health and food, new allies gained interest. Arguing for better access to nutritious food opened up recruitment channels throughout other social movements, and public health and "foodie"-oriented nonprofits answered the call.

Let's be honest: the healthy food frame brought more white people to the table. Political capital came with them. The disconnect between my interviewees' public and private accounts was not deception, it was strategy. And it works. It is the best tactic these neighborhood residents have for addressing retail inequality.

THE PUBLIC SIDE OF THE FOOD DESERT DEBATE

Starting in 2014, I began attending any public meeting or forum that might touch upon the food desert debate in Greenville. These events include the monthly meetings of the Southernside and West Greenville neighborhood associations.

Neighborhood meetings were supported by the city, which used Community Development Block Grant funding to pay staff to attend, provide logistical support, share information, and gather feedback. The meetings were slightly formal affairs where minutes were read and motions were seconded. In exchange for residents' efforts to attend and contribute to these meetings, the associations become eligible for small improvement grants from the city to pay for things like playground equipment and park benches. At a typical meeting, a police officer would deliver a monthly crime report, and a firefighter would announce how to obtain free smoke detectors. Politicians might make pitches and answer questions about their platforms. And usually, a couple dozen people attended. Larger, citywide proceedings drew crowds in the hundreds. Occasionally, controversial topics would arise and local media would attend. News coverage was helpful, and I cite it in this chapter where possible. These journalistic accounts enabled me to verify my observations as well as keep track of the media framing of the food desert issue.

I attended and took notes during roughly fifty such meetings and forums from 2015 through 2019. I went to more events than that, but some of them were social functions—like holiday parties and community dinners—that were more for building fellowship than conducting research.

I outline my methods here because my argument in this chapter hinges primarily on the public accounts I heard during them. Members of the neighborhood associations knew about me and my work—I generally became known as "the professor doing the grocery store study"—while at citywide forums, I tended to blend into the crowd. Whatever the venue, these were not secret gatherings. They were public and for a purpose: for neighborhood members to receive information from public officials and submit their feedback for the record.

Admittedly, the people I listened to at these gatherings are not statistically representative of their entire community. Public events attract a self-selected sample—the most politically mindful and time-rich members of the community. That they knew the time and place when these meetings were held was in itself an indicator of their civic engagement. They often had strong opinions (positive and negative) as well as the time and energy necessary to try and make their community a better place. Even if the demographics were skewed, though, the message they delivered was important and represented the concerns of not only themselves, but their neighbors and families. Their strategies can shed light on how social problems are solved in America today.

The public side of the food desert debate is also important because it offers a way to walk through the history of this struggle. Fighting for better services and amenities was a familiar battle to this side of town. The older Black residents of Southernside and West Greenville remember the civil rights movement vividly. Greenville, hometown of Jesse Jackson, civil rights leader and one-time presidential candidate, saw many protests, including some of the first lunch counter sit-ins. Southernside resident and city council member Lillian Brock Flemming was a member of the first graduating class to include Black students at nearby Furman University (where I teach). Keep in mind, she graduated in 1971. Segregation was not something she read about in history books. She lived it.

I will detail the particulars of Greenville in more detail later in the chapter. Until then, consider America's struggles with racism and poverty as the backdrop for today's fight over food access. The term *food desert* may be new, but the base issue—retail inequality—is not. The public voices I heard here in the 2010s echoed many of the rhetorical strategies of the 1960s.

The "Healthy Food" Frame

Frames help us organize what we see and hear. As I have noted in earlier chapters, particularly as I dug into media accounts, when we observe a pattern, *frames* help us answer, "What is this a case of?" But choosing the right frame is important.

Only the right frame will resonate with outsiders so that they understand and care about an issue. Community leaders who wish to motivate others to join their cause must find a frame that will "align" with the wider public's "interests, values, and beliefs" (Snow, Baker, et al. 1986: 464). Once adopted, the right frame can help leaders and members alike to draw the same conclusions and speak the same language. When trying to get a grocery store, the healthy food frame encouraged people to see distance to supermarkets as not just a drain on people's time and money, but also a drain on individual and public health.[2]

The healthy food frame already had a track record of success. The term *"food desert"* was coined in the west of Scotland in the 1990s, but it quickly took root in American politics. Advocacy organizations, like the Food Trust in Philadelphia, began promoting the idea that food deserts caused poor health outcomes through statewide and (later) nationwide campaigns. Their efforts paid off. The creation of the Pennsylvania Fresh Food Financing Initiative sparked a number of other statewide initiatives. And perhaps the best indicator that the healthy food frame got attention and spurred change was the passage of the federal Healthy Food Financing Initiative in 2010. It would provide over $200 million in grants and subsidies to organizations across the country over the following ten years, all pointed at healthy food access.

Frames also provide direction on what *not* to say. In Southernside and West Greenville, publicly voicing the healthy food frame meant keeping quiet about personal practices and beliefs that might contradict it. As discussed in chapters 3 and 4, distance was not the primary determinant of where people shopped, much less which items they bought when they did. Despite probing questions, hardly any of my interviewees viewed their current retail options as the cause of their health problems or believed that a new store would change their diet. A new store would make their lives much more convenient. However, "inconvenience" does not have the same political currency that "poor health outcomes" does. To be sure, 22 percent of the eighty-five people I interviewed told me—unprompted—that they wanted a new grocery store because it would help *others* in their neighborhood access a healthier diet. Their "not for me, but others" sentiment is admirable; it is also off-message. Best to keep to the simple line during public discussions.

The next step is to refine and condense the frame. During neighborhood meetings, whenever residents were given the chance to state their stance on the lack of grocery stores, the discussion nearly always drifted into a debate about which brand of store that served the region was the best. I witnessed this time and time again. The primary mid- and full-size grocery stores in Greenville at the time of my research included the Publix, Ingles, BI-LO, Sav a Lot, Walmart (both their Supercenter and Neighborhood Market storefronts), Aldi, and Lidl brands.[3] Some were more upscale (e.g., Publix) and others were discount providers (e.g., Sav a Lot). But again, the long-winded conversations debating their relative merits were not providing the sorts of clear talking points that politicians can act upon.

To keep things simple, more politically savvy community members began to teach their neighbors how to streamline their message. For example, when the longtime Southernside neighborhood association president, Mary Duckett, wanted the group to make a collective statement of their desire for a grocery store for the benefit of city representatives in attendance, she asked for a quick show of hands. What followed was a loud and lengthy debate about *which* store they should demand. I clocked the discussion, still going strong after ten minutes, turning over the pros and cons of each brand and their respective sizes, degrees of cleanliness, varieties of offerings, customer service, and so on. Their city council member, Lillian Brock Flemming, stood and quieted the group, "Keep it simple." She instructed her neighbors to just say, "'We want a store.'" Sensing confusion, she tried again, pausing between each word: "We need a grocery store." She implored the others not to get mired in the details, especially when speaking as a group. She, and her mother before her (Landrum 2019), had been fighting for the neighborhood for decades. She knew strategy.

Community leaders shifted the focus to which *type* of store. There was a clear difference between "good" and "bad" retail in the eyes of residents. When it came to asking for a grocery store, they reminded their neighbors that offerings had to be healthy. I saw this framing practice firsthand when I was invited to speak to a senior housing tenant association. One of the most vocal advocates for a grocery store was the group's president, Shirley, who asked me to come share what I had learned from my interviews and research on the topic.[4] (You may remember Shirley's plea for a grocery store at a community meeting in chapter 1). The group met in an old house that served as a community center. It was a lunchtime meeting and sandwiches and drinks were served on Styrofoam plates and cups. When we finished eating, I delivered a fifteen-minute presentation about the origins of the term *food desert* and the current attempts to fix the problem. I brought my recruitment materials, hoping to schedule in-depth interviews with as many attendees as I could.

After my short talk, when the conversation drifted predictably to a debate over the merits and flaws of every store brand in the area, I was unable to recapture the room's attention. Everyone had an opinion, and—being senior housing—no one was in a rush to adjourn. It wasn't my place to interrupt, so I sat and waited. After several minutes, the male director of the community center rose to speak. The chatter hushed as he calmly intoned, "People in Southernside want the same things that people in white neighborhoods want. We want healthy, fresh, and affordable groceries." Respectfully, the crowd nodded in silence.

This momentary lull seemed like a good point to pitch my research project and ask who might want to participate in an in-depth interview. I began by explaining that I wanted to learn their personal preferences—even if they might want something different than what other neighbors want. I held the floor for approximately fifteen seconds before the director stood again. He cleared his throat, looked to me, then looked to the crowd, steadily saying, "We want healthy, fresh, and affordable groceries." He knew how to give a sermon. Everyone seemed to catch on, nodding their heads in agreement. One feisty resident proclaimed that if a new store were too expensive, she would keep shopping at a Walmart three miles away. The director sighed, "Let's not lose track of the bigger picture. If something is five cents cheaper somewhere else, but you have to pay [bus fare] to get there, then it doesn't make any sense." Heads nodded. They got the message.

After I left the meeting, I looked for more information about the center director. I had seen him at a few neighborhood functions before, but at that point in my research I had not realized how important a figure he was in the community. He was the Reverend J. M. Flemming. Not only the husband of Lillian Brock Flemming, the city council member who had been keeping the Southernside meeting message on script, but also the president of the local chapter of the NAACP. Together, they were one of the most experienced couples in the neighborhood when it came to politics. These two knew what it would take to attract a store: consistent and simple messaging. Patiently and steadily, they were teaching their neighbors how to win at politics.

THE "HEALTHY FOOD" FRAME IN ACTION

Despite their refinement and practice of the healthy food frame, some residents still had a hard time applying it when it mattered. This is understandable. First, it is not easy: even professional politicians have a hard time staying on point. Second, residents had competing interests. Yes, they wanted a nice grocery store, and nice stores sell healthier foods. No, they did not plan to change their diets significantly or start buying healthier food if a new store came. They liked the foods they currently ate. Put together, what they really wanted was a store that offered their community the *opportunity* to buy healthy food, even if they might not personally take advantage of it. That argument is too complex to fit in a short soundbite. It also admits that they like to eat unhealthy food from time to time.

These competing interests—and the inconsistent messaging that could result—were rarely aired in public hearings about zoning changes or proposals for retail projects. At these events, residents spoke the most and their voice really could have an impact. Within the city limits of Greenville, getting permission to build or dramatically renovate commercial real estate in designated "redevelopment" zones required soliciting feedback from the neighboring communities and giving them a chance to ask questions and voice their concerns. A negative vote from the neighborhood did not automatically cancel a project, but it was an important strike against its approval.

Keep in mind, residents' skepticism toward new development was also the result of decades of struggle in Southernside and West Greenville. It had taken decades to pass a number of "down zoning" ordinances to keep pawn shops, tattoo parlors, bars, and "head shops" out of their neighborhoods. Those battles had been won. However, from residents' perspective, the fight was not over. If you wanted to do business in their backyard, you needed to answer their most fundamental question: "Do you care about *us*?" For developers to prove they cared, they had to address the community's concerns. Asking about the impact on neighborhood health was the litmus test that brought out business's true intentions.

In 2018, when out-of-state corporate developers stated their plan to build a restaurant on the edge of West Greenville, they came to the monthly neighborhood meeting to outline their designs. They brought posters with curiously vague architectural renderings and promotional materials that highlighted the jobs the building project and resulting restaurant would bring. Strangely, the lead representative of the group avoided mentioning the actual name of the restaurant for the first fifteen minutes of his team's presentation, instead repeatedly referring to the company's nationwide track record of building restaurants, giving the impression that they varied in style and offerings. Eventually, when he was pressed for specifics, he admitted that his corporation had one job: it built Burger Kings.

The health frame emerged quickly. When the floor opened to questions, a white woman stood and stated her "health concerns" about the food sold at Burger King.[5] A representative from Greenville County's Democratic Party came next. A Black man in his twenties, Jalen Elrod first mentioned his family's deep roots in West Greenville. It was immediately apparent he knew politics. He detailed his opposition to the project "from a public health perspective." The presenter countered, "I beg to differ that we don't sell healthy food," then implied that it was people who add "extra garnishes" that make their food unhealthy. Elrod folded his arms, unimpressed. He took a long pause, allowing the room to look his way, building anticipation. Then Elrod quietly snickered, smiled, and shook his head. In unison, the crowd turned their gaze back to the corporate rep. Visibly flustered, he switched tactics and asked the audience if anyone had a niece or nephew who might like a job.

The longest confrontation came from Viola, a Black woman in her fifties. Viola lived next door to the proposed site and, though she agreed more jobs in the neighborhood would be a positive step, she was more worried about trash and noise. She made no mention of the food Burger King sold. That wasn't surprising to me; when I had interviewed Viola a few months earlier, she admitted that she ate at fast-food or take-out options at least twice a week. In that private conversation, I asked what sort of food retail she'd like to see in West Greenville. She responded, "Maybe a pizza or sandwich shop, because from what I understand, pizza delivery don't come to this area, so we would have to go get it." In other words, Viola was not opposed to fast food, but to the discriminatory delivery practices of certain chains. What they sold was less important than their refusal to *accept her money* if she wanted to buy it.[6] After the meeting, I checked in with Viola. She told me she did not mind what Burger King sold, what she did mind was the consequences of living next to one: trash, noise, and traffic. At the end of the meeting, a vote was held: three in support of the project, thirty-seven against.

Jalen Elrod, who'd so effectively embarrassed the corporate representative in the meeting, spoke to a reporter from the local FOX affiliate afterward. On the news broadcast that evening, the young man argued that any potential jobs at Burger King would only pay minimum wage and that fast food was at the root of the poor health outcomes in communities like West Greenville. "Burger King does not provide healthy food options and lower-income communities are more enabled to suffer from obesity and putting a fast-food restaurant here would just contribute to that. . . . We would like to see something like a grocery store" (Styles 2018). He knew how to stay on message and leverage the political power of appeals to healthy food.

The healthy food frame served as a litmus test for people who wanted to do business in Southernside and West Greenville. Not all passed. When one business came to the neighborhood with plans to develop a small "mixed use" development on the edge of West Greenville, the project representative was caught flat-footed. She was asked about how her development would improve the well-being of the neighborhood. She showed renderings of a large building with retail on the first floor and condominiums on top. With residential units priced in $300,000s, it was clear her group was not targeting community members as buyers (the neighborhood's median household income was roughly $20,000 per year at the time). Sensing misgivings in the room, she insisted that the development would provide much-needed office space for area entrepreneurs. A resident questioned whether this meant some space would be open to the public, to which the representative stammered, "Yes, if you lease it." A groan flooded the room. The representative tried to recover and asked the crowd what kinds of businesses they would *like* the development to include. Eva, from the back of the room, yelled, "What about a grocery store?" Again, the representative was caught off guard.

From her printed materials, it was clear that the proposed commercial suites were less than two thousand square feet each. In a city the size of Greenville, no grocery store would move into such a small space. I knew this, the developer knew this, and it turned out that Eva knew this, too. I flagged her down after the meeting for a frank but friendly conversation. Eva, a forty-five-year-old Black woman, occasionally worked at a local recreation center where I use the gym, so I knew her a little better than most of my interviewees. When I pressed her why she asked about a grocery store in a space so small, she just shook her head, "It's in our neighborhood, but we can't even enter it." Eva knew the developer had no plans for a grocery store. She just wanted to make a point for the record. In public. And it worked. With that whiff of neighborhood opposition, the proposal stalled and was eventually withdrawn. In this case, the healthy food frame helped expose the myth that the project was "for" the neighborhood.

Retailers with more experience interacting with neighborhood residents were better prepared to pass this sort of healthy food test. Two gas station/convenience store chains served West Greenville and Southernside—one a large regional and the other a statewide chain. When the statewide chain wanted to tear down and rebuild one of their locations, a company representative sought a letter of approval from the West Greenville neighborhood association. He came to the meeting and made his pitch to the audience. Much of it described plans for new food offerings.

Clearly, this rep had been to community meetings before. He knew how to work the room. When questioned about healthy offerings, he quickly pulled out a rendering of the new interior design of the store, pointing to a refrigerated station that would "offer fresh foods, salads, sandwiches, and apples." He outlined the expansion of healthy food options in a quick and rehearsed fashion. Having passed their test, residents nodded in quiet approval. However, something interesting followed. Sensing the quiet in the room, he hinted that the chain's familiar favorites—even if unhealthy—would still be offered. Smiles and chatter spread across the room. Responding to this approval, he joked, "we move a lot of chicken tenders out of that location." And a wave of laughter rolled through the crowd. A reward for his honesty.

When the larger regional chain sought approval from the Southernside neighborhood to build a new location a mile away, its representative was similarly savvy about straddling residents' competing demands. He served as the chain's ambassador to the association, regularly attending its meetings and cookouts and donating gift cards for holiday parties. In his pitch, he was upfront: healthy options earned community goodwill, but unhealthy options paid the bills. During the Q&A, Southernside residents pressed for evidence that the store *would* stock healthy food. He responded by listing the "healthier" energy bars on the shelves and the bananas near the register. Asked whether they could add more fruits and vegetables, he responded with sympathy. His hands were tied, "Everybody says they want healthier food, but nobody buys it." I expected the audience to respond with frustration. Instead, they appreciated his willingness to tell the truth: most nodded and chuckled. Even the revered president of the association, Mary Duckett, stood up for him and playfully conceded that she mostly just purchased pizza at the chain's current locations. When an older, Black attendee urged him to reconsider and add fresh produce people could take home and prepare, the rep asked which specific items she would like to see. The woman, taken aback, had no ready answer. Eventually she admitted that, even if they heeded her request, she was unlikely to buy fresh produce for home cooking: "I don't even cook sometimes because my kids are grown." Once a retailer passed the healthy food test, residents felt free to be more honest about their personal food preferences. She summed up her feelings by saying she wanted the store to sell produce, "not for me, but for others."

Both of the chains' spokespeople had to clear two hurdles at these meetings. First, they had to address the issue of healthy food; that was nonnegotiable. Second, they had to tell the truth. By candidly conceding what their companies lacked in terms of nutritional offerings, they earned the neighborhood's respect. The meaning of food retail in South-ernside and West Greenville was not limited to the sum nutritional value of its offerings. By doing their homework and being honest, company reps could transform locals' perceptions of their chains from "bad retail" to "good retail."

THE CORE COMPLAINT: BAD RETAIL

The healthy food frame was not inauthentic or insincere. Residents were bothered by the dearth of healthy food retail in their neighborhoods. It just wasn't a concern rooted in a desire to overhaul their own diets. Their concern ran deeper than calories. These citizens were upset by the quantity and quality of what could be bought and sold in their community. The fight for a grocery store was a proxy for a bigger battle: retail inequality.

To get a better understanding of what motivates food desert residents to challenge retailers on what kinds of products they offer, it is more helpful to think of fresh fruits, vegetables, and whole foods as symbols. The *option* to buy these items—even if one chooses not to—signifies that one's community has value and worth. The inability to purchase them communicates abandonment and disregard. Thus the types of products and services offered by retailers are understood to reveal their intentions: do they want to make the community a better place, or do they just want to make money?

Listening to residents in private conversations and observing them in public venues, I learned the criteria for what divided good retail from bad in their minds. Much of it is obvious. Good retail is well lit, offers affordable as well as expensive options, and is receptive to neighborhood feedback. Bad retail caters to vice, invites loitering, and exploits the poor. Good retail is operated by and for the community; bad retail is not.

Although most of the criteria for good retail are obvious, some are not. The gas station chains mentioned above proposed new locations or significant renovations during my research. They secured neighborhood good will by showing up at meetings and listening to residents' requests. They were candid about their produce offerings, but they made other concessions. The statewide chain agreed to reduce their outdoor seating. The larger regional chain agreed to only sell beer in six-packs or larger. These concessions can seem counterintuitive. A lot of people would assume that a neighborhood would invite outdoor seating, where shaded benches and picnic tables might allow people to enjoy a meal during their lunch break. From the neighborhood's perspective, however, such amenities were a magnet for loiterers and litter. And to an outsider, selling beer in quantities no smaller than a six-pack would seemingly encourage more drinking. From the neighborhood's perspective, a person buying a six-pack was probably going somewhere; a person buying a single beer was going to hang around and drink it, or perhaps worse, panhandle in the parking lot to scrape up the money to get another one.

The representatives from both chains emphasized intentional design choices and how they reflected neighbors' preferences. They pointed out how their store layouts were designed to cycle people in and out quickly, rather than invite anyone to linger. They underscored their bright lighting as a way to improve public safety. They argued that their staff were trained to act as an extra set of eyes and ears for the police if they saw anything suspicious.

You may have noticed that loitering was a particular sore spot in West Greenville. As mentioned in the previous chapter, the historic Kash and Karry—once the only supermarket on the Black side of Greenville—was now represented in abbreviated name only (Kash & Karry) in the form of a small convenience store at the edge of the neighborhood. Whether in public or private conversations, the residents mainly described the current store as exploitative. In distasteful tones, they said it brought a steady traffic of people buying beer, cigarettes, and lottery tickets. At one neighborhood meeting, one resident asked the community police representative what could be done about the men who milled around the entrance. She called them a nuisance. "I want to be able to walk around and feel safe." She even told the audience that one man had approached her family, asking her daughter, "Are you working today?" They took it to mean the man thought the younger woman was a sex worker. It seemed to this woman that loiterers were drawn to bad retail like moths to the flame.

Once I began to weigh neighborhood complaints against their criteria for good and bad retail, I came to see their deeper frustrations more clearly. It wasn't about particular food items; it was about the long-standing effects of racism and poverty—and whether anyone was going to do something about it. When Southernside residents remarked that there was not a single business that sold vegetables within the neighborhood, but two that sold liquor, they were not necessarily saying that they wanted to make a salad. They were communicating their dissatisfaction with their consumer options. In a newspaper article about an old strip mall purchased and demolished by the city, Mary Duckett was quoted as saying the only acceptable development there "would be an enhancement to the neighborhood and vitally important to the neighborhood." She stressed that a nightclub or bar would be unacceptable. Whatever moved into the area should be similar to the nice options found on Main Street and the east side of town. Southernside and West Greenville, she argued, should be treated like "an extension of downtown," not just a dumping ground for cheap goods and services (Burns 2015).

Vacant storefronts were an eyesore; but residents did not want them occupied by just any business. This meant that new businesses with unfamiliar names weathered skepticism. When I reported at a neighborhood meeting in Southernside that a mini-grocery had opened in a largely empty row of businesses less than a mile from the neighborhood, Mary Duckett narrowed her eyes and asked me if it was another "scam store." I was confused. What did that mean? She explained that, in the past, stores that popped up in that particular location were there to "prey on poor people." I explained that it was a small Latino market that offered a limited variety of produce and fruits, plenty of dried and canned goods, and a wide variety of meats. Although it was clearly marketed toward a small but growing Latino population farther west of the city, the mini-grocery had a small aisle of refrigerated space exclusively for fresh food—something that nearby dollar stores lacked. Attendees shrugged with indifference. To them, it may have been new food retail, but it was not meant for them. During my interviews, no one reported shopping there. It went out of business within a year.

Even large-scale retail investment did not guarantee a positive reaction. When a small brewery and restaurant was proposed on the edge of the Southernside neighborhood, there was immediate pushback from community leaders. Social media posts from people who lived outside the neighborhood hailed the project: it would have filled an empty building and spruced up its surroundings with outdoor seating and fresh landscaping. Local media framed the development in positive terms, as an example of a renewed economic infusion in the area (Turner 2019). At the next neighborhood meeting, however, longtime residents were incensed. Mary Duckett critiqued its placement, next door to a homeless shelter that "ministered to men with addictions." Others at the meeting criticized its location just a few blocks away from the senior housing development (whose tenant association meeting I described earlier). The neighborhood's resident city council member, Lillian Brock Flemming, warned that the brew-pub would clog parking and bring noise late at night. At the end of the lengthy meeting, she stood, the crowd hushed, and Flemming walked everyone through the struggle for better retail, pausing between each sentence to draw out their affirmations: "We know what it used to be like. We don't want to go back to that. We've been trying for years to get rid of the liquor stores and the bars." When she mentioned how that location once housed a small grocery store, a person in the crowd interjected that she had worked at that store as a teenager. The irony of replacing a grocery store with a venue that sold alcohol added insult to the injury of the proposal.

In the following weeks, neighborhood sentiment settled securely on opposition. The proposed microbrewery would be in their neighborhood but not cater to their tastes or interests. Residents saw it as a venue for those who lived on the whiter, "revitalized" part of town to visit, carouse, and leave. The zoning board ruled that the business was technically allowed to operate at the site. Mary Duckett remained stalwart. If she had to, she claimed, she would charter a bus for protestors to go to the state capitol and testify against the brewery's alcohol license application. Neither the first retail battle nor the last they'd fight, this was a win for the neighborhood. They stalled construction, at least for the time being.

What makes retail "good" or "bad" is in the eye of the beholder. Some of the criteria seemed obvious (lighting, variety), others less so (outdoor seating, single-beer sales). Even potentially positive changes, like redeveloping an empty building into an upscale option, could be seen as intrusive and insensitive. The city was starting to change, and longtime residents suspected that the benefits of growth felt on the other side of town would not be felt by them. Real estate prices were rising, gentrification was beginning to accelerate, and if businesses wanted to open in their backyard, they needed to answer a bigger question: "Do you care about *us*? Did you care about *this* neighborhood and about *these* neighbors?"

Historic Origins of Retail Inequality

Southernside and West Greenville had changed a lot over the past fifty years. Up until the last decade, nearly all of that change had been for the worse. The corner stores and mom-and-pop operations had all disappeared. "Their" grocery store closed. What remained were largely undesirable liquor and convenience stores.

These transformations in retail options did not occur in a vacuum. Retail inequality is the modern-day consequence of past "color-blind" public policies that diverted resources away from city centers and carved up the remains in the name of urban renewal. The exodus of "good retail" can also be traced to transformations in the private sector. Originally built around manufacturing jobs, these neighborhoods withered when the jobs left town. Without much consumer buying power, residents left behind could not keep businesses from fleeing to build bigger stores on the periphery of town. "Bad retail" took their place and fed the decay, pushing down property values until they hit rock bottom: setting the stage for the gentrification that followed.

URBAN DECLINE IN POSTINDUSTRIAL AMERICA

There can be no gentrification *without* prior decline. The population of the neighborhoods I studied plummeted for decades until reaching its nadir in 2010 (see Figure 2). The jobs left first. By the 1970s, the occupational outlook in city centers had changed dramatically in the United States, "many blue-collar jobs that once constituted the economic backbone of cities and provided employment opportunities for their poorly educated residents have either vanished or moved" (Kasarda 1989: 28). The United States dominated the worldwide production of steel, iron, coal, and automobiles in the 1950s, but by 1980 relative shares in all these industries had dropped significantly (Perruci et al. 1988). For Greenville, this process played out in the textile mills.

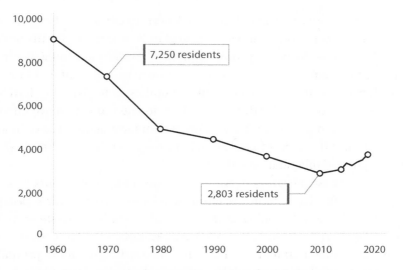

Figure 2. Depopulation of Southernside and West Greenville since 1960.
SOURCE: US Census and American Community Survey 5-year estimates.

Ironically, Greenville initially benefitted from geographic shifts in the industrial landscape. In the early 1900s, textile jobs had crept away from the northeastern "frostbelt" and toward the "sunbelt" where wages were lower and unions fewer (Bluestone and Harrison 1982). Greenville became home to a booming textile trade. The towering red brick mills—proudly bearing names like Monaghan, Poinsett, Judson, and Poe—were hubs of activity. The Woodside mill, located just across the train tracks from the West Greenville neighborhood, was one of the largest operations in the world. But, as the century wore on, globalization and mechanization eventually led to disinvestment and downsizing. By the 1980s, the biggest mills around here had significantly scaled down operations or closed altogether (Huff 1995; Connor 2017).

Manufacturing once employed 30 percent of the working residents of Southernside and West Greenville. That percentage was halved by 2000 and stands at roughly 10 percent today. The exodus of manufacturing jobs was profound across the city, but its western neighborhoods were hit hardest. These jobs had once supported an array of support and service industries. Without those paychecks, consumer buying power sank and retail left.

The expressions of urban decline in American cities varied by the types of jobs lost—automobiles in Detroit, steel in Youngstown. Yet the underlying lesson was the same: people cannot move as fast as capital. Business assets can be liquidated and reinvested elsewhere overnight, but humans take longer to untether from homes, families, schools, and churches. Houses and stores are harder to sell when no one wants to move into the area you're trying to leave. Those who remain have neither the economic incentive nor the means to repair and improve their homes. Wealth withers. Blight and dilapidation follow.

The deindustrialization of American cities hurt all residents to some degree, but Black communities fared significantly worse. This is because "color-blind" racism (Bonilla-Silva 2014) and capitalism operate as "interlocking systems" (Valdez 2011). We have capitalism to blame for the private sector abandonment of Greenville when it became more profitable to automate and ship textile jobs overseas. We have racism to blame for denying Black communities the wealth necessary to rebuild or escape their neighborhoods once decay took root. White households had comparatively more resources to flee to new suburban developments outside of town. And they had some help getting there. Local, state, and federal dollars paved the highways to reach them and subsidized the utility networks necessary to live there (power, phones, water, sewer, etc.). While the public sector was tearing down the deteriorating housing stock in Black neighborhoods, it gave white households with some wealth an off-ramp to start over elsewhere. Across America, a steady flow of "white flight" to the suburbs spanned the 1960s to the end of the twentieth century (Lloyd 2012).

In regard to food retail, the depopulation and wealth depletion of Southernside and West Greenville came at a particularly bad time. The retail industry was transforming. Even if businesses wanted to stay in the neighborhood, they could no longer compete. This is why grocers nationwide were shifting their business model to bigger stores, located on city peripheries, selling at higher volumes (Deener 2017). Hardware and other retail also expanded to the big-box store model and got farther away. The profit imperative at the heart of capitalism is the reason why the manufacturing jobs left *and* why the local stores collapsed. Add municipal disinterest and disregard along racial lines, and you get retail inequality. Black neighborhoods had no say in any of this. In the end, all residents could do was watch as the historic Kash and Karry, once the beacon of this neighborhood's reciprocal investment in the food system, moved from Southernside to a smaller location in West Greenville, then closed for good.

LEGACY OF RACISM

To say that Southernside and West Greenville residents were only upset about their current retail is to ignore the historical roots of the problem. It cast a shadow at public forums and meetings. Leaders and advocates for Southernside and West Greenville rarely mentioned racism at official gatherings, but they didn't have to: everyone already knew the story. It began long before the cloaked and "color-blind" version of racism we know today. The last lynching in the city was in 1947. The civil rights–era lunch counter "sit-ins" occurred downtown in 1960, the same year Jesse Jackson sparked the protest to desegregate the city's public libraries. It would be another decade before Greenville's public schools were desegregated (Huff 1995), and 2015 before Greenville County made Martin Luther King Day an official paid holiday (Bainbridge 2017).

None of this was abstract history to the older Black residents I spoke with privately and listened to at public meetings. They lived through it. For political reasons, they were careful about when and where to voice their suspicions that their poor retail options were a product of discrimination. But for anyone willing to look, the geography of racial inequality in the city was stark. The city's median household income in 2017 was roughly $45,000, but less than half that in the Southernside and West Greenville neighborhoods. Their side of town, near the banks of the Reedy River, was neglected before, during, and after the civil rights era. Population and housing units dropped along the way. Aerial photography of one square block in Southernside shows the difference in housing stock between 1955 and 2011 (Figure 3).

Some removals were due to the demolition of poorly constructed houses in the flood-prone area nearest the river. But it was also the kind of clearing that came with "urban renewal" in the 1960s and '70s.[7] That became even plainer when the same sites were later rebuilt with luxury residences in 2015. The irony of building $400,000 townhomes just blocks

Figure 3. Depopulation of Southernside from 1955 to 2011. SOURCE: City of Greenville, Historical Imagery Viewer; 1955 photo by Farm Service Agency; 2011 photo by City of Greenville.

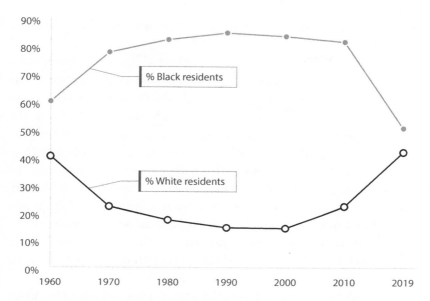

Figure 4. White flight and return. SOURCE: US Census and American
Community Survey 5-year estimates.

from where the city used to park its garbage trucks was not lost on residents who grew up there. The neighborhood was changing rapidly, reveal-
ing Southernside and West Greenville as classic cases of urban decline
leading to eventual gentrification.

Those left behind were generally Black households either unwilling or
unable to leave, especially so in Greenville. By 1990, the poverty rate for
families in Southernside and West Greenville hovered around 30 percent.
The outcome: racially segregated concentrated poverty. It wasn't until
property values hit rock bottom that white families came to see real estate
in these neighborhoods as worthy of investment again (see Figure 4).

The United States has a dark history of residential segregation enforced
by institutionally racist real estate practices. Banks have refused to grant
mortgages in predominately Black neighborhoods ("redlining"), and real-
tors have exploited white residents' fears of potential Black neighbors
in the coded language of "property values" ("block busting") (for more,
see Massey and Denton, 1993: 49–57). A recent investigation by the local
paper found racially exclusive neighborhood covenants—now illegal—still

embedded in the original property documents for homes throughout the city of Greenville (Davis 2018).[8]

After manufacturing jobs, the second-biggest driver of depopulation of this side of town was a pair of large-scale transportation projects. The first, a 1960s urban renewal style highway, the "Downtown Loop," was originally designed to plow through the neighborhood. That meant the city started cutting back on infrastructural maintenance or improvements in the Loop's proposed path. Whole city blocks were demolished to clear space on the northern bank of the Reedy River (Connor 2019). And the Loop was never built. The second major project, Pete Hollis Boulevard, was a six-lane thoroughfare for which the state Department of Transportation had to acquire and carve a path through residential Southernside. Roadway construction might seem unrelated to the issue of food deserts, but stories like these help put the residual frustrations in older residents in context.

And it's a sentiment shared across the nation's poor and nonwhite urban neighborhoods (Bayor 1988; Connerly 2002; Mohl 2000; Wilson 2009). Visually, the phenomenon of building highways and boulevards right through minority residential areas can be stark when you look at traffic maps of places like Camden, New Jersey (Cole and Farell 2006) or the former site of the now demolished Robert Taylor housing projects in Chicago (Biles 2000). As road crews cut through city cores, densely populated, urban, nonwhite communities are hemmed in between major highways and other impassable geographic features (lakes, rivers, rail yards, etc.) (Bullard, Johnson, and Torres, 2004).

Individually, it is difficult to prove that any particular decision to demolish houses or build a road is explicitly discriminatory. However, by viewing them through the lens of "color-blind racism," the consequences clearly affect historically Black communities in greater proportions. "Although these policies were seemingly nonracial, the line here between ostensibly nonracial and explicitly racial is blurred. For example, it could be asked whether such freeways would have also been constructed through wealthier white neighborhoods. In any case, they had a devastating impact on the neighborhoods of black Americans" (Wilson 2009: 29). Such projects have lasting effects on neighborhood residents. They divide and displace families and splinter communities. Decades later,

THE "HEALTHY FOOD" FRAME

residents' caution and skepticism toward municipal leaders should be of little surprise.

LEGACY OF PAST RETAIL BATTLES

Although retail inequality might seem to pale in comparison to injustices like police brutality or mass incarceration, it is no small matter. In America, full citizenship entails equal opportunity to buy whatever products and services one can afford, regardless of race (Parker 2015). Securing the simple right to buy food in the same public sphere as white Americans was the premise of the lunch counter sit-ins of 1960. The national civil rights movement included a number of "retail campaigns" that encouraged community members to "buy Black" by either patronizing Black-owned businesses or boycotting any establishment that only served or employed whites.

In the aftermath of the civil rights movement, opportunities for Black men and women to buy goods and services increased across the nation, but exploitative practices continued. Poor and minority neighborhoods came to be marked by "exorbitant credit fees, exploitative installment contracts, shoddy merchandise, wage garnishment, and nefarious sales practices, such as 'bait-and-switch' advertising, 'pyramid selling' and fraudulent door-to-door selling schemes" (Cohen 2003: 356). Eliminating these duplicitous practices means attacking "bad retail." True retail equality means equal access to "good retail."

In the 1990s in California, retail equality meant having movie theaters and coffee shops. The most famous example was spearheaded by former professional basketball player Earvin "Magic" Johnson. He excoriated the inundation of an "oppressive string of liquor stores, cash checking outlets, and mini-marts" (Simon 2011: 45) that left Black neighborhoods in Los Angeles without quality goods and services. Johnson called out retailers directly, "When they . . . come into urban America, they want to give us a second or third-rate store or second or third-rate customer service. We want everything [the suburbs] have. If you build a store in urban America, we want the same store that you build in suburban America. We want the same service" (Simon 2011: 51).

Which is to say, Black communities—especially those that bore the brunt of depopulation and displacement of urban renewal in the 1960s and '70s—have consistently expressed frustration about what they can and cannot buy in their neighborhoods. In 2015, I heard the president of the Greenville chapter of the NAACP, Reverend J. M. Flemming, instructing the members of senior housing association on public speaking and the need to emphasize that "people in Southernside want the same things that people in white neighborhoods want." It was obvious that he was not just talking about grocery stores. His grievance was the same as Magic Johnson's in Los Angeles and the same as the "retail campaigns" to "buy Black" in the 1960s. It is about fairness. It is about marginalized people asking the companies that want to do business in their neighborhoods, "Do you care about *us*?"

Why Health and Food Frames Work

That complaints about retail inequality got more attention and interest when they were reframed in the language of health and food was, for the residents of these food deserts, a bargain that came with costs. These rhetorical strategies work because they sidestep topics that those in power want to avoid—namely, racism and poverty.[9]

This tactic has produced results. When the White House Task Force on Childhood Obesity issued its report in May of 2010, it signaled that the food desert concept had fully arrived on the political scene. The federal Healthy Food Financing Initiative would come to subsidize and support improving access to better quality food in underserved areas across the country. A scholarly idea accomplished a significant social movement outcome.

To get to this point, the movement needed support. Lots of it. Of course, the people who live in food deserts have the most incentive to help. But what motivates outsiders? Why was the food desert movement able to recruit assistance from a wider base beyond the affected geographies? In chapter 2, I argue that media interest could be traced to increasingly accessible mapping technology, rapidly rising obesity rates, and the fact that the push to fix food deserts shared similar goals with other social movements. But it was the proposed solution to food deserts, a clear-cut goal to bring in more and better retail food options in order to remedy public health for underserved neighborhoods, that drew people to the cause and moved them to action. It certainly caught my interest; it is why I started this research.

Health frames have a proven track record when it comes to pulling the levers of research, funding, and legislation to fix problems in America.[10] Two other major social movements in the United States, campaigns to reduce intimate partner violence and homelessness, leveraged health frames over the past half-century, and their gains can help explain why communities with limited food retail would follow their path. At the same time, the past couple of decades have seen a proliferation of food-related social movements. Their loose "memberships" proved a base ripe for the push for more grocery stores. The food desert concept and the simple interventions that promised a quick fix created an opportunity for those interested in eclectic food issues—predominately white, middle-class Americans—to align with those affected by retail inequality.

Whether intentional or not, the health and food frames were clearly at play in the public forums and meetings when the discussion involved retail. And if these tactics worked, why *shouldn't* residents use them? I felt for them, and I shared their frustration over how long it had taken to get people's attention. They complained about the preponderance of shops that preyed on vice for decades, yet few outsiders cared. When they reframed the same complaint in terms of health and food, people (myself included) and the media started to listen.

SHIFTING THE FRAME TO HEALTH

Let's consider some prior examples of a social problem being reframed in these terms. What we now call intimate partner violence (IPV) and homelessness are both discussed in terms of public health, though previously, they were cast as private troubles with largely private consequences. Once they became framed as public health issues, the wheels of funding, research, education, and action began to turn.

Intimate Partner Violence

Today, the largest institutions devoted to measuring and reducing intimate partner violence are the Department of Justice and the Centers for Disease Control. Respectively, they frame the issue as a crime problem and a public health problem. Prior to the 1960s, the precursors of what became the "battered women's movement" advocated for the simple recognition of "battering" as an illegal act. At the time, hitting one's wife or girlfriend was not seen as immoral, let alone criminal, in the same way as hitting a random stranger was. The growing second-wave feminist movement pushed the criminal justice system to treat violence inside the home just as it would violence outside the home. They argued that male dominance was the root cause of violence against women, within and beyond the family home. As they put it, the personal is political.

At first, only the first of these two frames—abuse is criminal—yielded significant policy gains. Small reforms to the criminal justice system included evidence-based prosecution mandates as well as landmark legislation in the form of the Violence Against Women Act of 1994. The second frame—abuse is a product of patriarchy—floundered. Politicians were far more eager to appear tough on crime than tough on sexism.

Undeterred, movement members have continued to connect IPV to broader forms of gender inequality. They argue that violence against women is symptomatic of cultural values that teach men to exercise "power and control" over others. They debunk myths that abuse is limited to the actions of a few psychologically deranged individuals. Nonprofit women's shelters and rape crisis centers produce educational materials explaining how IPV is an entrenched social problem with broad consequences for the wider community. Despite these efforts, public acceptance of the patriarchy frame remains limited to academic circles and movement organizations (Kolb 2014).

Calls for reform beyond a criminal justice approach gained traction only once the issue came to be framed as a *public health problem*. In 1982, the surgeon general, C. Everett Koop, gave a lecture to the Western Psychiatric Institute arguing that we should diagnose and treat violence, particularly family violence, as a threat to public health (1982). Dr. Koop suggested that relative increases in morbidity and mortality across a wide degree of causes (suicide, homicide) might be related to family violence. *Something* was occurring inside private homes that was producing a more violent society. Along with IPV, he pointed to child abuse and elder abuse as shadowy phenomena onto which light must shine, no matter how taboo the subject matter. This was one of the first times a high-level governmental official identified interpersonal conflict inside the household as a social—not just individual—problem. In 1985, Dr. Koop convened a workshop on violence as a public health problem (US Department of Health and Human Service 1986).

In 1994, the Centers for Disease Control and Prevention (CDC) collaborated with the National Institute of Justice to conduct the first national survey on intimate partner violence, sexual violence, and stalking (Dahlberg and Mercy 2009). The CDC now recognizes "intimate partner violence (IPV) as a serious, preventable public health problem that affects millions of Americans" (Centers for Disease Control and Prevention 2019). The CDC's newfound jurisdiction over IPV is premised on its mandate to study injuries and how to prevent them. Yet, while intimate partner violence results in injury—both physical and psychological—its categorization alongside car accidents and playground safety is a far stretch from feminists' original analysis.

By the 2000s, the health frame was fully embedded in policy and research approaches. In 2006, the Robert Wood Johnson foundation and the Prevention Institute convened a seminar of leading scholars to chart a path toward a holistic, nationwide approach to reducing IPV. Their proposal urged "reframe[ing] the desired outcome of change as healthy behavior and healthy communities . . . [and] encourage new narratives about gender, power and relationships" (Parks, Cohen, and Kravitz-Wirtz 2007: 5). This was getting closer to the original plea from the battered women's movement to end sexism in all forms, but it aimed to make change by leveraging the more potent political capital reserved for improving public health and safety. Evidently, there is more political will for creating "healthy communities" than smashing patriarchy.

Homelessness

The fight to end homelessness is another social movement that experienced a surge in political capital once the problem was reframed in the language of health. The current usage of the term *homelessness* (and, more recently, *the unhoused population*) did not come into being until the 1980s. Before then, to be "homeless" was commonly understood as displacement via catastrophic disaster or war. As recently as the 1970s, Americans who lived in makeshift shelters or abandoned structures were deemed remnants of the Depression-era "hobos" and "tramps." They were seen as wandering vagrants foolishly recasting their destitution as freedom. Their struggles were dismissed as unfortunate, but also somewhat voluntary. The best solutions offered were soup kitchens and shelters where vagrants could be proselytized to—hear a speech about the value of hard work in exchange for a hot bed or a meal. So long as the problem had individualized causes, charitable solutions were the cure; politically, homelessness would not achieve large-scale governmental reform or social change until the early 1980s (Jones 2015).

The diagnosis of homelessness changed dramatically as the number of people living on the street began to increase in the 1980s. Images of people sleeping in parks and doorways was irreconcilable with any lingering stereotypes about happy, bindle-toting train-hoppers. Journalists and politicians began to search for a cause, which they found in "deinstitutionalization." A handful of influential studies funded by the National Institute of Mental Health linked the increase with the systematic defunding of psychiatric facilities (Jones 2015). In 1982, the *American Journal of Psychiatry* published an article entitled, "Is Homelessness a Mental Health Problem" (Bassuk, Rubin, and Lauriat 1984) traced to Reagan-era budgets and a social movement toward community care rather than institutionalization for the mentally ill and addicted. By the mid-1980s, homelessness was no longer seen as a choice. It was reframed as a consequence of exiling patients from mental health institutions, consigning many to the country's streets and jails.

The concept of deinstitutionalization was useful in ramping up political support to remedy the problem of homelessness. It cast the suffering of mentally ill people as involuntary and unfair. Sociologists call this process the "medicalization" of a social problem. By assigning deviant behavior a medical diagnosis—in this case, mental illness—the person who exhibits it is absolved of responsibility or blame. Thus, claiming that most homelessness could be traced to deinstitutionalization's effects on people with health problems meant the homeless were innocents who deserved political intervention. In their article, "The Myth of Pervasive Mental Illness among the Homeless," a team of sociologists argues that blaming deinstitutionalization also "individualized and depoliticized" homelessness in ways that lowered the possible electoral repercussions for politicians willing to intervene (Snow, Baker, et al. 1986: 420).

All of this diverted attention away from more entrenched social problems contributing to homelessness that would require more systematic and expensive solutions. For example, the economy dipped in and out of recession between 1980 and 1982. Unemployment hovered between 8 percent and 10 percent, inflation increased, and wages stagnated. Reframing the problem as a mental health issue pulled attention away from our beleaguered economy and callous approach to economic inequality. Put differently, "socioeconomic factors—such as the lack of jobs with decent pay, dislocations in the job market, and decline in the availability of low-income housing—tend to be ignored or discounted as the major causes of homelessness" (Snow, Baker, et al. 1986: 420).

Exactly how many instances of homelessness were caused by deinstitutionalization is a question for historians to answer. But the impact of reframing this situation is clear: Politicians were more eager to appear in favor of mental health reform than of alleviating poverty.

Costs and Benefits of the Health Frame

In these two cases, IPV and homelessness, framing the problems in terms of public health proved an effective social movement strategy.[11] Considering these examples sheds light on the strategy behind the fight for retail equality in Black communities. The issue gained little outside interest until the introduction of the food desert concept that focused on opportunities to buy healthy food. In American politics, there is more public willpower to study, legislate, and (hopefully) solve public health problems than to directly address the systemic inequalities that cause them, including patriarchy, poverty, and racism.[12]

SHIFTING THE FRAME TO FOOD

As mentioned in chapter 2, 29 percent of all media accounts about food deserts conflate the issue with other food-related social movements (food waste, food insecurity, local food, non-GMO food, etc.). That makes sense, as contemporary American culture is really interested in all things food (Johnston and Baumann 2015). And the confusion creates opportunities for recruitment. Focusing on shared solutions (more and better retail food options) enables leaders in food deserts to align with almost any other food-related campaign. By sidestepping the racial dimensions of retail inequality, the food desert movement can nonetheless gain allies interested in the similar outcomes. In the terminology of framing, this means putting more energy into "prognostic" frame alignment—*What should we do?*—than "diagnostic" frame alignment—*Who or what is to blame?* (Snow and Benford, 1988).

As a demonstration, I will outline the main food-related movements that have forged alliances with the effort to eradicate US food deserts. This is not an exhaustive census, but a way of showing how a multitude of related social campaigns share a similar prognostic frame. Though they also share a lot of goals, these campaigns nonetheless have important disagreements. Consequently, while the members of these movements bring a lot of political capital to the overarching fight over retail inequality, their priorities can distract from the issues food desert residents are really trying to solve.

Food Security

Food security is the movement most commonly conflated with the problem of food deserts in media accounts. Indeed, living in a food desert can certainly exacerbate food insecurity. And because new food retail opportunities will help reduce some food insecurity, advocates of each have some common objectives in their efforts.

Digging deeper reveals that food security cannot be fully addressed by increasing food retail options. If extra travel costs put groceries out of economic reach, then a closer store could help. But more stores cannot help the abjectly poor. For those well below the poverty line, living next to a grocery store rubs salt in their wounds: it only exposes them to inaccessible options. Further, even if a store could help fight against hunger, food security requires more than calories. People can get enough calories to meet their "dietary energy requirements" without being food secure (Pinstrup-Andersen 2009: 5). Food security requires knowing how and from where the next meal will come and having some say in what's on the menu; it also requires having consistent access to culturally appropriate sources of nutrition (Hamm and Bellows 2003). Attending to such a diversity of cultural tastes may not always satisfy food desert residents. Recall how Southernside neighbors were less than enthused when I informed them of the opening of a small-scale Latino market. To them, it was new food retail, but it wasn't *for* them. As such, it did not satisfy their neighborhood's wish for "good retail."

Food Justice

The food justice movement sets out to solve a number of problems within the production and distribution side of the food system. In general, this movement fights to ensure "economic opportunity, and community-based self-determination" (Broad 2016: 53) with regard to local food systems. Food justice advocates claim that because large companies control the way food is produced and sold in the United States, local workers and consumers are at their mercy. That is, factory farms and big-box stores and fast-food outlets and the people who plan school lunches put profits over individuals' well-being. This problem includes, but is not limited to, the modern phenomenon of large supermarket chains squeezing out smaller competitors, which, as we have seen, is such a thorn in the side of people living in food deserts. Putting grocery stores back in local communities is a solution on which both food justice and food desert movements can agree.

Store placement, however, is where the common concerns largely end. The food justice movement also fights against large agribusiness conglomerates that dictate the terms by which nutritional commodities are bought and sold on a global scale. Its members lobby for reforms that improve wages and labor practices of those who grow the food we eat. They argue that if profit is the driver of the food system, the health concerns of those who pick what we eat can suffer. People who live in and around farming communities should be able to afford the food grown nearby and have a say in how their lands are treated and used (Broad 2016). For members of the food desert movement, the primary concern is whether or not a nearby store sells quality offerings—not necessarily how they are grown or how its harvesters are treated. Many brand-name foods are produced by global corporations, yet food desert residents look for their products—not just generic options—on store shelves. Those big, recognizable names are a sign that the business owners see the locals as equal participants in the retail economy. Residents may not be able to afford to buy these brands, but they appreciate the respect conveyed when businesses at least give them the option of doing so.

Foodies

A more recent entrant among food movements, "foodies" see food as a "subject for study, appreciation, and knowledge acquisition" (Johnston and Baumann 2015: 51). However, who qualifies as a foodie is a subject of debate. The foodie identity is not defined solely by what one eats, but rather how one acts toward food before, during, and after its consumption. Foodies' modern form of cultural capital (Bourdieu 1984) is acquired through "omnivorous" tastes (Peterson and Kern 1996), which are both highbrow and lowbrow. Their motivations also vary. Some foodies use food to distinguish themselves from others, others' food choices signal their democratic ideals of inclusion and cultural diversity. These latter foodies (Johnston and Baumann 2015) share the most in common with food desert activists. Both groups see more and better retail food options as a means to make the world a better place. Both promote "ethical consumerism" or "lifestyle politics." This strategy requires members to "vote with their fork" and send a political message by "avoiding certain products and patronizing others" (Shah et al. 2007: 222).

Foodies who are motivated to use food as a means of distinction (Bourdieu 1984) share the least in common with food desert activists. Much like advocates of "slow food" (Portinari 1989), these foodies argue that identifying and consuming the highest-quality dishes is worth the extra time and money. Conversely, advocates for better retail in poor Black neighborhoods see foodie retail as catering mostly to white, middle-class newcomers. When a new farm-to-table restaurant opened on the edge of West Greenville (what the city's public relations office called "The Village of West Greenville"), few longtime residents registered its existence. It was nice, but it surely wasn't for them.

Sustainable Food

Advocates for more sustainable food production see large-scale corporate farming as not only bad for the earth, but also for our bodies. They argue that heavy reliance on chemicals and genetic modification in the production of the food we eat poses both known and unknown risks to human health. From their perspective, until we better understand the consequences of industrial farming, less intensive practices are best. These may not be as efficient, but movement members believe there is a benefit to smaller, local operations. Diversifying what is grown and where it is cultivated also creates a more robust food system. It is less profitable, but it is also less liable to cause a wholescale ecological collapse. Thus, sustainability is not solely an environmental concept, but also an economic and health issue.

THE "HEALTHY FOOD" FRAME

Members of the sustainable food movement share interests with those combatting food deserts on the basis that both see our current food system as headed in the wrong direction. They agree that local food production and consumption can keep money in the community. Thus, both can see the value of urban farms, school gardens, farmers markets, and community gardens so long as these efforts can help residents of food deserts save money, improve health, and improve their neighborhoods. And from a sustainability perspective, reduced transportation distances can translate to less energy spent getting people and products to and from the store.

The movements part ways whenever sustainable practices are seen as pushing prices higher or limiting options. Sustainability advocates balk at the idea of importing out-of-season foods from across the globe, yet the food desert residents I interviewed liked year-round availability. To them, abundance and predictability were markers of "good retail." Farmers markets may be a sustainable way to support local agriculture, but the premium costs can exclude low-income customers in ways that look not unlike other symptoms of retail inequality.[13]

Costs and Benefits of the Food Frame

By accepting the help of other food-related movements (food security, food justice, foodies, sustainable food), the effort to solve the food desert problem gained a lot of allies and political energy. All these groups may diagnose the cause of the problems within our food system differently, but they all agree that society can benefit from more and better food options. They also agree on neoliberal solutions to their respective problems, seeing retail reform as an appropriate vehicle for change. What gets lost in this combined effort is the significance of racial inequality embedded in the long-standing fight for better retail amenities. Southernside and West Greenville, like other Black neighborhoods in small cities across the country, are recovering from decades of public and private divestment. If things are going to turn around, they want a say in what "revitalization" will look like. Longtime residents of these places certainly agree with a lot of other food movements' goals, it's just that they *also* have their own priorities. This disjuncture helps explain why the public side of the food desert debate sounds so different than the private side. To recruit people who live outside the food desert, residents need to focus on where they agree (better food and better health) and downplay their differences regarding the root cause of the problem.

CONCLUSION

Interviewing individuals privately, I learned that their food purchasing and eating habits were shaped by complex dynamics bigger than money, transportation, and distance. The people I talked to also decided what, where, and when to eat based on their social capital, household dynamics, and durable taste for convenience. A retail intervention—like installing a supermarket in their community—would improve their life in a number of ways, but these individuals had no compelling interest in changing the way they ate or how they prepared food. Even those with health-related problems knew they *should* make changes to their diet, but their tastes were real; new retail options would not change their embodied preferences or their life circumstances. So why did "healthy food" come up so often at public meetings and forums? And why did members of largely white, middle-class social movements suddenly gain interest in the long-standing problem of retail inequality in Black neighborhoods?

In this chapter I have attempted to put the strategies of the food desert movement into historical perspective. It is not the first movement to shift its frame toward health in order to garner political capital and potential allies. This tactic achieves results. Is it the best approach? In many ways, yes. Complaining about bad retail has only yielded a few small victories in the past—like Magic Johnson's movie theaters and coffee shops. But complaining about *unhealthy* retail kickstarted state and federal programs that have distributed hundreds of millions of dollars in grants and subsidies. Combining the issues of health and food brought even more newcomers to the table. Whatever their differences regarding how the food environment came to be, they could agree on a future marked by more and better food retail.

Now we know why people inside food deserts are speaking out. It's time to see how well outsiders are listening. Let's shift to the perspective of the problem solvers—those new allies working through food-related organizations, speaking at public meetings, local food conferences, and Tedx

Talks. I attended these events, talked to the activists, and even worked on a local farm for a month to test the viability of local farms as a solution to the food desert problem. These helpers sometimes had limited or incomplete knowledge about the lived experience of the people in Southernside and West Greenville, but they were heavily and genuinely invested in trying to improve the food system.

6 The Problem Solvers

By 2010, as the food desert concept began to catch more people's attention, a considerable number of people came to the table to help. Nonprofits and organizations answered the call to improve access to healthy and affordable food in areas of need. They came with good intentions and a number of ideas—some new, some old. It is important to learn more about these problem solvers' perspectives in order to understand why they choose to pursue particular types of solutions. At the very least, if we want to improve the lives of people living in food deserts, we should probably know more about the people who are already trying to help. Their interventions may not be able to change the way people eat, but some of their efforts might alleviate food desert residents' core complaint: the dearth of "good retail" in their neighborhoods.

To understand the goals and motivations of those trying to improve food options, I talked to farmers growing crops on urban city lots, organizers of community gardens, directors of farmers markets, and owners of gas stations. I attended seminars and symposiums on the "local food system," watched local TEDx Talks on how to improve options, and had coffee with people trying to implement new ways of distributing healthy food. Some of these efforts experienced modest success, others dissolved and disappeared.

Successful or not, the people behind these interventions are part of the story of retail inequality in America. They are the ones trying to stock the shelves with fresh and whole foods so that nearby residents can fill their shopping baskets with more nutritious items. Their motivations vary, from altruism to profit. Some were "food desert activists," intentional in their desires to increase access to nutritious offerings. Others did not sign up to fix the food desert problem but were "unwitting bystanders": identified in the media accounts surveyed in chapter 2 as the types of people who *could* be part of the solution.

All of the people described in this chapter saw improving access to better food as a good thing. They openly and honestly wanted to improve the variety, freshness, and quality of food in Greenville, South Carolina. They are the "problem solvers."

I was drawn to this group because I used to be a full-time problem solver myself. In my mid-twenties, I was a Peace Corps volunteer in Paraguay. My job was to learn an indigenous language (Guarani) and teach basic beekeeping skills to farmers in a rural village for two years. Technically, I was an agricultural extension agent, but in more practical terms, I just tried to improve the living condition of the people around me. The beekeeping techniques were not particularly advanced—the modern Langstroth beehive has been around for over 150 years—but they could be scary (like capturing wild hives in the forest). Getting people to adopt these practices required trust and patience. Logical arguments and technical proficiency were not enough; I had to meet the farmers where they were and show them a feasible path forward. During that time, I also developed a new relationship with food. There were no retail supermarkets in that remote area, yet we had an abundance of whole foods.

Fast forward to 2014, when I began my research on food deserts—unaware that the complaints in Southernside and West Greenville were really about retail inequality—and hoped to investigate the feasibility of meeting locals' needs with "local food." The neighborhoods were in the city, but there was farmland as close as ten miles away. In retrospect, I was a perfect example of why so many food desert initiatives fail. My white, middle-class privilege combined with my Peace Corps experience had helped me develop an interest and passion for locally grown food, so when I heard people talking about the lack of grocery stores, I assumed that they wanted what I wanted. I had good intentions; I just did not yet understand the everyday realities of the people I was trying to help or what made small-scale farming economically feasible in America. Eventually, I would figure it out. I was still smart enough to know that I couldn't be sure I had a full picture unless I talked to people who grew food for a living, too.

To assess the potential effectiveness of local food and the myriad other initiatives in action at the time, I will weigh their strategies to provide more nutritious food against the everyday realities of residents that I outlined in chapters 3 and 4. People who live in areas without grocery stores face considerable challenges to obtaining healthy food. Their circumstances, that set of six factors including their perceptions of the food environment, their economic situation, and their transportation options, as well as their social capital, their household dynamics, and their durable taste for convenience, are a mix of opportunities and potential pitfalls.

Trying to increase consumption of healthy food without attending to these circumstances simply won't work—no matter how well-intentioned the effort. A better approach would be to rethink the desired outcome. Remember, food desert residents may not want or be able to easily change the way they eat, but they still want the respect that quality food retail options signify. Food desert residents want retail meant for *them*. Not as outsiders see them, but as they see themselves.

FOOD DESERT FIXES

If you attend a community forum or presentation about how to make healthy food more accessible and affordable, you'll learn that everyone has a better idea. Whenever I discussed my findings with city leaders and policy makers about how hard it was to solve the food desert problem, I was invariably asked, "Has anyone in Greenville ever tried X, Y, or Z?" After a few years of surveying the initiatives and efforts in the area, my response became rote: "Yes, they have." The names and logos were unique to Greenville, but the general tactics were the same as everywhere else.

The spectrum of food desert solutions can be divided into five general categories. These include efforts to (1) buy directly from farmers, (2) provide nutritional education, (3) establish urban agriculture, (4) improve donated food options, and (5) install retail interventions. All were tried in Greenville in some shape or form during my research. Whether they succeeded or failed depends on the outcomes you expect of them.

Buying Directly from Farmers: Greenbrier Farms

Back when I started this project, I wanted to find a way to funnel local food into food deserts. On paper, the idea has promise. When farmers sell their goods directly to customers, they do not have to pass on the costs of shipping, brokerage, and distribution to them. Farmers can get a greater portion of the profits, and customers can get more competitive pricing. And Greenville county is peppered with small and mid-size farms. There are over three hundred working farms within an hour's drive of the city.[1] It seemed plausible that rerouting food from these farms—a relatively quick and convenient solution—could work.[2] I made a trip out to Dacusville, South Carolina, about a dozen miles from the food deserts in Southernside and West Greenville, to see what I could learn.

Greenbrier Farms, a two-family operation, was one of the most popular stands at the downtown Greenville farmers market at the time. When I told the owners about my research project, they quickly agreed to let me work for free in exchange for behind-the-scenes access. I was on sabbatical and I wanted some fresh air. Labor costs were one of their greatest expenses, so an extra set of hands was an appealing offer. I offered to work full-time for a month, and they agreed to be open and honest about their daily routine. Some of the labor on the farm was lightly mechanized (tractors helped clear land, plow soil, and build beds) but most of what I did was manual (hand planting, harvesting, and weeding).

The Greenbrier brand is built around its owners' personalities. Chad Bishop runs the vegetable operation; his wife, Amy, the agritourism side; and their partner Roddy Pick heads up beef and pork production. They are a charismatic trio. On market days, Chad has instant advice on which lettuce to buy, "The buttery is smooth, and the green leaf has a little crunch . . . get both and that way you'll have different colors and textures." Roddy can explain how "intensive grass-finishing" makes for a better steak. For customers with questions about hosting a fundraiser or wedding on the farm, Amy already knows which views your guests will remember most.

Amy's role is significant. For small operations like Greenbrier, selling food is no longer enough to make a living. Many depend on events and tours to survive (Barbieri and Mshenga 2008). Amy oversees the farm's professional kitchen, walk-in coolers, and wood-fired pizza ovens. These are located just steps away from a retrofitted barn with modern amenities (bathrooms, sound system) and rustic touches (hay bales, exposed beams). These resources help the farm diversify its cash flow and leverage all aspects of the business. For example, weddings and dinners can take place during lulls in the growing season, allowing for year-round income. Farm events, like Greenbrier's live music series, cross-promote their vegetable and meat operations. When Roddy's slow-smoked brisket is served at restaurant pricing, Amy can charge for the ingredients, preparation, and the ambiance of their surroundings. As Chad put it during a presentation on farm branding at a "local food" educational seminar, "you can't make any more money than growing it yourself and selling it hot on a plate."

The farmers intentionally developed their marketing savvy. They came to farm life already equipped with sizable business skills. All three had college degrees and were on track to live out comfortable white, middle-class lives. Chad previously worked in sales, Amy was in real estate, and Roddy ran logistics for a successful corporation. But then came the Great Recession in 2008 and their previous plans became both untenable and unfulfilling. They were looking to move away from their office jobs and toward something different and more meaningful. They knew they might not make as much money, but they hoped that their new careers would earn them—as Roddy put it—"a quality-of-life wage increase."

I saw the appeal of this life instantly, even though I already had a great job. One of the ironies of my privilege is that it leads me to take my circumstances for granted. In my case, I work at a university, with tenure, and have total control over what I teach and research. My workplace is safe and clean. My colleagues are smart and helpful. Amid all these benefits, I was nonetheless incredibly jealous of Chad, Amy, and Roddy. Their workplace drew me in. Greenbrier is expansive, breathtaking. A majestic red oak towers over rolling pasture. There just aren't many places like this anymore in the United States.

For all their simple beauty, small farms are businesses. Farming at this scale is a complicated business, and the unpredictability of droughts and pests is stressful. Large corporate agriculture has acquired and consolidated most of the country's family farms. The industry has changed so much over the past century that small farmers can no longer compete on cost. Chad could never sell a tomato cheaper than Walmart; Roddy could never win a contract to supply McDonalds. So they compete on a different playing field.

Local farms like Greenbrier differentiate their food offerings by emphasizing the more intense labor and care that go into their production. These create intense flavor and quality, but at a price residents of food deserts cannot afford. Take tomatoes, for example. At the beginning of each season, Chad plants individual seeds in starter trays; first he pokes a popsicle stick into sterilized soil, then drops in one seed at a time. Six weeks later, he and his staff transplant the heirloom varietals into raised beds (that's what I did for my very first eight-hour shift). Soon after, they pile-drive stakes into the rows at ten-foot intervals and trellis them with string. They eventually will guide the growing plants in and out of the twine so that it supports their stalks and heavy fruit on their way to ripeness. Nearly all of this work is done by hand, which adds to Greenbrier's costs and the quality of its end products. Chad's tomatoes can be sold at a farmers market for three times the cost of supermarket tomatoes.

The same is true for Roddy's steaks and chops. He brings recently weaned steers up to full weight with an intensive paddock-shifting operation. Based upon the head count and total weight of the herd (accounting for daily growth), Roddy can calculate the square footage of pasture needed for each day of grazing. Each morning, his staff create an electrified quadrant adjacent to the previous day's paddock. The new area will have waist-high fresh forage that draws the steers in. It requires micromanagement, but it brings the meat to market faster and tastier than passive grazing. Ostensibly, Roddy sells beef, but the real star is the quality of the forage. As he put it, "I raise animals but essentially I grow grass"

Like Chad's tomatoes, Roddy's product is qualitatively different than the beef sold in most supermarkets and fast-food restaurants. His pasture is chemical and pesticide free. His steers are slaughtered in a "certified humane" facility. Roddy's beef is a specialty product. He can't compete on price, so he competes on quality.

Spending a month on the farm, I learned that the Greenbrier's business model, like other local farms that sell directly to customers, was about more than food. The vegetables, meat, and agritourism functioned like a three-legged stool, each leg supporting the other. On the whole, farms like this solve a lot of problems. Their approach to cultivation is better for the soil, the water, the animals, and the local economy. But these methods are expensive. To balance the books, these farmers need to sell at a premium. Their primary customers are people like me willing to pay extra for a tomato, I visit farmers markets for the experience. In short, I enjoy the idea of local food and small farms as much as the food itself.

Even though the people I interviewed in Southernside and West Greenville placed a high value on freshness, Greenbrier cannot change where they buy food or what they eat. This isn't Chad, Amy, or Roddy's fault. They are "unwitting bystanders": depicted in media accounts as a possible solution for a social problem decades in the making. Greenbrier is their business, and they are just trying to make a living. My food desert interviewees understood why the goods at farmers markets were expensive, and they did not begrudge farmers for charging what they could. Instead, my interviewees saw the weekend market as an event for the city's white and more affluent residents—more of an excursion or an outing, not a primary food source. It wasn't like a grocery store where you could get all you need in one trip. That was the kind of retail they felt they deserved.

Buying Directly from Farmers: Markets, CSAs, and Food Hubs

That Greenbrier sold high-end, specialty products that food desert residents likely couldn't afford does not invalidate the entire direct-to-consumer model. In theory, shortening the distance (literally and figuratively) between producer and consumer should also reduce product cost. If local farmers using more conventional methods could get more affordable foods straight to neighbors in Southernside and West Greenville, it would go a long way toward improving their retail options and budgets.

During my research, the Greenville county area had four initiatives in place to help people buy food directly from farmers. There were "Healthy Bucks" vouchers at the downtown farmers market, Community Supported Agriculture (CSA) programs, a mobile nonprofit farmers market, and the beginning phase of a "food hub." All were intended to reduce the cost and increase the availability of healthy, locally grown food. With the exception of the CSA programs, all were partially funded by grants.

Farmers markets have increased in popularity dramatically since the passage of Public Law 94-463, the Farmer-to-Consumer Direct Marketing Act of 1976 (Brown 2002). This federal legislation funded financial, technical, and marketing support for these markets, using public funds to help American farmers. As solutions go, farmers markets generally do increase geographic access to fresh food for people in food deserts (Wang, Qiu, and Swallow 2014).

At the downtown market, the City of Greenville provided considerable logistical support. It helped set up tents and tables, pick up trash, manage traffic, and advertise the market. The market's organizers understood the relatively higher prices at these stands and tried to assist low-income residents as best they could. They were food desert "activists" in the sense that they took clear steps to reach out to the city's poorer residents. They placed the market just a few blocks from the bus transfer station, making it more accessible to people without vehicles. They also accepted payment via Electronic Benefits Transfer (EBT) cards that enabled people to use money received from their Supplemental Nutrition Assistance Program (SNAP) or Temporary Assistance to Needy Families (TANF) accounts.

The most high-profile assistance program at the market was the "Healthy Bucks" campaign for people receiving SNAP benefits (Payne et al. 2013). In South Carolina, eligible participants could buy a $10 voucher for fruits and vegetables for just $5. Marketing materials for Greenville's downtown market encouraged people to use the program to "double your bucks!"[3] Yet there were limitations: customers were limited to one half-price coupon per week, and it took multiple steps to obtain one. Farmers had to attend a training session on how to accept the payment.[4]

Various local farms—including Greenbrier—also sold shares in or subscriptions to their Community Supported Agriculture (CSA) programs (Brown and Miller 2008). For prices ranging from $200 to $400 (paid upfront), customers would receive an assortment of farm goods on a weekly or biweekly basis over the fourteen-week growing season. These were available for pickup at the farms themselves or at centrally located points in the city. Farmers liked CSA programs, which helped shift the farm's economic risks and income variations to the consumer. Customers liked CSA programs because it enabled them to "vote with their fork" and show their support for local food.[5]

For those who had trouble getting to the market or a CSA drop-off point, another local nonprofit organized a "mobile farmers market" (Robinson et al. 2016). Just like it sounds, this market trucked fruits and vegetables into the Southernside and West Greenville neighborhoods on a biweekly basis between May and September. The mobile market accepted EBT payment and participated in the "Healthy Bucks" program.

At first, the mobile market was poised for success. These food desert activists won a $10,000 grant from a statewide funding source to purchase a walk-in trailer that could house shelving and refrigerated cases. Its representatives came to Southernside and West Greenville neighborhood meetings and solicited feedback on what products residents wanted to buy. When my students and I surveyed the mobile market's customers, most buyers reported significant support for the mission of the organization and appreciated its investment in the community. But few of those buyers lived in Southernside or West Greenville. They traveled, usually by car, to buy from the mobile market (we calculated their median distance traveled at 2.5 miles). These folks could just as easily have driven to a grocery store, a CSA pickup, a regular farmers market, or even a local farm. After two years, the mobile market eventually stopped coming to these neighborhoods.

A small "local food" mini-grocery set up shop less than one mile from the Southernside neighborhood a few years before I began my research. A for-profit venture, it started small and thrived over the years, quickly expanding to over six thousand square feet of retail with plans to add more. The owners of the mini-grocery straddled the line between food desert activism and being unwitting bystanders. They claimed to be providing access in a food desert in their promotional materials and business grant applications, but they were primarily devoted to helping local farmers. For small-scale growers in the area, their store was a lifeline: it bought from all nearby farms, no matter their size, selling their products at premium prices that nearby residents could not afford. As a result, when my students and I surveyed over five hundred of the mini-grocery's customers over a four-year period, we learned that nearly all their customers were driving in from other parts of the county. Less than 10 percent lived within a mile of the store. I confirmed these findings in my interviews with nearby residents. The vast majority had never heard of the store; those who had were predominately white, middle-class, and had moved to the area within the past five years.

Another effort to help people buy locally grown food was the development of a regional "food hub" to be placed in an empty warehouse between the Southernside and West Greenville neighborhoods. Food hubs are mediators, and they may help local residents indirectly. This project— dubbed "Feed and Seed"—was to have a small retail counter for unprocessed and prepared foods, but primarily serve as a "means of aggregating and distributing food by pooling food products from a number of smaller farms and delivering them to grocery stores, schools, hospitals and restaurants" (Cleveland et al. 2014: 27). Food hubs can inform growers what buyers want, and steer buyers to potentially cheaper products from local producers. Because small-scale farmers lack the distribution and processing abilities of corporatized agriculture, food hubs can increase their profits while also lowering prices for nearby institutions and businesses. The Feed and Seed project went an activist step further, including job training and vendor space for local entrepreneurs in its plans.

Unfortunately, this plan to help the community became another victim of gentrification. A nearby development was planned to include the food hub with healthy retail (which residents liked), but also vendors that served alcohol (which residents did not). Pitching the project as a way to sell fresh foods in the area helped the developers secure neighborhood support during the project's planning phase. However, when a restaurant pulled out for its own financial reasons, the project designers changed the mix of occupants: Feed and Seed was out. Rather than include demonstration vegetable gardens and offer culinary training, the development would instead feature exclusively expensive items, like high-end coffee complete with barista service.

Nutritional Education

Another popular approach to helping food desert residents is teaching them how to eat healthier. Most lessons focus on making better choices from among prepared options when eating out or stretching the household dollar in home cooking. "Teachable moments" arose frequently in my observations. For example, when a local hospital presented a health assessment of Greenville county, an audience member asked about how to remedy high obesity rates. A local nutritionist stood up and offered some activist advice of how people could cook healthy and delicious meals on a budget. She believed it was possible to teach families how to improve their diets within their economic means.

In this way, educational initiatives in Greenville varied from informal to highly institutionalized. A few small groups sought to change people's diets through occasional seminars, open potlucks, and group outings. Among these, one endeavored to gain adherents to the "paleo" diet (Cordain 2010). The group's founder, having experienced physical benefits from adopting the diet herself, was motivated to teach others that eating foods "as close to their natural state as possible" could be healthier and more economical than eating at restaurants. She led classes on food preservation and encouraged others to save money and eat healthier. During her interview, she told me how anyone could engage in some form of preservation: "freezing food when it is in season and blanch them and freeze them . . . that would be food that you would have for the winter." No matter how zealous she was, the organizer was an unpaid volunteer with job and family obligations. She told me that she wanted to be more of an activist, helping people in food deserts, but admitted that her group was small and had difficulty getting its message out. Not one of my interviewees in Southernside or West Greenville knew it existed.

Educational campaigns integrated into local institutions were more effective. The local hospital system, in partnership with the developing food hub, offered nutritional assistance to parents of children in local Head Start agencies (Head Start is an early education program for kids living below the poverty line). In Greenville, one pilot program delivered fresh fruits and vegetables to Head Start parents, then taught them how to prepare meals with these ingredients at home. All the ingredients were sourced from local producers, and this "farm to belly" meal kit was offered at no cost twice a month during the school year. By the end of its inaugural year, the activists had notched a small victory: children included in the program scored higher on tests about nutrition that asked whether a given dish was healthy.

LiveWell Greenville undertook a larger scale effort. The local public health activist organization developed a labeling campaign—"LiveWell approved"—to signal the healthiest items at schools, local parks, and recreational facilities inside food deserts and beyond. Its marketing campaign was part of a nationwide movement to "nudge" people toward eating healthy through product placement, lighting, and signage (Bucher 2016; Escaron et al. 2016). By integrating their work into other institutions, health organizations like LiveWell had a more extensive reach. School cafeterias in particular have a lot of potential for changing eating habits; they determine the dietary options of children at least once a day during the school year.[6]

The institutionalized solutions may have a broader reach, but much of the rhetoric I heard in food-related seminars and workshops during my research still focused on individualistic strategies. Whether in a nutritionist's contribution at the hospital's health assessment presentation or in the words of a Whole Foods representative at a TEDx Talk in Greenville— "Instead of buying pineapple chunks, buy the whole pineapple and cut it up yourself!"—the drumbeat of advice was consistent: With desire and instruction, even people living in food deserts can stretch their dollars and eat healthier. Sociologists are more likely to propose structural solutions like the LiveWell and Head Start programs; my interviewees in Southernside and West Greenville appreciated individual approaches. Many of them, for instance, remembered their parents or grandparents saving money by growing and preserving their own vegetables. Few respondents canned food, yet they had positive associations with the idea of buying seasonally and in bulk. When I asked why they didn't make good on that inclination, they typically responded they did not have the time, equipment, or know-how—they were echoing the individualist advice I heard from experts.

To explore the feasibility of preserving less expensive local food with tried-and-true water bath canning methods, I signed up for a course with my local agriculture extension agency (operated by the nearest land grant institution, Clemson University). The challenge I posed to myself was to preserve a healthy staple food that was cheaper than what could be bought at Walmart. The canning course had a small registration fee but included a free recipe guide and a copy of the famous *Ball's Blue Book* (Harrold

2015). Equipped with this knowledge, I set up my experiment in the most favorable scenario possible. I would make pasta sauce.

I chose pasta sauce because my family eats it regularly and tomatoes have sufficient acidity to making canning it easier. Canning requires glass jars and metal bands, but at least hypothetically, these can be reused and shared. The unavoidable costs were materials like the single-use sealing lids and spices. For tomatoes, I drove ten miles to a conventional farm (not organic) to buy one hundred pounds at the peak of the season. With bulk pricing, I paid 50 cents a pound for enough fruit for a year's worth of sauce.

In the end, I was able to preserve thirty-two pints of sauce (512 ounces) for a total of $70 in raw materials, or 13.5 cents per ounce. That sounds cheap, but this form of food desert activism is doomed from the start: the end product was still *three times* more expensive than the cheapest, generic, store-bought pasta sauce. Even if I excluded the costs of equipment, transportation, and energy, I still couldn't save money by preserving food. I had hoped that maybe an educational program using local food could work. But it didn't. And it was probably for the best: my idea would not have improved the retail options in their neighborhood, either.

Urban Agriculture

Where good food is hard to find, why not grow your own? This type of problem solving can start small (kitchen gardens); involve groups (community gardens); or take over an entire lot (urban farming). This is another long-standing food access strategy that would have been familiar to my older respondents in Southernside and West Greenville. The federal government, for instance, encouraged people to grow "victory gardens" during World War II as a means to fill gaps in nutrition supplies (Miller 2003). Indeed, with a patch of dirt, some sun, water, and seeds, people can grow basic vegetables with little training.

In Greenville, two small operations offered consulting advice to homeowners on how to establish and maintain a small plot. The first contacted me when he learned of my research. Not a food desert activist, he was more of an unwitting bystander: Because he owned a business selling vegetable seeds, his services are part of the larger debate on how to increase home food production. He argued that a big barrier to home food production was an unlikely culprit: the grassy lawn. "We consider them beautiful . . . but there could be tons of food production going on [there]." He acknowledged that his services were out of the price range of most food desert residents but pointed out that basic gardening information was available at any public library. With a small amount of time and money, he believed that food desert residents could adopt low-maintenance, cost-effective growing strategies, like planting edible perennials to augment and diversify their food intake.

Midway through my research, another home gardening consultant contacted me to ask if I knew any groups or neighborhoods where he could fruitfully volunteer his services. He was strongly considering entering into food desert activism. He used the space-intensive techniques that marked an emerging trend among urban farmers who grow on leased and borrowed land.[7] He wanted to show people how to transform open space to grow basic crops, including ones that could be stored for a long time, like some squashes and root vegetables. With his expertise, he believed he could teach others how to produce enough for themselves and donate their surplus harvests to local food banks, pantries, and homeless shelters.

Not everyone has their own space to grow food, though. Renters in apartment complexes are seldom allowed to alter the landscaping. For them, community gardens become a more attractive option.[8] In Greenville, Gardening for Good offered technical assistance and materials to groups of people who wanted to begin a collective plot. During the time of my research, the organization was actively looking for spots in Southernside and West Greenville (that is, they were food desert activists). Its leaders would help neighborhoods build raised beds, explain a few different strategies for collective gardening, and leave the community responsible for weeding and watering. Individuals could manage their own plots, or the work could be done collectively. Throughout, organization representatives were available to answer common logistical questions (Should there be a fence? Will people steal food? What happens if someone forgets to water?).

Initiatives like these encourage people to grow their own food for their own consumption. Its leaders believed that it could help people eat better and spend less. They also believed it could change tastes. When interviewed, members of these organizations all expressed a version of the sentiment, "If you grow it, you'll eat it"; they hoped that when people invested time and energy in gardening, they would be more willing to consume its end product.

Other problem solvers tried a bigger approach. During my research, two urban farming operations were present in the Southernside and West Greenville area. One, Reedy River Farms, was an unwitting bystander: a for-profit entity that maintained its neighborhood operation for nearly five years before moving to a more rural location. The other, a nonprofit, had much more activist goals but failed midway through its first season.

Urban farming is not easy. The primary challenge is the cost of land. Urban real estate costs more per square foot. In response, urban farmers often look for free or donated land. Both of the Greenville urban farms found landowners willing to grant temporary usufruct of small parcels. One of the organizations paid a yearly lease of $1, contingent upon buying its own liability insurance, the other secured permission from the county parks and recreation department to work on an unused public land overrun with weeds.

Neither of the urban farms was even an acre. Which is to say, urban farms are small and easy to miss. There are no tractors. There are no grain silos. At a distance, the farmhands could be confused for a landscaping crew. The crops are smaller, too. This is because urban operations are better suited to smaller, efficient, faster growing crops, like salad greens, carrots, beets, and radishes. Broccoli can take three months to mature, meaning a single harvest per season. Lettuce, on the other hand, can be planted and harvested continually, producing consistent yields.

The urban farms' motivations can be easy to miss, too. Past research has shown that urban farmers sometimes have different goals than nearby residents. For example, in the aftermath of Hurricane Katrina, the organizers of a new urban farm in New Orleans wanted to offer fresh, seasonal produce for residents whose grocery stores had been forced to shut down. The problem was that locals wanted year-round access to the staples of their cultural cuisine—the "holy trinity" of celery, bell peppers, and onions. These don't grow year-round in Louisiana's climate. The urban farm organizers wanted to do the right thing, but their goals conflicted with the preferences of the people they were trying to help (Kato 2013).

In Greenville, the owner of the for-profit urban farm was aware that his operation was in a food desert but figured solving the problem of food access was beyond the scope of his enterprise. That others saw his operation as a possible source of produce for the people who lived near his plot was rather beyond his control. He simply wanted to make a living growing food. From his perspective, "urban farming on leased land was the way to get into it with the least amount of financial investment and low overhead expenses . . . less risk." He wanted to work with his hands, outside, and build a business that sold directly to consumers (including restaurants). The first time he saw his farm mentioned on a local menu, he was overwhelmed with relief, "I thought to myself, 'Wow, I can't believe this is working.'"

Greenville's nonprofit urban farm had more explicitly activist goals. It had secured a $50,000 start-up grant via a soil and water conservation agency. In its application materials, it featured its location "in the middle of a high need USDA designated food desert." The site, adjacent to a charter school, was owned by the parks and recreation department. Farm managers hoped to use the garden as an educational tool for students and ultimately source the school's cafeteria. It did harvest some salad greens, but when historical land use records indicated the soil might have been contaminated from a former industrial plant, it was forced to shut down.

When it comes to increasing food production in Southernside and West Greenville, the challenges are many. Whether the problems are perceptual (Americans' inability to see front lawns as spaces for growing anything but grass) or logistical (getting neighbors to take turns watering the community garden), transforming the food system is difficult.

Improving Donated Food Options

Media accounts often conflate the issues of food insecurity and food deserts (roughly 18% of accounts in my database, according to the analysis in chapter 2), though they are different phenomena. People who are food insecure are not regular participants in the retail food market. Some are priced out of supermarkets entirely; others need a little assistance to get through the month. The farther people drop below the poverty line, the less retail access impacts their dietary choices. The donated food environment—what others give, swap, or trade—on the other hand, has a clear and direct effect on what they eat. Increasing the nutritional value of those options *can* impact health outcomes. It won't change a community's status as a food desert or ameliorate retail inequality, but it can improve the lives of the most vulnerable.

To assess the quality of donated food, first you have to find it. Its venues rarely have advertising budgets. In Greenville, they were embedded in church basements, community centers, child care facilities, senior housing, and service providers frequented by the poor. The people in the most need had to traverse a haphazard circuit across the city to get to all of them. At some locations, clients could get hot plates, others offered only brown bag lunches. A few provided cardboard boxes filled with a week's worth of calories.

The majority of pantries near Southernside and West Greenville were stocked by donations from a local food "rescue" organization, Loaves and Fishes, founded in 1991. Its mission is to retrieve soon-to-expire goods from local supermarkets and deliver them to pantries across the area. Organizations like these accept millions of pounds of produce, dairy, frozen meats, prepared foods, and canned goods across the country (Schneider 2013). However, despite the director's activist desires, the bulk of Loaves and Fishes' donations still fell under the category of "breads and sweets."

During her interview, the director explained the dilemma of combatting hunger with unhealthy food. "Yeah, we get a lot of Krispy Kreme [donuts]." She had mixed feelings about this. From her perspective, withholding food or dictating what her clients ate was too harsh an intervention. She would like to offer more healthy items but found that they were in less demand. "We had asparagus. . . . That was the hardest stuff to move. . . . We don't have any problem getting rid of bananas. Those are the easiest thing to get rid of . . . but asparagus, just killed me." Sweets may not be healthy, but they will be eaten. They won't require storage or cooking. They won't have time to go bad. For the director, fresh foods her clients did not want had a second problem: they took up considerable agency resources. The longer it took to disburse this produce, the more valuable refrigeration space it occupied.

Once food pantries receive deliveries from organizations like Loaves and Fishes, they have to organize, store, and distribute the food. The two most popular pantries in Southernside and West Greenville were both located in traditionally Black churches. They both had a minimal staff of volunteers who balanced competing desires. They wanted to be fair and minimize waste, which meant giving everyone a mix of high- and low-demand items.

Pantry volunteers knew their clients' tastes and schedules well. During their interviews, they explained that meat was very popular (ground beef was the most requested). Most fresh vegetables are also in demand, but because they often arrive in the form of bag salads on the brink of spoilage, they must move quickly. Cakes and cookies were highly sought-after, but easier to manage because of their shelf lives. Over the course of the month, staffers noted, people on fixed incomes and public assistance exhausted their monthly benefits. Demand for the pantry's services increased each week of each month.

The director of Greenville's soup kitchen, Project Host, also saw serving healthier food as an uphill battle. She wished she could be a source of exclusively nutritious food, but such activism was a luxury she could ill afford. First, she was limited by the ingredients donated during any given week; second, her clients were less than interested in healthy meals. When characterizing her organization's menu, she explained, "Is it really healthy? No. . . . We are healthier than what we used to serve in the soup kitchen. But we are also donated all the sweets. . . . We use whole wheat bread instead of white bread, but if I quit serving a dessert, there would probably be a revolt."[9] The daily lunch meal consisted of two soups (one tomato-based, one cream-based), a salad, a fruit, a sandwich, and dessert. The organization's large garden out back occasionally allowed for a featured vegetable dish. However, healthy items were placed on a side table; If they were automatically doled out in the serving line, there would be waste. "I tried to serve green beans once that were not cooked to death, and no one ate them."

There is significant potential in using donated food to improve the healthiness of the food environment. As of 2019, 10.5 percent of the US population lives below the poverty line, making for a captive audience relying at least partially on food pantries and soup kitchens. Because healthier food is more expensive per calorie, improving the quality of donated food would help people stretch their budgets for other items, like paper products and cleaning supplies. Put in the context of retail inequality, these savings could also be put toward occasional trips to nicer stores, helping poorer residents feel like equal participants in American consumer culture—at least, from time to time. That was the strategy adopted by my interviewees who visited pantries and soup kitchens. Nonetheless, just because it is free does not mean people will eat it. As shown in chapter 3, there was a robust secondary trading market in food pantry items in these neighborhoods; even people who experienced food insecurity still gave away unwanted food to friends and family.

Retail Interventions

The most commonly discussed solution to the food desert problem is a retail intervention. That is, inserting better-quality food retail in places where they don't exist. These can range from making changes inside convenience stores, to starting up small markets, to recruiting full-sized supermarkets. In Greenville, I observed all of these efforts to improve the food system during my research. By the end, I learned that selling healthy food is a difficult business and just because residents state they want new stores does not mean they necessarily plan to change how they shop or what they eat.

The largest-scale activist effort I witnessed was undertaken by the City of Greenville's Community Development Division, aimed at recruiting a supermarket to the edge of the Southernside neighborhood. The City had previously purchased a dilapidated strip mall, demolished it, cleared the land, and put out a "request for proposals" from commercial developers (City of Greenville 2014). To document the site's potential, an outside consultant was contracted to conduct a market analysis and give a public presentation of his findings. His report suggested that the west side of Greenville could support not one but two grocery stores of up to 25,000 square feet each. Armed with this information, City leaders expressed hope that a developer might fill the void left by recent supermarket departures.

Unfortunately, no one took up the City's offer. The site was large (2.06 acres), but not quite large enough. Even small grocery stores (less than 20,000 square feet) that operate under brands like Aldi and Lidl still require a parcel of at least 2.5 acres. It would be five years before a large supermarket came to Greenville, and even then, it would choose a site on the more affluent east side of the city. It was even farther away from Southernside and West Greenville than existing options.

In the meantime, two separate activist efforts tried to build a small-scale community market in West Greenville. These retail interventions were meant to address simple and basic needs at affordable prices. There would be no pharmacy, deli, or bakery, just the fresh and staple foods dollar stores and convenience stores didn't carry.

The first was spearheaded by a local woman called to action when she read a *Greenville News* piece about nearby food deserts. A former Walmart produce department manager, she felt she could help create a healthy retail option for her community. She modeled her proposal on a retail intervention underway in Chester, Pennsylvania, called Fare and Square: the only nonprofit grocery store in the country at the time.[10] During her interview, she stressed a focus on affordability, not "pushing healthy food on people if that is not what they wanted." Unfortunately, her goal "to empower the community by offering fresh, healthy, and affordable food choices" never came to fruition. She had put together a board of directors and was in the beginning stages of the paperwork to obtain 501c3 nonprofit status. But her grant application was rejected by a local funding agency. Three years later, the Pennsylvania market she had tried to emulate, Fare and Square, sold to a for-profit entity. Public health researchers later found that it had failed to divert nearby residents from supermarkets farther outside of the city (Yao et al. 2019).

The second market did materialize, but only lasted a year. The same activist organization that operated the nonprofit mobile farmers market in Southernside and West Greenville built a "brick and mortar" storefront on the edge of West Greenville. Like its mobile venture, it accepted EBT payments and offered a "Healthy Bucks" coupon to increase SNAP recipients' buying power. It sold a full complement of fresh, dried, and canned foods (albeit with very limited variety of each). Store managers made repeated attempts to solicit feedback from neighborhood residents about which products to sell. Despite positive feedback and thanks from the neighborhood for investing in their neighborhood, it closed. There wasn't enough business. The people I interviewed liked the *idea* of the store, but its small selection meant they would still need to do additional shopping at a larger venue to meet all their needs—it took two trips, including one that made it abundantly clear they could get the same products at lower prices from a bigger retailer.

More modest efforts were underway in the three primary gas station convenience stores in the area. Efforts to increase the availability of healthy food in these types of outlets is a popular strategy because they already have a presence in food desert neighborhoods (Adams et al. 2012). In the previous chapter, I outlined how food retailers needed to pass the "healthy food" test if they wanted to earn neighborhood good will and—more importantly—secure approval for their plans to build and remodel stores. At these meetings, business representatives often referred to their efforts to sell more fresh fruit by placing it near the register as evidence they wanted to increase consumption of healthier items. These three chains varied greatly in their number of stores, and each faced unique challenges to selling healthy food. I interviewed corporate officers at all three business and learned that wanting to sell healthier options and getting it on the shelves are two entirely different things.

The largest regional gas station chain had over eight hundred stores in eleven different states. It was a new entrant into the Greenville market, but earned positive feedback from the neighborhood associations because of their willingness to take steps to reduce loitering, as outlined in chapter 5. I spoke with the chain's real estate acquisition manager. He explained that outsiders who thought his chain could solve social problems facing unique neighborhoods simply did not understand its business model. His employer was an unwitting bystander in the food desert debate, because the size of its operation actually made it more difficult to add healthy items to specific stores. Their production and distribution systems could not be tailored to meet the needs of individualized store formats. All their stores in all eleven states were the same size with the same layout. This uniformity increased efficiency and profitability. Even the location of individual items on store shelves were designed at corporate headquarters. Vendors (Coca Cola, Lays, etc.) paid "slotting fees" to feature their soft drinks and snack foods in prime retail locations.[11] Individual store managers had little leeway.

This regional chain sold some healthy food—mostly prepared salads and sandwiches—for three primary reasons. First, the corporation's long-term business plan included depending more on food and beverage sales than gasoline; or, as the regional manager put it, "to be looked at more as a restaurant that sells gas than a gas station that sells food." Second, offering a variety of food made it possible to accept payment via EBT cards. According to state guidelines, in order to accept SNAP and TANF benefits from customers, a store must sell a certain combination of (1) dairy products, (2) breads, grains, (3) fruits and vegetables, and (4) meat, fish, and poultry, and (5) cereals. Once EBT eligibility is secured, customers can use their accounts to buy bottled sodas and bagged snacks if they like. Third, even if it cut into profits, selling healthier items earned good will: "You are constantly hearing feedback to get it, but you never have the sales." Even if the healthier options did not sell well, they improved community relations. This willingness to engage with the community transformed the company's reputation into "good" retail. And that positive image made it easier to receive permits to build and renovate new stores.

The next gas station chain, a smaller statewide venture, also saw selling healthy food as a short-term cost, long-term investment. In the business terminology of their executives, this chain wanted to offer more "immediate meal solutions" that "minimized dependency on the fuel offer." They sought to entice a wealthier clientele to frequent their stores on the way to and from work. For the owners, dabbling in food desert activism was a long-term strategy. Offering fresh salads and ready-made sandwiches was a way to differentiate the atmosphere of their stores from their smaller competitors. Fresh food also had a greater profit margin because this chain owned its own food production facilities, meaning they could prepare food from raw ingredients rather than depend solely on third-party vendors. Selling more expensive items was also a way to be seen as "good retail" by nearby neighbors even though they may not be the target customers: "We went through a period where we lost a good bit of money doing this, but we felt like that [wealthier] consumer is going to come."

This statewide chain had eighty-one stores, and it was not bound to identical formats like their larger competitor. Each location could be tailored. The statewide chain could also move more quickly through the research and design phase of food offerings; for example, a new sandwich could go from idea to store shelf in three to six months.

The smallest chain had more flexibility in their offerings, but still faced the biggest hurdles to selling healthier options. Ironically, its vice president was the most activist executive among these three case studies. He explained how his multi-county-wide chain had thirty-six stores, most of which were in Greenville County, including one a half-mile from the West Greenville neighborhood. He outlined how their smaller numbers allowed him to develop personal relationships with his food and beverage distributers. If he wanted to change an item, he could pick up the phone and have the new item on the next delivery truck. If necessary, he could make changes on his own. For example, when he first decided to offer bananas, local distributors were not equipped to store and deliver them (bananas need to be stored at different temperatures than other refrigerated or frozen goods). Undaunted, the vice president bought bananas himself and had store managers pick them up at his office.

Being smaller allows for micromanagement of stores within the county-wide chain, but there are still limits. For a brief period, he was in talks with a local nonprofit to stock vegetables from their farm operation. He even agreed to place them in a cooler near the register: "I told them, 'I'll give you prime real estate. I'll give you 'Boardwalk and Park Place' if you can get me the stuff.'" However, despite his willingness to forego some profits, the opportunity cost became too great. For one, inserting new products into the store's square footage is a zero-sum game. Adding healthier items means removing other, better-selling ones. In addition, as a food retailer, he needs consistent deliveries. His customers expect a constant supply of familiar options. If the store starts selling produce, customers would expect to see the same amount and type delivered every week, year-round. Local nonprofits couldn't promise deliveries as consistently as food distributors. For a small chain with locations across only a few counties, the prospect of empty shelf space was just too risky.

Retail interventions are, of course, representative of just one category of proposed solutions to change the way people in food deserts eat. But like the others, they run up against the everyday realities of the people they are trying to help. Interventions that reduce retail inequality may appear to fail because they do not change residents shopping or eating habits. But that misses the point. Food desert residents want options. Just because their circumstances make dietary change impractical does not mean they are undeserving of investment and improvement in their neighborhoods.

PUTTING FOOD DESERT SOLUTIONS TO THE TEST

The people I interviewed in Southernside and West Greenville wanted better retail. When the food desert concept came along, they discovered the political power of the "healthy food" frame and watched the influx of food desert activists. Others who operated in the fields of health and food were identified in media accounts as problem solvers, too, but most were unwitting bystanders just trying to make a living. Put together, these groups share an interest in increasing the amount and quality of nutritious food in underserved areas. And neither could realistically transform the way people in food deserts eat. Their proposed solutions just didn't fit within residents' current circumstances (outlined in chapters 3 and 4). Applying those realities to these attempts can enable us to see more clearly why they have failed and will continue to fail. This process is important. It is the last step before seeing the issue with clear eyes: the food desert fight was about something bigger than food.

Perception of Food Environment

For a solution to work, residents must know about it. However, real visibility requires more than just a physical presence. It also needs to fit within the cultural habitus of nearby residents. It must offer the type, quality, and variety of food that they know and like. Otherwise, it will be invisible in plain sight.

"Bad retail" is seen, but unseen in this way. The food desert residents I interviewed were upset and frustrated by their nearest convenience store options. They viewed the older and smaller convenience stores as run-down and exploitative, especially compared with the stores they remembered from decades past. They were sick and tired of businesses profiting off of their neighbors' bad habits by selling primarily alcohol, lottery tickets, and cigarettes.

Likewise, being considered "good retail" was a necessary, but not sufficient, step toward changing diets. Residents were pleased by the regional and statewide gas station chains' efforts to offer a few fresh options, a gesture that transformed these venues into "good retail." Still, being grateful for the attention didn't translate to buying fresh produce. People wanted the *opportunity* to buy a salad, even if they didn't buy one. The food desert residents I interviewed didn't consider gas stations places to buy grocery items, but places for snacks and drinks.

Farmers markets were similarly visible but invisible. My interviewees saw them primarily as a novelty: good for an excursion, but not to stock their cabinets. They liked the *idea* of buying locally grown food and believed it was fresher because it spent less time on a truck. They just couldn't afford to pay more to support local farmers. The people I interviewed who shopped heavily at farmers markets and felt strongly about diversifying the local food system were largely white and middle-class residents. Longtime residents (predominately Black) were not "against" local food, they just had other more immediate concerns.

I saw the clearest example of this disconnect at a local TEDx event in downtown Greenville. It was titled, "Thought for Food: Alleviating Greenville's Food Deserts," and the moderator for the evening was Russell Stall, the former director of a local nonprofit who years later would be elected to the Greenville City Council. He introduced the event—featuring a representative from Whole Foods—by saying, "We have scores of local farms selling healthy and culturally appropriate food to [our area], but some are being left out." It was clear that the moderator had a genuine passion for service and had committed his professional career to making Greenville a better place. However, his remarks showed that he had fallen into the same trap I had at the beginning of my research. I genuinely thought local food could be the answer. Early on, I did not yet realize that those being "left out" (residents of Southernside and West Greenville) never really demanded local food, and the people who could seemingly sell them this food (local farmers) never volunteered to serve it to them at a price they could afford.

Small local farmers cannot compete with large-scale corporate agriculture; they do business on a different playing field. Unable to guarantee uniformity in shape and ripeness, they play up the quirky nature of their heirloom varietals. Unable to produce chicken cheaper than firms with vertical business operations, they charge premiums for their free-range and humane production methods. And by marketing their products to the highest end of the market, they effectively make themselves invisible to those trying to stretch their dollar as much as possible.

Many local farmers, especially younger ones, are passionate about their work and want to leave the world a better place. All the owners of Greenbrier Farms—Amy, Chad, and Roddy—left their office careers for work they saw as more meaningful and less sterile. They, like the current mini-resurgence of farming among younger adults (Ackoff, Bahrenburg, and Shute 2017), were influenced by writers like Michael Pollan (2007) and Wendell Berry (1977). They want to solve some of the world's problems, but they cannot solve all of them. Running a farm is a really tough business. Their direct-to-consumer sales may reduce costs, but not enough to help food desert residents.

Economic Resources

No matter the problem, an effective solution must target the population that both needs and can benefit from it. In food deserts, this is a narrower segment than portrayed in media accounts. The USDA Food Access Research Atlas, for example, identifies census tracks without supermarkets that have a high enough rate of poverty and a low enough rate of access to transportation. The media then report that the total population "lives in a food desert." But this paints too broad a brush.

A more accurate calculation would only include the number of people for whom the extra transportation expenses put healthy food out of their price range. This excludes the truly poor, who are not full-time participants in the retail food market to begin with. For them, living next to a grocery store only means being closer to items they cannot afford. Similarly, families with enough economic and transportation resources are not absolutely constrained by the distance to existing stores. They already have access, so they are unlikely to change their diets if newer stores move closer.

This leaves the people most affected by the lack of a grocery store: those who live above the poverty line but are still struggling. Households earning between 100 percent and 125 percent of the poverty line are described by the US Census as "near poor." When I began my research in 2014, roughly 20 percent of Southernside and West Greenville fell into this category. And if activists want to overhaul diets, this group must be the target market; they are the residents for whom new retail options might meaningfully change eating habits.

Right now, this group, the near poor, finds "local food" largely out of range. All the potential savings built into the direct-to-consumer model are still not enough. And the local farmers set premium prices and sell mostly to wealthier projects not because they want to gouge anyone, but because their small-scale profit margins are exceedingly thin. Even the most successful farmers at the Greenville downtown farmers market rarely made more than $30,000 in annual income.[12]

Conventionally grown local food has potential, but primarily during harvest times. Greenville County has a number of mid-size conventional (i.e., not organic) farms. It was from one of these that I bought tomatoes at 50 cents a pound to conduct my canning cost experiment. But even these farms' cheapest prices at peak production only barely beat supermarket prices, especially considering the transportation costs of an extra trip to buy them. Locally grown food might be higher quality, but the near poor have more pressing priorities.

Again, we find that efforts to "nudge" the near poor to buy healthier foods through product placement or labels ignore the zero-sum nature of their food budgets. Nearly all of the participants in the retail food market that I interviewed were able to find their way to a grocery store at some point each month. Persuading them to buy healthier options at convenience stores or snack bars only takes away from their food budget when they eventually get to the grocery store. Even if "point of purchase" marketing initiatives show increased sales of bananas or carrot sticks in one location, there is no evidence that these customers do not already buy these products at supermarkets—at a lower price. As a case in point, when supermarkets move near convenience stores, research has shown that nearby residents continue to purchase the same snacks and drinks as before, just from the new grocery store instead (Allcott et al. 2019). Prodding people to buy healthy products in a new location does not convince them to consume foods they did not eat before; it sends them to another venue to buy the items they already eat.

Expecting small-scale convenience stores to sell fresh foods at affordable prices is not feasible, either; at least not at the prices the near poor are able to pay. Take the example of the small county-wide gas station chain, whose vice president was in talks with a local nonprofit to feature locally grown produce in the "prime real estate" next to the cash register. He was willing to engage in food desert activism, even if it cut into some of his profits. Soon, though, he realized the opportunity costs were too great. To understand why, consider what it would take for him to be able to sell fresh vegetables. The local farmer would have to sell at a lower wholesale price than a direct-to-consumer retail price, the vendor would take shelf space away from more profitable (unhealthy) items, and the buyer would still have to pay higher prices than what could be found at a supermarket. Three levels of sacrifice. Too many to make it work.

Transportation

For those without cars who depend on rides, or those with a car but struggling to pay for the cost of wear and tear, shopping trips are special occasions. They do not have the luxury to scavenge for deals at multiple outlets. They need food, but they also need toilet paper. They need milk and cereal, but they also need soap and cleaning products. In short, they need one-stop shopping.

There is only one venue that sells all of the above: supermarkets. Essential household items are not for sale at farmers markets and are too expensive at convenience stores. You can get detergent at dollar stores, but you cannot get your prescription filled too. Drug stores sell trash bags, but they don't have any fresh food. That leaves only one suitable outlet.

There are grocery delivery options, mostly run by third-party operations, where the seller takes care of the transportation problem. However, that adds a layer of labor, which drives up costs. The same goes for "meal-kit" services. They are convenient. They are time-saving. And they are expensive. The more hands that touch food before it gets to the consumer, the higher the price. None of my interviewees thought delivery or meal-kit services were worth the added costs, including most in middle-class households.

Public transportation is another possible remedy to those without cars. Effective bus or subway service can enable multiple trips at affordable rates. But the service must be extensive, frequent, and rapid. Even if the bus system in Greenville doubled the number of its routes as well as the frequency of its departures, it still could not match the convenience of the informal ride network in Southernside and Greenville. My interviewees who relied on rides from others were picked up at their doors, delivered directly to the storefront, and helped with their bags—all features unlikely to mark public transit. Remember, those with minor mobility issues need help getting bags from shopping cart to trunk to cupboard. Those with disabilities have even greater needs. Yes, they can qualify for paratransit, but it is slow and unable to deliver equally personalized service. For a transportation solution to work, it will have to be at least as convenient as the one they have carved out for themselves on their own.

Social Capital

The conventional wisdom on food deserts too often depicts residents as passive victims to their food environment. This is not true (Reese 2019). The informal ride network they created was a case in point. These arrangements did not just happen, they required cultivation. Sometimes the payment was direct and in cash, other times it was more indirect. A nephew who drives his aunt to the store does not do so because he expects her to return the favor. Instead, his sense of obligation is built on his membership with the family: they help each other. This is how social capital functions. It is assistance based on promises of reciprocity. But for all this to work, riders needed to be flexible.

For residents without cars, the art of getting rides hinged on their ability to be ready to go when their drivers are. The rider did not dictate the exact time they could shop. If their drivers worked, shoppers had to be ready to go out after their shifts ended. They needed to be able to tag along when their drivers said so. All this means that solutions to their shopping needs must be available during regular hours, nearly every day, and year-round.

Consistent availability is one thing that direct-to-consumer farmers markets cannot offer. These markets operate on fixed schedules—a few hours a day, once a week, during the growing season. My interviewees struggling to stay in the retail food market could not schedule their lives that precisely. When their money came in, they went shopping. Waiting four or five days for market day was unrealistic: other expenses would inevitably creep up and hijack their plans.[13] Community gardens offer more flexibility, but only during the growing season.

The advantage of grocery stores is that they can serve as refrigerated holding pens for food when the customer is ready. For residents without cars, that means when their drivers are ready, too. Because the informal ride network cannot guarantee arrival time, food desert residents need retail venues that open early and close late.

Household Dynamics

Acquiring healthy food is one thing, preparing it is another. Traditionally, home cooking was made possible by two things: a nearby grocery store and a full household eating the same food at the same times. Whereas a single trip to the store to cook a single meal is uneconomical, buying ingredients to cook a meal that feeds many mouths saves time and money. Add enough people to the table and factor in an additional round of leftovers, and cooking at home begins to get cheaper and quicker (per meal) than rounding everyone up to eat out. In short, supermarkets enable cooperative meal planning, preparation, and consumption. But cooperation needs people.

The home-cooked meal is simply not on the table for most American families (Bowen, Brenton, and Elliot 2019). Over a quarter of American households consist of only one person. One in every seven adults lives alone. From my interviewees, I learned that solo dwellers saw raw vegetables as a challenge—it was hard to use them all up before they spoiled. In 1960, the average household size was 3.3, now it is roughly 2.5. But even larger families that live together increasingly eat apart. Different work schedules can mean different meal schedules. The modern invention of "kid food" adds another layer of obstacles; one meal for parents, another for children. Of course, parents ultimately control what their children eat, but buying raw vegetables that kids might refuse poses economic risks for those who can least afford them (Daniel 2016).

Unsurprisingly, Americans spend considerably less time in the kitchen today than in decades past. Some of this is due to appliances that can speed up the process, but the biggest influence is a shift toward eating food prepared outside the home. Roughly a third of all calories consumed are from foods prepared by others (Smith, Ng, and Popkin 2013). This estimate is conservative, because it doesn't account for pre- or par-cooked food that is simply heated up at home.

In most cases, relying on food prepared by others is the logical and even economical choice. There is no evidence that food desert residents are less knowledgeable about cooking. People with higher incomes actually consume more fast food than people with lower incomes (Fryar et al. 2018). It is not that household members are lazy or irrational. Quite the opposite. The coordination necessary to make home cooking work has just become too difficult. Eating food prepared by others saves time and money.

These same household dynamics also show why encouraging people to grow or preserve food is unlikely to work. Gardening is labor intensive and requires collective effort. Community gardens solve some, but not all of that problem. First, my interviewees saw neighborhood gardens as only tangentially related to their year-round diet: a good thing for the neighborhood, not something to survive on. Second, freshly harvested food is perishable, meaning it must be prepared or preserved within days of purchase. These deadlines are daunting for people living alone, people balancing hectic and irregular work schedules, as well as those living together but eating apart.

Taste for Convenience

Food desert activists need to be patient. Eating habits will not change overnight, or even in a few years. American's taste for convenience will likely take generations to change. This is disheartening, but it can also give us hope. This is a taste largely of our own making, and so what has been done *can* be undone. Changing tastes will not reduce retail inequality, but improving health is still a worthy goal.

First, we have to overcome some daunting biological, cultural, and material obstacles. The biological aspect is something that makes most sociologists uncomfortable. We would much rather document the health impacts of income inequality or how the material world shapes the development of cultural values than account for how taste buds work. However, our bodies are material, as is our food. Access and exposure to different kinds of food can change the tastes we pass on to our children; not just through socialization and embodiment, but through small but consequential shifts in how their bodies respond to different flavors, ingredients, and quantities.

As I've explored in earlier chapters, our innate cravings and aversions—hardwired via evolution—are now being manipulated by advanced food processing technologies (Katz and Sadacca 2011). The not-so-secret dirty secret of supermarkets is that they are filled with processed items that appeal to our innate biological cravings of salt, sugar, and fat. Mothers that acquire these tastes can act as "flavor bridges" and pass them on to their offspring (Mennella, Jagnow, and Beauchamp 2001). The quality and quantity of food exposed to infants can create lifelong epigenetic changes in how our bodies respond to it later on (Gluckman and Hanson 2009). In short, we changed the food system, and now the food system is changing us.

Nor is the durable taste for "convenience" foods I found among my interviewees unique to food deserts.[14] It is a nationwide phenomenon. Many of my interviewees only used their stoves, ovens, or microwaves to warm pre- or par-cooked food unless it was a special occasion. Most Americans, across income and geography, enjoy and eat fast food.

Yet, biology is not destiny; it may set us in particular directions, but we have the ability to course correct. Adults' tastes can and do change, usually coinciding with changes to their economic and social circumstances. That is, the "conditions of existence" (Bourdieu 1984: 178) that shape our preferences shift over time. Access and exposure to certain foods are part of these "conditions," too. Our individual tastes are our own, yet they are shaped by external social forces. To change them will take time, a long time, but not forever. To say that pre- and par-cooked foods prepared by others will always be as popular as they are today is short sighted. Humans have agency. We have the power to eat differently. We ate differently in the past, and will likely eat differently in the future. Historically, the only constant is change.

CONCLUSION

To understand why initiatives in food deserts are unlikely to change the way people buy and eat food, we need a more scientific approach. We need to identify and understand far more about the people whose behavior we're trying to change, and we need to identify and understand far more about the people designing and implementing the interventions. Whether they volunteered for this task or were lumped into this category by others, they both are cast in media accounts as the problem solvers. I found that their methods and goals varied, but their work fell under five main categories. They hoped that they could improve access and affordability by buying directly from farmers, providing nutritional education, using urban agriculture, improving donated food options, and creating new retail options. Even if they cannot directly change the way people eat, their efforts to improve access to better food should be applauded. The mobile farmers' market operators who wanted to truck vegetables directly into the neighborhoods; the consultants who wanted to teach people to start kitchen gardens; the "local food" mini-grocery that offered a lifeline to small farmers; and the well-meaning former produce manager who read a newspaper article and tried to start a nonprofit—these people were not in it solely for the money, they were trying to make the world a better place.

Media accounts may point to local farms or convenience stores owners as possible fixes, but they might think twice if they understood the economic challenges those businesses face. Policy makers who see local food and "point-of-purchase" retail interventions as ready solutions might think differently if they actually talked to the people running farms and gas stations.

Many food desert solutions will be hard-pressed to change residents' purchasing and consumption habits. They overlook the everyday realities of living in these neighborhoods. Those resources and constraints first outlined in chapters 3 and 4 offer a framework to assess the viability of proposed remedies. Any workable idea must account for residents' perception of their food environment, economic circumstances, transportation options, social capital, household dynamics, and taste for convenience. It must be visible within residents' habitus, target the "near poor," provide for one-stop shopping, be available morning until night, make healthy eating efficient, and be willing to play the long game—dietary change takes time.

Now that we see how current efforts will not work, it is time to reconceptualize the food desert debate and find ways to actually help these neighborhoods' residents. This means acknowledging that, like anyone, these locals want better retail, regardless of whether they can support those businesses themselves. They want investment, but only from stores that will act as partners. For now, they require help getting to and buying the goods and services they need, as well as political support while they work to improve the options nearby. And even though the fight was never only about food, they will still need help if they want to prepare healthier options at home. We can help. We just need to design solutions that meet our neighbors where they are—we need to help them design the interventions that will actually improve their lives.

7 A Path Forward

This is a book about retail inequality, race in America, and how we misunderstood the food desert debate. And by "we," I mean the scholars, the media, the policy advocates, and the politicians who decided that we knew best what the people who lived in these neighborhoods really wanted. We need to be held to account—myself included—for initially framing this issue around health and food when it was really about respect and fairness.

Urban food deserts are not randomly distributed in America. They are the legacy of public and private sector abandonment of the urban core decades ago. When investment shifted toward suburban development and infrastructure, these neighborhoods were left behind. White residents with resources fled to build intergenerational wealth elsewhere. Remaining retail withered, unable to compete with the newer and larger options just outside of town. The continued loss of manufacturing jobs left homes vacant and storefronts empty. Racially segregated and concentrated poverty settled into these hollowed out remains.

Now white residents are coming back, retail too; but the newcomers riding this wave of gentrification do not know what these neighborhoods went through. They are unaware of the past fights to push out the liquor stores and the pawn shops. They do not understand why longtime residents would object to a brand-new brewery or a mixed-use development

For decades, Black men and women in these neighborhoods have been screaming into the void for better retail. One day, they finally discovered a rallying cry that caught outsiders' attention: healthy food. It caught mine. I heard their complaints about the lack of a grocery store and I started dreaming of ways to bring "local food" to the community. This is the trap of the healthy food frame. I could only imagine solutions that whet my appetite, too. For me, with my white, middle-class tastes, fighting for "healthy food" was a way to do good for the neighborhood and also cater to my own interests. Looking back, I see how my rush to the local food solution was really just the safe way out. My privilege blinded me: it wasn't about fruits and vegetables, it was about racism and poverty.

Looking back, I still marvel at how a term with a first official mention in a 1995 British taskforce report could become the theoretical foundation for a multimillion-dollar federal funding initiative in the United States less than two decades later. The passage of the Healthy Food Financing Initiative marked an astounding accomplishment for a wonkish policy concept. But the subsequent decline of the food desert concept also makes me sad. In many ways, I still wish it were true. I wish we could improve health with a solution as simple as putting a new store in an underserved area. But now research has shown that the usual set of interventions do not change the way people eat. I suspect we will keep trying. I just hope we can put more focus on the real remedy residents were asking for: retail equality.

The adjacent neighborhoods of Southernside and West Greenville unfortunately represent the textbook case of how this sad story has played out in small cities across the country. The economy of Greenville, South Carolina, underwent these painful transitions in its economy and redistribution of retail after the decline of its textile industry. Manufacturing jobs that once constituted a third of all employment now employ less than one-tenth of working adults. Roadway projects—one planned but never built ("The Downtown Loop"), another that bisected residential areas (The Pete Hollis Boulevard)—depopulated and disconnected these neighborhoods. City residents today see these communities as historically Black, and they are. But they were less racially segregated half a century ago. White residents once represented 40 percent of these neighborhoods. But most left for the suburbs. By 2010, only 15 percent of Southernside and West Greenville were white. This contraction caused the population to drop to one-third of what it was in 1960. Without people or consumer buying power, local businesses lost their customer base.

Retail inequality doesn't happen overnight. The mom-and-pop stores that dotted their neighborhoods were the first to vanish. The historic Kash and Karry, remembered fondly by longtime residents as "their" store, closed soon after. The quality and selection in these stores may not compare to today's standards, but that wasn't the point. They were a tangible signifier of the neighborhood's worth. And now they are gone. A smaller supermarket replaced it a mile away, affectionately referred to as the "Baby BI-LO," but it closed in 2013. The local paper started running features on the food desert problem and referring to this side of town as the "Unseen Greenville." These were the precursors to my entrance in this field of research in 2014. The food environment had hit rock bottom. Speculators were beginning to enter the market. Opportunity and tension were in the air.

When I started researching food deserts, I was not a stranger to the Southernside community. I had worked with its neighborhood association for years to try to stop the state's Department of Transportation from tearing down a bridge that connected them to a neighboring community on the other side of the railroad tracks. We lost that battle, but during that time I came to learn of their frustrations about the lack of a grocery store in the area. I kept in touch by showing up at city and county meetings advocating for funds to rebuild the bridge, and I began attending meetings and public events that addressed the lack of food options. I expanded my scope to include an adjacent neighborhood called West Greenville. They shared a similar history of demographic change and also were without easy access to healthy food.

Being new to the debate about food access helped me see the field with fresh eyes. I was not a public health researcher or a geographer. I was not invested in any particular study or set of findings. But my newness also set me back: having no stake in any particular solutions, my own tastes and preferences blinded me to the shortcomings of the one that appealed to me the most: local food. When I signed up to work at Greenbrier Farms in Dacusville, South Carolina, to test out its feasibility, I was naive. It took a month of hard work before I learned my lesson. But I had to start some-where, so after I finished my stint planting tomatoes and corralling steers, I did what any academic would do: I read every single thing written about food deserts I could get my hands on.

I learned that the first comprehensive studies of food desert inter-ventions in the early 2000s yielded positive results. New grocery stores seemed to have a small but clear impact, especially for the most vulnerable residents. This created a sense of hope for those looking at the correlation of poverty, geography, and eating habits. We knew (and still do) that the poorest areas have the fewest grocery stores. We knew (and still do) that the poorest areas also have the worst health outcomes. Perhaps it was the lack of stores causing their health problems. Right?

Soon after, support for the concept started to thin. The first tell-tale sign was when businesses intentionally built to solve the problem started to fail. Media accounts of grand openings framed these ventures as long-awaited sure things. But the supposed pent-up demand for fresh fruits, vegetables, and whole foods rarely materialized. They built it, but the shoppers didn't come. Large corporations made big promises of inserting fresh and healthy food in their existing stores, too; sadly, many of those never materialized. Nonprofits and community ventures fared better than strictly for-profit initiatives, but their success rate was lower than expected. Still, business closures are not enough to indict the concept of the retail intervention. After all, stores go out of business all the time. Sell-ing food is a tough business. More research was needed.

Academics started to flag the shortcomings inherent in the food des-ert concept starting in 2011, especially when studies began to adopt more comprehensive methodologies. New research used pre- and post-test designs, relied on longitudinal rather than cross-sectional data, and com-pared the eating practices of neighborhoods getting new stores against those in demographically similar "control" neighborhoods whose food environments went unchanged. The results were disheartening. After community leaders, commercial outfits, and the federal government had invested so much time and energy into improving healthy food access, this food desert fix wasn't producing the dietary change they wanted.

Retail interventions were not the only solutions out there. Other ini-tiatives, like farmers markets subsidies, nutritional education campaigns, community garden initiatives, and refashioning convenience store layouts were also tried. But none of *these* efforts could definitively show dietary change, either. By 2017, the consensus within the scholarly community had changed dramatically. We could not reduce food purchasing and consumption practices to a few variables like price and proximity.

The media did not get the memo. News accounts continued to refer to pre-2011 research that suggested that distance determined diet. The durability of causal narrative is important, because it shows just how powerful the food desert concept was at the time. Despite a growing body of research questioning the idea, the conventional wisdom hardly budged. To show this, I reviewed 389 news articles, transcripts, wire-feeds, press releases, and op-eds published on food deserts from 2011 through 2017. The majority referred to older studies while ignoring newer findings; others repeated claims that had never been proven in the first place. For example, 33 percent of these accounts claimed that food desert residents rely on convenience stores and fast food for the bulk of their diets. Yet, a quick review of the research (old and new) shows that this is simply not true. Yes, food desert residents buy snacks and drinks at convenience stores as well as the occasional last-minute grocery item, but they do not depend on them for their dried, canned, and fresh items. Yes, food desert residents eat a lot of fast food, but so do Americans who live near supermarkets. Fast-food consumption, in fact, increases with wealth. Despite this evidence, these misperceptions persisted in news media.

Media accounts reflected how muddled and confusing the food desert debate had become. For example, food deserts are routinely conflated with other food-related issues, most notably food insecurity. While the two are related—especially among those who cannot afford any extra travel costs— they are different problems with different causes and require different solutions. Those surviving well below the poverty line have troubles that a closer store cannot solve. Yet nearly one in five media accounts during that time used the terms *food deserts* and *food insecurity* interchangeably.

As soon as I began my comparison of the academic literature with media accounts I knew I would need to talk to people in Southernside and West Greenville to find answers. (Surprisingly, only a few books out there do this.)[1] I went to people's homes and asked straightforward questions. I talked to people with or without cars, with or without jobs, with or without family and housemates. Some of these people I already knew through my work with the community; others I found through connections I made attending neighborhood meetings. I sat with them in their kitchens and dining rooms and we talked about what was in their cabinets. I asked them what they thought of existing stores and how they decided what to purchase, prepare, and eat. Afterward, I would calculate the precise driving distances between their homes and nearest grocery stores; but during our conversations I wanted a deeper understanding of what they thought about their retail environment. If they had grown up in the neighborhood, what were their early memories of the stores that had since closed down? How had the neighborhood changed? How did they feel about it?

I do not claim my sample is statistically representative, but I did learn how living in different circumstances can make dietary change feasible or infeasible. By the end, I interviewed eighty-five residents of Southernside and West Greenville and came to see the logic behind their choices. Their food practices are governed by a set of everyday realities, many of which were out of their control and unlikely to change anytime soon. I finally began to see why most food desert solutions have not worked.

The first set of realities are familiar to those who follow the food desert debate: perception, economics, and transportation. The second are rarely mentioned, but deserve closer attention: residents' social capital, household dynamics, and their taste for convenience foods. These realities can make or break their ability to access fresh food, prepare it, and consume it.

In regard to perception, I expected residents to be unsatisfied with their current options. However, their frustration ran deeper. It was grounded in both the past and present. Looking back, it was easier to get food in the neighborhood forty years ago than it was today. This was progress? Looking around today, we can see other areas of the city were getting new stores. Why must their side of town be the depository for bad retail?

Lack of money excluded some residents from participating in the retail food market. They relied on food pantries and soup kitchens to meet their dietary needs. Residents hovering over the poverty line straddled the retail and non-retail food markets; buying most of their food in stores while using donated food to make it through the end of the month.

As for transportation, those who had working vehicles had a number of options from which to choose. Their regular travels to and from work, family, worship, and appointments caused them to cross paths with more stores than outsiders would assume if they looked only at their residential addresses. Those without cars may have lived near bus routes, but they generally saw the public transportation system as inconvenient and impractical. For those with mobility problems, the bus ride was the least of their problems: it was the stairs, curbs, and the parking lots that made transit impractical.

While many media accounts depict food desert residents as passive victims to their food environment, they are wrong. Those with limited food budgets swapped and shared food with others. Those without cars found rides. These workarounds were not easy, but residents used their social capital to open up new opportunities. They cultivated an informal ride network that was more convenient than the bus, cheaper than taxis, and driven by familiar faces. Of course, there are limits to what social capital can provide, but it is still a resource worth examining.

Even if we can help people overcome their economic and geographic barriers to access, though, more daunting obstacles to dietary change remain. Being able to buy groceries and being willing to cook them are two different things. While cooking at home does not guarantee a better diet, the food desert concept is *built* upon the idea that lack of fresh and whole foods leads to poor health outcomes. Meanwhile, decisions about whether to cook or consume prepared food were made with individuals' household dynamics in mind. Food that is pre- and par-cooked is faster to consume and requires minimal cleanup. Small households, single parents, and adults living alone do not have enough mouths to feed at the same time with the same tastes to justify the time and effort necessary to cook meals from scratch. Sometimes, thawing and heating ready-made meals is the more logical choice.

There is also a rational explanation for food desert residents' taste for convenience foods. They, like *all* Americans, have developed a durable preference for them. The food environment has changed with the advent of new food processing technologies, ingredients, and techniques. Decades of exposure to unhealthy foods and deprivation from healthy ones has changed both our cultural tastes and our bodies. These new tastes for convenience are of our own making and will likely take generations to be undone.

In the food desert debate, the importance of dietary tastes and preferences cannot be overstated. Tastes are embodied, slow to evolve, and personally felt. This point was utterly clear among my interviews: The residents liked what they ate, knew they should probably eat a little healthier, and had no intention of changing their diets dramatically. Even though a grocery store would make it easier, quicker, and less costly to cook meals from scratch, my interviewees admitted that closer access to healthier food was unlikely to change their mealtime routines. Their diets were entangled in their other everyday realities that were not going to change in the near future.

Once I was convinced that a new store would not change the way people buy and eat food, I finally gained the confidence to explore the food desert concept as a political strategy: a talking point that can get the attention of local officials and white, middle-class allies. Not everyone in the neighborhoods I studied were savvy political actors, but some were. Watching them teach their neighbors how to use the language of public health was a political science masterclass. From this new perspective I finally understood why the people I interviewed talked so differently about food in private than they did in public. At neighborhood meetings and forums, "healthy food" was front and center. Residents lamented the lack of grocery stores and the saturation of fast food franchises. In private, however, they rarely mentioned the health impacts of not having a supermarket; they enjoyed what they ate and confided that a new store would not likely change their dietary practices. The fight over food deserts wasn't really about food.

Adopting the healthy food frame had its drawbacks, though. It did bring a number of new allies to the table, but it also set up a lot of their efforts for failure. In Greenville, a mobile farmers market struggled to attract customers and eventually stopped coming. The same nonprofit opened a "brick and mortar" market that subsidized healthy purchases but eventually had to close due to lack of business. Nearby residents liked the *idea* of these ventures, but they did not plan to change their eating or shopping habits.

Failed food desert interventions pose a problem for these neighborhoods. Using public funds to subsidize investment in their neighborhoods is contingent on results. And if those goals are measured in health outcomes and business viability, further funding becomes less likely. This is the problem with the healthy food frame: it assumes food desert residents are ready to pounce at opportunities to buy nutritious offerings at a moment's notice. But they cannot: their eating practices are nested within their existing circumstances. They want better retail even if their personal circumstances preclude their ability to take advantage of it. They want retail restitution for the historical neglect and abandonment of their neighborhoods.

MAKING IT RIGHT

So what now? Reinvestment in neighborhoods like Southernside and West Greenville will take at least a generation to restore their past population levels. Area improvements (sidewalks, parks) also have unintended consequences: amenities that make neighborhoods more attractive also drive up housing costs, potentially displacing the same residents we are trying to help. There are measures to ameliorate the impact of rising property values like homestead exemptions and inclusionary zoning practices, but I will leave large scale urban planning policy debates for others to discuss. Instead, I am interested in smaller, more practical steps that we can take today with existing resources at hand. I will focus heavily on improving food options, but the same strategies can be applied to achieve other forms of retail equality. The first three proposals do not require any resources, they outline ways of rethinking the food desert concept, why activists were so drawn to it, and how to design solutions that meet people where they are. The last four do require some financial help, but at a fraction of the cost of building a new store or expanding public transportation. They amplify the efforts of existing local businesses and resources and—more importantly—keep the money in the neighborhood.

Move the Goal Posts

Undoing retail inequality will take time and cost money. We need to be clear at the beginning about what this kind of investment can and cannot do. In the case of food retail, if subsidizing new outlets can improve health outcomes, so be it. But that should not be the goal. Instead we should justify programs like the Healthy Food Financing Initiative via their more indirect and non-health-related impacts. Some benefits will not be quantifiable. And that is okay. Making up for past wrongs is the just and fair thing to do. No single solution can solve all of the world's problems; just because economic subsidies and incentives likely cannot overcome the most difficult obstacles to changing the way people eat does not discount the other benefits they offer. They still need to be celebrated and supported.

Helping people buy food from farmers offers a lot of potential benefits. Buying locally produced food can reduce costs—maybe not enough to beat the prices at Walmart, but the direct-to-consumer model introduces its own efficiencies into the retail food market. It also supports the local economy; the money customers spend will ultimately be reinvested in their area via the goods and services that farmers buy and the labor they employ.

Local food also reduces environmental externalities. These savings are not directly felt by food desert residents, but the opposite—degrading the environment—comes at a cost that we will eventually have to pay. Over the month I spent at Greenbrier planting tomatoes and corralling steers, I saw a clear effort at sustainable practices that larger corporate agriculture and livestock operations largely avoid. The owners lived on the land they farmed. Their children played in its fields. They were invested in the health of its soil and water. Improving their land was a means to produce a high-quality product as well as preserve it for future use.

Educational efforts to teach people how to eat better are, similarly, an investment in our future. In an era where eating food prepared outside the home is now the new normal, fewer parents are teaching these skills to their children. The next generation of families that engages in home cooking and food preservation will need help from nutritional advocates. Cooking is both a cognitive and an embodied skill. The end result needs to be satisfying, both rationally and emotionally. Logical appeals to work with raw ingredients and whole foods are not enough. Unhealthy, processed food will always be cheaper and easier in the immediate short term. Yet the costs in time and money will be worth it if we consider the long-term yields of better health and maintaining the cultural legacy of regional foodways.

Urban agriculture serves a number of important functions, too. Seeing how a seed can become a meal is to connect with our history as a species. Even if one is disinclined to eat bell peppers, the sunk costs of a community garden can increase the appeal of those bell peppers in the eyes of those who tended the plants over time. Growing involves physical activity and allows people to see their neighbors from a perspective other than behind window blinds. If organized enough, communal urban gardening can yield large amounts of food. Perhaps not enough to move residents to change their eating patterns, but sufficient to produce healthy alternatives during the growing season.

Improving the donated food environment is an ethical imperative. Humans need food to survive. To deny it to the hungry is cruel and inhumane. The least we can do is make free food more palatable. This will require higher-quality healthy foods as well as unhealthy foods. The latter is equally crucial, no matter how counterintuitive that sounds. Food pantries and soup kitchens would love to get their clients to eat healthier items, but they are constrained by the ingredients they have and what their clients actually want. For all the hardship facing those living below the poverty line, should we begrudge them their taste for something *they* want every now and then? Those experiencing food insecurity are trying to meet their basic needs; once those are settled, we can design more ambitious dietary goals.

Lastly, even though I have been critical of the retail interventions attempted in Greenville and across the country, they still deserve applause. They may not have been able to change the way people ate, but they invested time, energy, and money in communities that have long been ignored. It is not their fault that the everyday realities of the people they are trying to help made it too difficult for them to take advantage of these offerings. These businesses and nonprofits tried to use food as a vehicle to do good. Instead of blaming them for failing to change the way people eat, we should move the goal posts to celebrate their other achievements.

Be on the Lookout for Irresistible Concepts

The rise of the food desert concept helped draw attention to neighborhoods in need, but distracted outsiders from the deeper root causes of the problem. To not make the same mistake again, we need to identify the generic processes of how social scientific concepts can rise to such popularity and influence. As outlined in chapter 2, our receptivity to it was rapid and understandable. There was a crisis. Obesity rates for adults were on the rise, and the lifelong implications of childhood obesity pulls at our heartstrings. The correlation between obesity and poverty is real. While it is ironic that those with the least weigh the most, comparing the price per calorie of unhealthy food vs healthy food is a fairly easy route to understanding. Eradicating poverty was apparently too daunting a task, though, so something else would have to stem the crisis.

Geographic arguments are compelling. Some say that the current state of accumulated global inequities all boils down to geographic luck of developed regions' earliest settlers (Diamond 1997). Maps have helped us solve public health outbreaks, like cholera. Spatial analysis has been boosted by the proliferation of accessible Geographic Information System (GIS) software. What once required mainframe computers can now be done on a laptop. However, just because it is now easier to map social problems does not mean we should be quicker to accept that geography-based approaches can solve those social problems.

This is what happened with another irresistible concept: "broken windows theory." Its appeal persisted in the public imagination long after academic research showed its flaws. The "CompStat" approach to police incident mapping was named the hero of the reduction in crime in New York City in the 1990s. We now know that crime rates were dropping all over the country, including areas that did not adopt the strategy. Broken windows theory only fell out of political favor when it was used to justify the overly authoritarian (and often racist) strategy known as "stop and frisk." But even then, the case against the theory was only that it was executed too harshly. I still hear cops refer to broken windows theory as gospel at neighborhood meetings in Southernside and West Greenville to this day.

To be on the lookout for the next irresistible idea, we need to remember the conditions necessary for the rise of the food desert concept. First, it appeared during a period of crisis, making for an eager audience. Two, its advocates were able to communicate it with newly accessible mapping technology. Three, reframing retail inequality as a health and food issue attracted new allies (middle class, white) who were more willing to tackle the symptom than its larger root causes (racism and poverty).

Recognize the Everyday Realities of the People Who Live in Food Deserts

Selling healthy food is not always economically viable in food deserts. Residents often lack the necessary density and buying power to keep them in business. These ventures may fail, and when they do, we should not blame the community for failing to support them. People who live in food deserts are unable to change their diets overnight when a new option is made available. This isn't their fault. Dietary behavioral change is difficult. And slow.

To understand just how daunting a task it is, consider the following thought experiment: What if we had the resources to deliver a free box of fresh fruits, vegetables, lean meats, and whole foods to every doorstep in a food desert? Problem solved, right? Not so fast. For this free box to be acquired and utilized, it must also fit within the six realities of the recipient households. Think of each of these realities as individual switches in an electrical circuit. To get the current all the way to the bulb, all switches must be flipped to the on position at the same time. A single closed circuit can disrupt the flow.

First, to transform this box into a consistent set of meals, the contents must be culturally familiar. By familiar, I mean foods that residents have had before and know how to prepare. The residents would have to trust the delivery system, too. This is the lesson I learned about residents' perception of their food environment when they told me that they would never seriously consider buying fresh food at a gas station. To them, gas stations weren't places to shop for fresh ingredients. Second, even if the individual items are culturally familiar and come from a trusted source, they must be able to fit together to form a whole dish. If the potential combination of ingredients is unclear, the utility of the box becomes less visible—it's like being handed a set of keys without being told what they unlock.

So a free box of healthy foods solves most of the economic challenges of food desert residents. For those who could not otherwise afford it, the box enables access; for those who already could, the box provides convenience.

Remember, those living well below poverty cannot take advantage of new retail options no matter how close, and those well above already have the means to buy healthy food should they choose to do so. The poorest among us might have trouble preparing the contents if they also lack the necessary kitchen space, equipment, and basic essentials to engage in home cooking. Thus we see again that a free box would have the best chance to change dietary practices among the "near poor." For them, it is the extra transportation costs to travel outside the food desert that make healthy food unaffordable. Still, a free box would not eliminate all of their travel costs.

That's because homes need other items: toilet paper and cleaning products, for instance. Free food boxes would be a remarkable service for food desert residents, but they would still have to go shopping at some point during the month anyway. A free box would enable them to shop at stores that do not offer fresh food—like dollar stores—which would make their lives much easier. However, cooking requires more than just raw ingredients. Households still need recipe-specific spices and seasonings, for example. Coordinating their purchases with the arrival of the box requires a level of planning that's difficult for families in precarious circumstances, especially considering the time-sensitive nature of perishable food. In short, people with few transportation resources (public or private) need one-stop shopping, and if they need to cook the food in their box soon after its delivery, then they will also need on-demand travel, the one service the informal ride network cannot provide.

Food desert residents are resilient. Like everyone else, they have agency and will design innovative solutions that many outsiders fail to recognize. The informal ride network allowed people to trade promises of reciprocity to get to stores within a five-mile radius at least once a month. Even though these rides came at a cost—economic and emotional—they provided door-to-door service that no public transportation system could match. The only drawback was that shoppers could not demand a precise pickup date and time. The drivers in the system had their own lives and obligations. For a free box of healthy food to help, the delivery schedule would have to be predictable and the contents would have to be able to last until the drivers in the network were ready to go to the store for the ancillary items.

And even then, how would you get people to see preparing food as worth the effort? If we could find a way to deliver free, fresh (for at least a week), and culturally appropriate food boxes to people with enough predictability that they could coordinate their other shopping around them, we still would have flipped only four of the six circuits necessary to transform the contents into a meal. Household dynamics are the fifth circuit. Are there enough mouths to feed at the same time with the same tastes to justify home cooking? Single mothers with children, for example, would most likely use the box to make one dish for themselves and another for the younger ones. A free food box would reduce the economic risks of children rejecting unfamiliar foods, but the coordination of times and tastes would still be tricky. For the 28 percent of American households that consist of only one person, preparing meals from scratch (and cleaning afterward) would still take longer than consuming food prepared outside the home.

That brings us to the sixth, possibly most stubborn circumstance: taste. Would people want to eat a meal from the box? While fresh and healthy ingredients would seemingly solve all the problems of our current dietary practices, tastes are hard to change. The interaction of culture, biology, and access to particular foods over the last few decades has produced a durable taste for convenience—and not just in food deserts. When people say they like the food they eat, we should believe them. When people say they aspire to like new and healthier foods, we should help them. When people fail to take advantage of our efforts to change the way they eat, we should keep trying.

The food environment has undergone serious structural transformations of our own making. Designers of processed foods have learned how to manipulate our responses to food and make products that are difficult to resist. In some cases, foods have changed how our bodies respond to them with lasting and intergenerational effects. Flipping all six circuits on the way to better diets will take a lot of work and resources. Most importantly, it will take a lot of time. We need to be patient.

Subsidize Informal Ride Networks

Because it is hard to get good retail to move into poorer neighborhoods, residents will still need to find a way to get the goods and services they need. Helping them access those things will require transportation. Current policy discussions typically weigh the costs and benefits of expanding public systems to move people, but those are expensive projects for smaller cities like Greenville.

For the time being, successful solutions will need to capitalize on residents' existing strengths. The informal ride network in Southernside and West Greenville was impressive. It provided door-to-door service, drivers would often wait until shoppers were finished, and drivers and neighbors often helped people with mobility problems get groceries into and out of the trunk, even into the shopper's cupboards. No public transportation can match this service; it shouldn't try. Instead, a more effective solution is to keep the money in the neighborhood and subsidize the network as is.

In 2019, the Department of For-Hire Vehicles (2019) in Washington, D.C., announced that it was offering residents up to $10 vouchers to use its "Taxi-to-Rail" program for rides to grocery stores, libraries, and recreation centers.[2] Rail systems—while very efficient—face "last mile" problems like shipping and distribution systems. Even though subways and light rail can deliver passengers from stop to stop, getting people who live farther than a comfortable walking distance to utilize them is a challenge. Yes, people with cars can "park-and-ride," but they already have travel options. Buses can fill this gap, but creating new bus routes is expensive. So the transportation department in Washington, D.C., decided to outsource the solution to local cab companies.

Instead of paying taxi drivers, why not direct the money to the people already providing the rides? These nieces, nephews, cousins, and friends-of-friends know their riders well, norms of reciprocity encourage them to offer good service, and paying them directly keeps the money in the neighborhood. Drivers could cash in their vouchers at retailers, which could request reimbursement from the City. Good retail might be more willing to locate nearby if businesses knew the City was facilitating the transportation of customers to their storefronts.

Subsidizing the informal ride network would both take advantage of and strengthen food desert residents' social capital. Those who paid for rides would be able to stretch their monthly budgets and no longer feel like a burden to others. Medicaid already has programs to reimburse those who act as caregivers for their relatives. A twenty-first-century "fares-for-food" ride program could accomplish similar goals. Paying people to help their neighbors is an ethical and efficient choice.

Skeptics will quickly point out the risks of misuse for personal gain by both drivers and riders. What if food desert residents just use the service to buy junk food? What if drivers keep the money and strand their riders? While there are means of preventing abuse, such as limiting the products riders could buy and requiring drivers to undergo rigorous certification, these regulations are not worth it. They would only make the program less flexible and undesirable. At some point, the benefits of means testing and strict oversight reaches a diminishing rate of return. This is not a luxury service; we are just helping people spend money at local businesses.

Harness the Potential of Nonprofits and Donated Food

In areas with high rates of poverty, people straddle the retail and non-retail market to get the things they need. A much higher percentage of my interviewees consumed donated food in the past three months than reported experiencing food insecurity. This means that they rarely turn down an offer of donated food just in case they might need it. Donated or subsidized food can also free up people's budgets for other retail or when bills come due.

The current business model of food retail (where they locate, what they sell, at what price) is not well suited to people hovering near the poverty line. A handful of retail interventions in food deserts have thrived economically, like Brown's Super Stores in the Philadelphia area (Singh 2015), but they are few and far between. Small operations in urban areas with higher real estate costs cannot compete on price with their larger competitors on the periphery. The market has failed our core communities.

This was clearly evident with the business failures and unfulfilled private-sector promises soon after the peak of political interest in food deserts in 2011. Shortly after the rollout of the Healthy Food Financing Initiative and the federal "Let's Move!" campaign, scores of well-intentioned businesses shut down, citing low customer demand. National retailers, like Walgreens, made sweeping promises about stocking stores in food deserts with healthier fare. It didn't happen. Why? Because for-profit enterprises need to make profits.

The clearest example of the financial challenges food deserts' retail interventions face can be seen in the recent closure of the Shop 'n Save in the Hill District of Pittsburgh. This store, built in 2013, initially received over $700,000 in public funds as well as a donation of $1 million from the owner of the Pittsburgh Penguins NHL team to subsidize its construction. It was the focus of intensive research by the RAND corporation, which surveyed residents before the store opened in order to measure its effect years later. Ultimately, the Shop 'n Save failed to divert neighborhood residents away from their familiar, but further shopping options. It closed down for good in 2019 (Dubowitz and Wagner 2019).

The lesson from these unfortunate stories is that if we want to sell healthy options in food deserts, we need to make a choice: do we want new stores to solve a social problem or make money? In some poor communities, you can't do both. Relying on ethical consumerism is not a long-term solution. "Vote with your fork" efforts that ask customers to pay higher prices to prop up for-profit businesses in their communities is too much to ask. People will make occasional symbolic purchases to show their support, but when it comes time for a big shop, they will get a ride to a supermarket on the edge of town.

From the trial and error of retail interventions over the last ten years, we have learned some interesting lessons. A few survived the wave of failures, after all. These were more often nonprofit and community-driven ventures (Brinkley et al. 2019) where store managers had lower pressure to make immediate profits and could be patient while the community adapted to their presence. We also saw that involving neighborhood stakeholders in the planning and design of a new store will tap into locals' social networks and serve as a form of free advertising. In short, the assistance to small stores can't stop with grants and subsidies; the support must continue indefinitely. These stores may not drastically change the way people eat, but that should not be the goal. They will provide the "good" retail that market forces siphoned away, and that is what matters.

Partner and Pair Existing Resources

For food desert residents to be able to take advantage of new retail opportunities, their offerings must fit within their existing circumstances. In other words, the goods and services need to be familiar and affordable, enable one-stop shopping, be open long hours, enable efficient consumption, and accommodate local tastes. Most food retail initiatives only address two or three of these requirements, and that is why residents don't rely on them. By pairing solutions and creating partnerships between businesses, we can multiply their effectiveness. Below I will outline how this could work to make it easier to sell healthy food, but the same concept applies to other businesses. If good retail isn't economically viable on its own, subsidize its work with another non-competing business that its customers also frequent.

I learned the art of pairing through my interviews with people who organized farmers markets. To make everyone happy, they had to set restrictions on who could sell goods. Primarily, they tried to reduce overlap. For example, shoppers want eggs, but if too many farmers sell them, none can sell enough to make money. Customers might be initially happy because competition drives down costs, but lower profits too much and sellers stop coming to market. Organizers tried to minimize direct competition between farmers and maximize the diversity of offerings across the market: with some selling eggs, others milk, others tomatoes, others salad greens, and so on. That way all the farmers can go home with empty trucks, full wallets, and—importantly—excitement about returning the following week.

One way communities might partner complementary vendors could involve placing fresh food stands near dollar stores. In many food deserts, after the local grocers left, discount dollar stores took their place. Residents often perceive these shops as blocking better retail from coming back, and there have been some recent efforts to limit their entry into poorer communities (Donahue and Mitchell 2018). Instead of threatening moratoriums, municipalities could negotiate for outdoor vending space for fresh food stands. A single trip to a farmers market is inefficient and costly for those without transportation, but a combined trip to a stand selling fresh food *and* the dollar store could enable one stop shopping. It won't overcome the constraints set by residents' household dynamics or their taste for convenience, but it can make food shopping easier.

Dollar stores sell dried goods, canned goods, cleaning supplies, and household items that you can't find at a farmers' market. They have parking and ample roadside visibility. Fresh food markets can offer items you can't buy in a dollar store: fresh fruits, vegetables, and whole cuts of meats (not just deli slices or frozen sausage). The expense of buying from farmers markets is amplified by prohibitions on reselling food bought wholesale and geographic constraints on how "local" farms need to be. If you waive these two restrictions, you can drop stands' prices considerably. Fresh vegetables and frozen "family packs" of meat need not be locally sourced. Conventionally grown food is cheaper still. While an individual has little need for twenty-five pounds of onions, resellers can buy in bulk and sell in small quantities to customers outside the dollar store after they have bought their dairy, frozen, canned, and dried foods inside.

Convenience stores are also a potential partner. They are accessible, located in or near urban food deserts, and already possess the infrastructure (parking, refrigerated space, cash registers, etc.) to sell food. Near Southernside and Greenville, there were three different gas stations with c-stores. Each attempted in some small way to offer healthier items, but only the statewide chain would offer future partnership possibilities for improving food access.

The flexibility of c-stores to set aside floor space for fresh items depends on the size of their business. The smallest gas station and c-store operation in Greenville was primarily a county-wide business with less than forty stores. Its offerings were limited to what food distributors were willing to deliver. The chain's owner wanted to sell more nutritious items, but he could only sell what could be delivered and stocked on his shelves, and space was at such a premium that sacrificing more profitable (and less healthy) items was too risky.

The multistate, regional chain had hundreds and hundreds of c-stores under its portfolio. It could also harness greater profits by cooking and preparing its own food and delivering it to stores with its own fleet. Not relying exclusively on third-party food providers would cut out an additional layer of costs. However, vertically integrated c-store chains work best when every store format is identical. This uniformity increases efficiency, but also eliminates any possibility of special offerings tailored to the tastes of specific food deserts.

This leaves mid-sized chains as the best candidate for partnering with a healthy food initiative. In Greenville, the locally owned statewide chain was large enough (more than eighty stores statewide) to support its own food commissary and distribution divisions, yet small enough that it could adjust its offerings depending on neighborhood need. Company representatives visited neighborhood meetings and became familiar figures. Local organizations wishing to increase the consumption of healthy food could work with mid-size chains to prepare and produce items in these chains' own commissaries. Because these chains have their own delivery fleets, these items can yield higher margins than selling food cooked by third parties. Given that selling fuel is the least profitable component of gas station c-stores, providing fresher options in food deserts might be a viable business strategy.

Meal-Kit Cooperatives

My last suggestion will not address residents' core complaint: retail inequality. It will instead be directed toward those who want to change what they eat. Even though the fight over food deserts was about more than food, we still need to help those trying to improve their diets. They are doing their best in a food environment not of their own making. Facilitating healthier eating will require getting them more involved in the act of meal preparation. Convenience foods can be healthy, but they are more expensive. There are too many incentives for the producers of pre- and par-cooked food to sacrifice our health for their profit. This is not just a problem in food deserts—although it is felt more acutely in them.

Consumers do not yet possess enough nutritional knowledge to understand how a dish prepared by others is qualitatively different than one we prepare ourselves. Nutritional labels are a start, but listing calories and grams, even spelling out the names of processed ingredients, isn't enough. Who knows the meaning of the multisyllabic processed ingredients in the list? Even those who do are unlikely to know what their long-term significance is to our health. If we understood what they meant, we might change the way we eat; but we do not, and so we are not.

The nightly, home-cooked meal, à la Norman Rockwell, is a myth that too often serves to blame women for failures in our food system (Bowen, Brenton, and Elliot 2019). The dynamics of today's smaller households, with their uneven work schedules and competing tastes for "adult" and "kid" food, make the traditional grocery store model of buying raw ingredients and preparing them at home an almost impossible undertaking. These demographic and cultural changes have been decades in the making.

Instead, for those willing to try to cook at home, we should try to recreate the circumstances that make food preparation the cheaper and quicker choice. Cooperation among households offers a tantalizing idea: if coordinating tastes and schedules is too difficult in single homes, what about community meal prep?

The act of cooking is perhaps the easiest, most enjoyable part of eating at home. The real work is the travel and the shopping and the chopping and the scrubbing. A pot on a timer can boil with minimal attention; measuring ingredients requires direct focus. Collective meal prep can make cooks more confident and cooking more efficient. Their appeal is evident in the rise of subscription-based meal-kit shipment programs, but those are too expensive to be a realistic solution to the food desert problem.

A possible, workable vision might include public health organizations or food-based nonprofits connecting existing social networks with ingredients, know-how, and prep space. A community organizer could identify and recruit residents, likely through preexisting associations like neighborhood organizations or Bible study groups. A piloted program would have to offer incentives in the form of subsidized food and free training. Menu decisions and recipe choices could be collaborative, so that participants could express their tastes and preferences and realistically hope to have them heard. Allowing people to have their say is crucial. "Food swap" experiments that organize exchanges of food rarely succeed because people want direct control over what they eat (Fitzmaurice and Schor 2019). Nutritionists with ample experience can help the co-op develop healthier versions of familiar dishes that can be tailored to individual households' size and tastes (Reicks et al. 2014). Together, the group could plan a week's worth of meals (including leftovers) with simple ingredients.

Early incentives (free food and training) could help draw in participants, with membership contingent upon individuals and pairs taking turns to purchase the ingredients from bulk wholesale club stores. That drives down costs per meal and eliminates the financial risk of food waste. Remember, for a small household, a whole head of broccoli is a race against time, and a dish that calls for 1 cup of florets is not worth a trip to the store. However, three heads split among a dozen people lowers costs and everyone gets only what they need. Dividing shopping duties also relieves pressure for those without transportation; they would still have to tap into the informal ride network, but with less frequency.

The next step, preparation, requires space and equipment. All of the homes where I conducted interviews of food desert residents had two things in common: the nearest grocery store was miles away, and a church or community center was much closer. While the kitchens of my poorest interviewees were sparsely equipped, professional-grade equipment was within walking distance. The task of the community organizer is to put residents in touch with existing resources where they live. In some cases, they might need to apply for grants to upgrade equipment and storage capacity to meet sanitary standards for food handling. Either way, investments in equipment and training would stay in the community. Further, bringing existing sites up to health standards for food preparation creates business opportunities. Certified shared kitchens or "culinary incubators" can offer local food entrepreneurs some space to prepare their value-added products before bringing them to market.

Developing recipes, acquiring ingredients, and securing work space will be the easiest part of collective meal-kit prep. Convincing people to work together and prepare meals together will be the most difficult. Cooking with others outside the home is not a familiar practice. The advantages pile up quickly, though. Preparing two to three meals at once is much faster than starting from scratch each evening. Working as a group makes the transfer of nutritional knowledge more efficient. Developing new skills is easier when people can watch and learn from each other in person, too: Trying to debone a chicken via a printed handout is intimidating; the pressure drops when you see you're not struggling alone. Which is to say, for those with little experience in the kitchen, cooking together can boost confidence.

Collective meal prep can solve a lot of problems in food deserts. It is a solution that is both old and new. To start, it will require grants and subsidies, most of which are already available. Community-based nutritional education is not novel, nor are initiatives that support collective kitchen space as a means to boost local food entrepreneurism. What is new is getting people to purchase, measure, chop, and pack meals together.

Solutions like this will not fix all the problems that food desert residents face, but it can make some things better. It can offer cost savings to the near poor who cannot afford the up-front costs of bulk purchases. It can improve diets by offering healthier takes on familiar dishes. It can expand human capital in the form of cooking skills. It can create local business opportunities by upfitting communal kitchen space. It can reduce food waste by pooling and dividing ingredients. It can relieve some of the pressure on the informal ride network. It can re-create the efficiencies that larger households enjoy for home cooking.

In the end, meal-kit co-ops are just one way to spur dietary change in America's underserved neighborhoods. We will need many. We will need to continually monitor successes and failures, making tweaks and overhauling plans and gathering resident feedback. For this or any other attempt to improve their lives to work—to really work, in lasting ways—we need to meet people where they are, tap into their existing resources, and offer them a fighting chance to make the most of their existing retail options. One day, if we reinvest in these neighborhoods, better retail will come and validate residents' worth as equal consumers in a vibrant community.

Epilogue

WINS AND LOSSES

The hardest part about researching retail inequality is knowing when to stop. The neighborhoods of Southernside and West Greenville were transforming rapidly throughout my research. White residents were moving back in and new businesses were opening to cater to their tastes and preferences. Longtime residents had not succeeded at getting a grocery store to come to the neighborhood, but if you wanted to get coffee, take a yoga class, or drink craft beer, your options were expanding.

To bring you up to date, I will detail the demographic changes that have occurred in Southernside and West Greenville, the city's efforts to right past wrongs, the battle over retail that rages on, the new business model of Greenbrier Farms, and the latest and least expected factor shaping the food environment: COVID-19.

THE TRANSFORMATIONS OF SOUTHERNSIDE AND WEST GREENVILLE

Throughout this book, I document the demographic changes in Southernside and West Greenville dating back to their population apex in 1960 (roughly nine thousand residents) down to their nadir in 2010 (less than three thousand).[1] Over the past ten years, the population has begun to rebound (the steady stream of new residents has raised the population by about 16%), though these neighborhoods are unlikely to return to their original composition. In 2014, their combined population was 72 percent Black, and just five years later, it was 51 percent Black. By all indications, as soon as 2025, these will no longer be "minority-majority" communities.

The new households popping up in Southernside and West Greenville are not only whiter, but much wealthier: the percentage of households in the neighborhoods earning over $100,000 jumped from 5.2 percent in 2014 to 23.1 percent in 2019 (all figures are in 2019 dollars, adjusted for inflation). During that same time span, the median household income has been pulled up from $17,705 to $36,167. On the surface, this should be a good thing, just like the decrease in the poverty rate from 43.3 percent to 20.5 percent. However, a closer look at community statistics reveals the untold story of "revitalization" in Greenville, South Carolina: the beneficiaries of these changes continued to be divided along racial lines. While the median household income among Black households on the west side of town had improved to reach $23,698 in 2019, that still paled in comparison to their white neighbors' earnings of $74,674 in that same year.

Thus, the transformations of Southernside and West Greenville are bittersweet. There is less blight, vacant homes are quickly refurbished, and people are starting to move back in. For the Black residents who waited out the bleak years, the reward is a flood of demographically different neighbors who do not know their community's history nor what they went through. Half a century ago, white families fled. When things hit rock bottom here, a new generation of white families arrived to take advantage of rock-bottom property values. Now the neighborhoods have returned the same racial proportion that existed in 1960, just with even wealthier and more educated white residents. The retail described as "coming back" is coming back for these newcomers' tastes and needs.

RIGHTING PAST WRONGS

I have tried throughout this book to document how supposedly color-blind policies and projects can have racially discriminatory outcomes. This provides the crucial context for why Southernside and West Greenville residents were so frustrated by what should have been welcome redevelopment. They were tired of being forgotten and neglected. Past governmental decisions about where to build roads and infrastructure had made their communities obsolete; like other postwar American cities, they had watched as the public sector enabled the growth of suburbs and private investment followed. Divestment and draining manufacturing jobs left the urban core high and dry. Today, as Greenville is touted as a city on the rebound, it remains to be seen whether local officials will be able to right past wrongs.

The City of Greenville's attempt comes in the form of Unity Park.[2] The sixty-acre project is proposed for location on the dividing line between Southernside and West Greenville, partially using land once used as the municipal public works and garbage truck parking lot. When completed, the $60 million endeavor will feature an environmental restoration of the Reedy River and a statue honoring Lila Mae Brock, a historical figure in the community (and mother of Lillian Brock Flemming, Southernside's city council member and political coach). In short: Unity Park is the city's official apology for the systemic racism and poverty these communities have suffered in the past.

I welcome the new park, though it also worries me. Now that public money is improving areas around the site (with paved roads, buried power lines, bike paths, and improved lighting, for instance), real estate speculators are circling the area. When I attend neighborhood meetings, I regularly ask people whether they have received an unsolicited call or letter offering to buy their homes for cash. Everyone has. When state and federal governments decided to invest in the suburbs, they created new pathways for building intergenerational wealth there. Now that they are doing the same in the urban core, locals and others have to wonder whether area improvements, like Unity Park, will drive up property values and ironically displace the people for whom this gesture is meant.

To its credit, the City of Greenville has created a number of policies and programs to prevent displacement. Having acquired land around the park, the City set up the Greenville Housing Fund, which will funnel public and private dollars to increase the number of residences for sale and rent at less than market value.[3] You may remember the aerial photos in chapter 5, showing entire neighborhood blocks of homes bulldozed and removed after 1955. The housing fund has proposed rebuilding homes on that same spot, among others. The program also offers loan support for those who need help repairing their homes.

ZONING BATTLES

The fight over good retail continues to this day. Longtime residents of Southernside and West Greenville want businesses to engage with them, offer goods and services that cater to their preferences, and treat them like valued consumers despite their limited economic means. As detailed throughout *Retail Inequality*, residents made the most of their limited opportunities to interrogate business representatives and try to learn whether they wanted to make the community a better place or just make money. As in gentrifying areas around the country, the fight over retail inequality is taking place in zoning board hearings and alcohol licensing panels. For those fighting to retain control over the type and quality of retail in their neighborhoods, bureaucratic red tape is often their last line of defense.

In chapter 5, I documented a few success stories. In West Greenville, a politically savvy resident, Jalen Elrod, was able to wield the "healthy food" frame to secure neighborhood opposition to a proposed Burger King. In Southernside, a determined neighborhood association president, Mary Duckett, threatened to travel to the state capital to lobby politicians to prevent a new brewery from opening near a senior housing project. But these victories were fleeting. The designers of the Burger King project took advantage of the fact that their building footprint straddled two adjacent lots with different zoning restrictions. By moving the building to the less restrictive portion and the parking lot to the more restrictive one, they were able to bypass zoning requirements that necessitated neighborhood feedback and move forward with the restaurant. And though the brewery project was halted, another sprang up a half mile away two years later. Once I spotted the "coming soon" signage while out for a bike ride, I called Mary Duckett. Normally the first to know these things because she kept tabs on local liquor license applications, Mary was surprised. Right away, she wanted to rally the troops for a tough fight: the new brewery was replacing a restaurant that had a liquor license before closing. Stopping it would be nearly impossible. But she was undaunted. Her moral crusade was not about temperance—she confessed that she enjoyed a margarita on special occasions—it was about fairness. Why did so many businesses want to serve alcohol in *this* neighborhood?

To help its underserved neighborhoods weather the storm of incoming development, the City of Greenville is experimenting with a new type of zoning strategy. South Carolina currently forbids mandatory "inclusionary zoning" requirements that force developers to set aside a portion of their planned commercial and residential space for use at below-market rates, so, in addition to establishing the Greenville Housing Fund, the city has opted to implement form-based zoning.

Form-based codes are a variation on traditional zoning. They place more emphasis on factors that influence the character of public spaces in order to shape a neighborhood's identity. The recently adopted code for Unity Park Neighborhood District (UPND) applies to a 360-acre area covering the lower third of the Southernside neighborhood (including 60-acre Unity Park). The UPND code has been rigorously designed to foster a walkable urban center that will protect existing residential areas from inappropriate infill and redevelopment. The code is intended to "promote affordability" and maintain the "character" of the neighborhood.

Will it work? I hope so. Am I optimistic? Not really.

GREENBRIER FARMS

In chapter 6, I describe my experience working on a local farm to see whether "local food" could be a solution to the food desert problem. Looking back on my naive thinking in 2014, I'm still surprised at how hopeful and optimistic I was about leveraging nearby agriculture to change the way people ate. After interviewing eighty-five residents in Southernside and West Greenville, I now know that the local food solution is impractical and infeasible—for both the producers and would-be consumers. The everyday realities of food desert residents are insurmountable. The economic pressures on small farms are too intense. The idea looks good on paper, but it won't work in practice.

Since then, I've kept up with the owners of Greenbrier: Chad Bishop, Amy Bishop, and Roddy Pick. Although they were pioneers at the downtown farmers market in Greenville, their field became crowded by new competitors selling similar products. In 2018, looking to diversify, Greenbrier applied for a special state permit to grow hemp in order to meet the growing demand for cannabidiol (commonly abbreviated CBD) for medically approved use. Growing hemp requires drastically different farming methods than the small-scale organic processes for which Greenbrier was known, and so the owners leased forty acres of conventional farmland a few miles away and toiled an entire summer to produce their first harvest.

Greenbrier also got into the restaurant game. The owners, partnering with a local chef, opened "Fork and Plough," a farm-to-table restaurant on the northeast side of Greenville. I was surprised that they got into that risky business, until I remembered that farming entails a host of its own economic uncertainties. Starting a restaurant might be daunting to some, but if you've been able to manage the threat of droughts, floods, hail, frost, pests, blight, and tax hikes, the risks of running an eatery seem relatively less scary.

But the toughest business challenge they had to overcome was also the one they least expected: COVID-19.

COVID-19

I completed the first full draft of this manuscript on March 11, 2020. You may recall that was the day that actor Tom Hanks announced that he had been diagnosed with the novel coronavirus we have come to know as COVID-19. For me, that was the day the pandemic suddenly felt very real and very close. I was visiting my parents in New Orleans and began to worry about the safety of air travel back home to Greenville. I was scared about my father, who had recently undergone surgery to repair a broken hip. I was concerned about my students at Furman University, who had just been told not to return to campus. My spouse called, worried about losing her job. My daughter was upset about not being able to see her friends face-to-face. And just when I thought things could not get more disorienting, I went to the grocery store. Walking up and down the aisles, confused by the empty shelves and lack of toilet paper, I started to question whether my conceptualization of dietary behavior in this book would still be applicable in a post-COVID world.

People's dietary decisions are mired in a complex web of everyday realities. On March 11, 2020, many of those realities began to suffer a jolting shock. And people's eating habits changed as a result. Reversing a decades-long trend, people started spending more money in grocery stores than in bars and restaurants (Clayton 2020). Market research showed decreases in eating out and increases in cooking food bought at grocery stores (Redman 2020). In other words, we saw a resurgence in what I call the "traditional grocery store model." Why? Because people's circumstances changed. Whether or not these produce permanent shifts our dietary practices, inside food deserts and out, depends on how long these COVID-19 changes last.

Perception

Eating habits are shaped by what options people perceive to be available to them. Being open and being seen as preferable are two different concerns. Shelter-in-place ordinances and restrictions on indoor dining created an immediate change in the type and number of places where one could purchase prepared food. However, opening doors to customers does not mean they will want to come in. Fear of infection can make trips outside the home less attractive even though the dishes on the menu remain the same. Restaurants can ease those fears by communicating their safety measures, but how diners respond is never a given.

Money

The rapid surge in unemployment caused many people in the United States and beyond to revisit their budgets, implementing household austerity measures and rethinking the purchase of food prepared outside the home. Those already in poverty faced increased competition for donated items as food pantries attempted to meet crushing demand (Kulish 2020). Emergency increases in the Supplemental Nutrition Assistance Program (SNAP) benefits made more grocery items available to those who straddle the retail and donated food markets (Coello 2020), but temporary relief will not produce lasting changes in diets. Healthier food is more expensive per calorie, meaning fresh and unprocessed foods will be out of reach for more people until the economic crisis ends.

Transportation

Public transportation systems saw a steep decrease in ridership once reports of COVID-19 began to emerge in cities across the country (Baskar 2020). This was due to service restrictions as well as fear of infection from usual riders. Although public transportation is regularly considered a solution to the food desert problem, the pandemic revealed some of its shortcomings in helping the people who need it the most.

Social Capital

With bus and subway systems becoming less viable, informal ride networks—like the one I detail in chapter 4—may prove to be a more resilient strategy to provide access to food than previously imagined. Although passengers in the same vehicle put each other at risk of infection, getting rides from the same driver each time can reduce the number of people one interacts with on a monthly basis compared to public transportation. In times of crisis, social networks can become an even more valuable resource. As public goods and services are restricted, many people are forced to rely on friends and family to fill the gap: something residents of food deserts have already learned to do out of necessity.

Household Dynamics

Likely the biggest cause of the increase in the "traditional grocery store model" can be found in the reshuffled household dynamics during COVID-19. Many parents lost their jobs or were forced to work remotely. Many children were forced to take classes online and had their recreational activities canceled, losing access to the meals often provided in those settings. Put together, more people together in the same place at the same time made home cooking a more viable option. It may take longer, but as financial insecurity increases, so does the incentive to spend time to save money. Tasks that once seemed inconvenient—meal planning, preparing, and clean up—become new forms of freeing up family budgets for other needs.

Taste for Convenience

The extent to which COVID-19 changes eating practices will not be measured in grocery store spending or reports of home cooking. The real test will be whether people change what they buy and how they prepare it in the long term. As I show in chapter 4, my interviewees—even those without cars—were generally able to get to the grocery store (if they participated in the retail food market). It was just that getting to the store and choosing to buy whole and unprocessed foods that require home preparation are two different things.

Most Americans have a durable "taste for convenience." That is, before COVID-19, the rich and poor alike preferred pre or par-cooked foods that required minimal preparation, storage, and clean-up. This would not be a problem if all convenience foods were nutritious enough to be part of a healthy diet. Some are. However, foods that are convenient *and* healthy cost more. The cheapest are the least nutritious but easiest to consume; unlike home cooking, these are mostly about reheating and assembling, microwaving cellophane-sealed trays or making a sandwich. If COVID-19 has nudged Americans to substitute convenient home versions of foods they used to order at restaurants and take-out venues, it's still unclear whether it has permanently shifted their dietary practices.

Changing diets is hard. Retail interventions in food deserts were unable to do it. But that does not mean it is impossible. Tastes can and do change. In this book I offer a model of taste that accounts for our biology, our socialization, and our material access to food. COVID-19 has already caused clear shifts in access; if public health restrictions last long enough, they might change the dietary practices that we pass on to the next generation. After all, as a nation, we ate differently in the past, and we'll likely eat differently in the future. We created the conditions that ushered in our current tastes, it may just take a pandemic to produce the conditions necessary to usher in new ones. The only constant is change.

Appendix

FOOD DESERT MEDIA DATABASE

Date	Title	Source
1/23/11	"Food deserts" challenge local area residents	*Richmond Times-Dispatch*
3/1/11	Pitt's Berg Center develops scorecard that measures food security in city communities	*University of Pittsburgh News Service*
3/3/11	Emanuel applauds 5 new Chicago grocery stores in food deserts	*Daily Herald*
4/5/11	Parents must be in charge on childhood obesity	*The Philadelphia Inquirer*
4/26/11	Nebraska lawmakers advance bill to encourage new health-food markets in "food deserts"	Associated Press Newswires
5/11/11	Finding an oasis in a nutritional food desert	*Abilene Reporter-News*
5/11/11	SD has higher rate than the national average of people with low access to healthy food	Associated Press Newswires
5/25/11	Heineman vetoes of Nebraska food desert and horse racing bills survive override attempt	Associated Press Newswires
6/2/11	Food deserts found amidst plentiful local food supplies	*Virginia Farm Bureau News & Resources*
6/7/11	"Food desert" public policy forum set for June 15 in Omaha	UNL News Releases
6/8/11	Perception and nutrition education	*Daily Camera*
6/10/11	Save the Children asks, "How do you choose your plate in a food desert?"	*Save the Children*

Date	Title	Source
6/15/11	Kendall College joins with Fresh Moves to address food deserts in Chicago	Targeted News Service
6/22/11	Roots of good health; farmers market for Flushing	New York Daily News
6/27/11	Healthy eats hard to find in Duval County, study shows	The Florida Times-Union
7/11/11	Food deserts in America: If you build a supermarket, will they come?	CNN Wire
7/13/11	Obesity crisis: Does a lack of grocery stores make poor neighborhoods fatter?	The Oregonian
7/13/11	Programs cropping up across USA to address "food deserts"	USA TODAY
7/19/11	Retailers line up to replenish food deserts	Gannett News Service
7/20/11	Chains and Michelle Obama team up on "food desert" stores	Reuters Health E-Line
7/20/11	Michelle Obama launches attack on US food deserts	Agence France Presse
7/20/11	Wal-Mart, SuperValu joining First Lady to boost food initiatives	Dow Jones News Service
7/21/11	Big retailers make pledge of stores for "food deserts"	The New York Times
7/21/11	Effort could bring more healthy retailers to Kern	The Bakersfield Californian
7/21/11	First lady, grocers vow to build stores in "food deserts"	Washington Post
7/23/11	Michelle Obama attacks "food deserts" to combat child obesity	Asian News International
7/25/11	Many parts of W.Va. considered to be in food desert	Register Herald
7/25/11	Task force to address lack of healthy options	The Atlanta Journal-Constitution
7/26/11	Mayor Emanuel announces plan	Targeted News Service
7/27/11	Healthy oasis: The First Lady makes a case for good-food access	Pittsburgh Post-Gazette
7/28/11	Local grocers snubbed for Whole Foods	The Detroit News
7/29/11	Corner-store program brings healthy food to the masses	The Philadelphia Daily News
8/4/11	Wendell Pierce, of "The Wire" and "Treme," to open groceries in New Orleans "food deserts"	Washington Post
8/5/11	Utica's garden grows greener	Hamilton College News
8/7/11	Fresh Moves brings fresh fruits and vegetables to Chicago's West Side	NBC Nightly News
8/12/11	Oasis in a food desert	City of Madison News

Date	Title	Source
8/14/11	It's hard to swallow. Nix "food desert" tag for 3M NYers lacking store	New York Daily News
8/17/11	Families struggle in "food desert" as programs end	Daily Herald
8/19/11	DCCK to deliver produce to D.C. food deserts	Washington Post
8/24/11	Health workers plant oasis in an East-side "food desert"	The Capital Times & Wisconsin State Journal
8/25/11	Fresh & Easy opens in S.F. Bayview-Hunters Point	SF Gate
8/25/11	SF neighborhood considered "food desert" gets new grocery store	The Houston Sun
8/31/11	The Rachel Maddow Show transcript 08/31/11	MSNBC
9/5/11	Maywood Market exemplifies grocery stores' struggles in "food deserts"	Chicago-Tribune
9/9/11	Philadelphia is creating a healthier "food desert"	The Philadelphia Daily News
9/13/11	City receives $20,000 grant to advance urban agriculture	Kansas City infoZine
9/19/11	Food deserts bloom around Lima	The Lima News
9/22/11	PBS NewsHour for September 22, 2011	PBS
10/12/11	Life in food desert can be fattening	Ventura County Star
10/12/11	Oregon's obesity crisis: Seeking solutions in the design of cities and suburbs	The Oregonian
10/13/11	USDA supports diverse food access through farmers market promotion program grants	United States Department of Agriculture
10/19/11	Five myths about healthy eating; from food deserts to Tony the Tiger.	Washington Post
10/22/11	In our view: Cheers & jeers	The Columbian
10/25/11	First Lady Michelle Obama on making a difference in cities with food deserts	The White House
10/25/11	Mayor Emanuel announces three dozen new and expanded grocery stores	City of Chicago Press Releases
10/26/11	U.S. first lady promotes new grocery stores for America's "food deserts"	Xinhua News Agency
10/28/11	A market for, and by, North-East Central Durham	The Herald-Sun
11/1/11	UCLA helps convert East L.A. corner stores from "food deserts" into healthy food oases	UCLA Newsroom
11/17/11	Mayor Emanuel joins community members at new Save-A-Lot store in city of Chicago	City of Chicago Press Releases
11/25/11	Errol Castens column	Northeast Mississippi Daily Journal
11/30/11	Bipartisan group introduces public-private plan to expand healthy food options	Original Press Release

Date	Title	Source
12/18/11	Goochland farmers help residents in "food deserts"	*Richmond Times-Dispatch*
12/25/11	Community garden shrinks food desert	*The Commercial Appeal*
1/27/12	Community gardens get funding boost	*The Hartford Courant*
1/29/12	Loss of Food Lion store adds to food desert strain in Lynchburg	*The News & Advance*
1/30/12	78,000 area residents live in food wastelands	*Springfield News-Sun*
1/31/12	Communities learn the good life can be a killer	*The New York Times*
2/25/12	Philabundance to open a grocery store in Chester	*The Philadelphia Inquirer*
2/28/12	NJ's largest city combats "food desert" phenomenon with first new supermarket in 20 years	Associated Press Newswires
3/12/12	New supermarket for underserved Camden	*Philadelphia Business Journal Online*
3/14/12	Super (market) news! 4.5M in tax breaks for W'bridge store	*New York Daily News*
3/15/12	D.C.'s food deserts	CNN Wire
3/20/12	The Global Body, part 3: Developed world city—Los Angeles	*Australian Broadcasting Corporation*
3/27/12	ShopRite proposed for city triggers traffic study	*Baltimore Business Journal Online*
4/3/12	Pendleton County healthiest in state, McDowell County least healthy, researchers say	*Charleston Gazette*
4/8/12	Local residents in food deserts yearn for greater access to fresh food	*Northwest Indiana Business Headlines*
4/9/12	Fork in the road: Community gardens aim to bridge food desert gaps	*The Times*
4/10/12	Fork in the road: Grocers in underserved areas find challenges, opportunities	*The Times*
4/18/12	Do food deserts matter? Do they even exist?	*Washington Post*
4/18/12	Studies question the pairing of food deserts and obesity	*The New York Times*
4/21/12	When the supermarket is a mile away	*The New York Times*
4/24/12	Access to healthy foods	*The New York Times*
4/25/12	Green carts bring urban residents healthy options	*Washington Post*
4/28/12	A food stamp paradox: Starving isn't the issue—it's access to nutritious foods	*Deseret News*
5/1/12	What will make the food desert bloom?	NPR: *All Things Considered*
5/9/12	City warming up to idea Port Jeff ferry move	*Connecticut Post*
5/9/12	Have California schools cracked the code on obesity?	*Washington Post*

Date	Title	Source
5/13/12	Ignoring obesity builds roadblocks to better health	*Daily Camera*
5/14/12	Food desert tied to obesity, unhealthy community	*The Commercial Appeal*
5/24/12	The food desert conundrum	*The Commercial Appeal*
6/4/12	Madison grocer has plan to serve "food desert"	*The Wisconsin State Journal*
6/6/12	Mobile oases for food deserts	*The Commercial Appeal*
6/9/12	Access to healthy food must be part of the fight against obesity	*The Boston Globe*
6/11/12	Will Philadelphia's experiment in eradicating "food deserts" work?	*Washington Post*
6/15/12	There grows the neighborhood	*Fulton County Daily Report*
6/20/12	Planting fresh produce in D.C.'s "food deserts"	*Washington Post*
6/22/12	Proximity to healthy foods doesn't matter: Price does	*Washington Post*
7/2/12	New grocery store has competitors scrambling	*The Washington Post*
7/16/12	Mobile grocery store aims to address "food deserts" in urban Kansas City	*Kansas City Business Journal Online*
8/30/12	In Philadelphia, a bounty of opportunities to eat healthy—and local	*The Philadelphia Daily News*
8/30/12	Proposed food co-op in Bennington brings criticism over grant	*Bennington Banner*
9/9/12	Fed up in food battle residents push Walgreen to add on a grocery store	*New York Daily News*
9/12/12	US shoppers showing appetite for stores offering fresh foods	*dpa International Service in English*
9/27/12	Conference focuses on increasing South Carolinians' access to healthy food options	Associated Press Newswires
9/29/12	Anderson downtown neighborhoods a "food desert"	*Anderson Independent-Mail*
9/29/12	Upstate experts say collaboration key to healthy, nutritious food access for the poor	*Anderson Independent-Mail*
10/1/12	Farmers market food truck to bring fresh, local produce	Associated Press Newswires
10/1/12	Minneapolis marketing executive Haberman to speak at South by Southwest	*Minneapolis/St. Paul Business Journal Online*
10/5/12	Southdale neighborhood may get grocery; the county executive wants a feasibility study	*The Capital Times & Wisconsin State Journal*
10/9/12	Bay Area residents tapped to fund West Oakland grocery store	*San Francisco Business Times Online*
10/19/12	Lingering post-Katrina problem: In a food-crazy city, some have limited access to groceries	*Global News*

Date	Title	Source
10/25/12	Neighborhood's popular fruit trees on chopping block	*The Capital Times & Wisconsin State Journal*
10/26/12	Organic grocery opens in downtown Lynchburg	*The News & Advance*
11/15/12	Bottom Dollar opens in Brewerytown	*The Philadelphia Inquirer*
12/7/12	CNN interview with Cory Booker	CNN
12/15/12	Yes Organic Market needs more than a name change	*Washington Post*
1/7/13	Finding ways out of a "food desert"	*Reading Eagle*
1/8/13	A healthy diet is difficult, but possible for many Reading residents	*Reading Eagle*
1/14/13	City considers solution to Beacon Hill "food desert"	*Kansas City Business Journal Online*
1/25/13	The East End is not a "food desert;" the grocery store obsession is an unrealistic distraction	*Charleston Gazette*
1/30/13	The East End really is a "food desert;" a grocery store would provide another anchor	*Charleston Gazette*
2/2/13	Camden Garden Club's eviction could worsen plight in a food desert	*The Philadelphia Inquirer*
2/7/13	Mississippi House approves bill to bring relief to "food deserts"	*The Commercial Appeal*
2/12/13	Deal paves way for SR grocery living wage coalition, city settle	*Press Democrat*
2/19/13	Cory Booker touts Newark's newest super-market, says city's food desert is shrinking	NJ.com
2/19/13	NJ's largest city combats "food desert" phenomenon with another new supermarket	*Washington Examiner*
2/19/13	UC researchers study how to pinpoint "food deserts"	*Cincinnati Business Courier Online*
2/25/13	Putting expired foods to good use	*Boston Globe*
3/7/13	Truman Medical Center moves step closer to opening full-service grocery store in "food desert"	Associated Press Newswires
3/13/13	Harwell leads walk to address lack of access to healthy foods	Associated Press Newswires
3/19/13	Camden unveils plans for 1st full supermarket in 30 years	*The Philadelphia Inquirer*
3/19/13	Pick up your shovel; grow a better city	CNN Wire
3/22/13	"Treme's" Wendell Pierce opens first Sterling Farms grocery store	*Times-Picayune*
3/28/13	Programs bring fresh produce to "food deserts"	*The Washington Post*
4/16/13	Programs deliver fresh food to consumers' doors	*Evansville Courier & Press*
4/21/13	What role should government play in combatting obesity?	*Wall Street Journal*

Date	Title	Source
5/14/13	"Junk food" bill sparks debate	*Wisconsin State Journal*
5/16/13	New grocery store attracts crowd	*Press Democrat*
5/22/13	Veggie might music big seeks healthy food options in needy nabes	*New York Daily News*
6/13/13	"Food desert" moves closer to getting an oasis	*Kansas City Business Journal Online*
6/18/13	C-plus rating for Mass. on health	*The Boston Globe*
6/22/13	A south Minneapolis "food desert" is about to gain its own natural foods grocery store	*Star-Tribune*
6/26/13	Growing healthy habits, and hope, in Paterson	*The Record*
6/27/13	Uptown normal not a food desert	*The Pantagraph*
6/28/13	Atlanta is in top 10 of U.S. cities with "food deserts"	*The Atlanta Journal - Constitution*
7/11/13	Wheel healthy produce-laden van to visit uptown "food deserts"	*New York Daily News*
8/1/13	Lack of produce drives mobile grocery project	*Pittsburgh Post-Gazette*
8/14/13	Fund started to get healthy products to Colorado grocers in food deserts	*Denver Business Journal Online*
8/17/13	Farmers' markets bring bounty to urban food deserts	*The Boston Globe*
8/29/13	Elgin approves incentive for new Butera Market	*Chicago Daily Herald*
9/6/13	Three Pathmarks closing, leaving 238 jobless	*Philadelphia Business Journal Online*
9/10/13	S.F. supervisor blasts Fresh & Easy for closing Bayview market	*San Francisco Business Times Online*
9/14/13	With Wal-Mart veto, DC mayor puts city's poor ahead of rally cry for working poor	*Washington Post*
9/19/13	Empty Bowls funds help purchasing of produce	*Bowling Green Daily News*
9/24/13	Bearing fruit city harvest promotes healthy choices in bodegas	*New York Daily News*
9/26/13	Nation's first nonprofit supermarket to open in Chester	*The Philadelphia Inquirer*
10/9/13	Camden Council advances supermarket plan	*The Philadelphia Inquirer*
10/17/13	Hill District finally gets a supermarket; mayor discusses his future strip project	*Pittsburgh Post-Gazette*
10/22/13	New truck helps food bank produce	*Times Record News*
10/27/13	Oregon county hopes to produce corner groceries with healthier products	Associated Press Newswires
11/8/13	Churches take on challenge of feeding region's hungry	*Pittsburgh Post-Gazette*
11/15/13	Community lab talks Broome County food insecurity	*Pipe Dream SUNY at Binghamton*
11/24/13	An Oasis of Groceries	*New York Times*

Date	Title	Source
12/1/13	CNN Heroes: An all-star tribute	CNN
12/3/13	Some Houston stores are immigrant family business	*Houston Chronicle*
12/31/13	Pedal to the metal for healthy foods	*The Journal Record*
1/4/14	Thousands in Sioux City and millions across country endure "food deserts"	*The Journal*
1/6/14	Second inner-Loop Wal-Mart to open this month	*Houston Business Journal Online*
1/14/14	$3M damage estimate from water-main break at shopping center	*The Philadelphia Inquirer*
1/20/14	Effort to getting grocery stores into "food deserts"	Associated Press Newswires
1/29/14	Group aims to fight obesity	Associated Press Newswires
2/2/14	Large swaths of Topeka labeled as "food deserts"	*Topeka Capital-Journal*
2/3/14	PBS NewsHour for February 3, 2014	PBS
2/8/14	Federal farm bill to alleviate food deserts	*Pittsburgh Post-Gazette*
2/11/14	Key Food closes in Newark, leaving residents in "food desert"	NJTV News
2/14/14	Study finds grocery hasn't changed area's health	*The Philadelphia Inquirer*
2/16/14	Healthier grocers arrive, but old eating habits stick	*The Washington Post*
2/19/14	Healthy food from the ground up	*Sarasota Herald-Tribune*
3/10/14	Charity outreach seeking rural W.Va. volunteers	Associated Press Newswires
3/10/14	One more Dominick's location yet to sell	*Chicago Business Journal Online*
3/20/14	NC legislator to discuss food deserts	*The Washington Times*
3/25/14	Foods Co. opens new store in East Oakland "food desert"	*San Francisco Business Times Online*
4/1/14	Program hopes to trim bad habits	*New York Daily News*
4/3/14	Hunger in the land of plenty	*San Angelo Standard-Times*
4/9/14	Fresh veggies a FAVE downtown; van makes healthy food available to many	*The Evansville Courier*
4/17/14	Florida's efforts to cut smoking show results	*Tampa Bay Times*
4/17/14	S.L. school district gets federal fitness grant	*Deseret News*
5/1/14	Sterling Farms grocery, co-owned by Wendell Pierce, closes after just one year	*Times-Picayune*
5/2/14	Low income lifestyle stresses child development	University of New Hampshire
5/5/14	Wilder Foundation converting retired Metro Transit bus into mobile grocery store	*Minneapolis/St. Paul Business Journal Online*
5/6/14	Sterling Farms to close flagship store in Marrero	Associated Press Newswires
5/31/14	Raleigh area churches open nonprofit grocery store	Associated Press Newswires

Date	Title	Source
6/2/14	WakeMed opens Farmer's Market in southeast Raleigh, a "food desert"	*Triangle Business Journal Online*
6/6/14	An eyewitness account of Cuba's shocking wretchedness	*National Post*
6/11/14	Farm town on Colorado plains now a "food desert"	Associated Press Newswires
6/25/14	Starting a revolution in West Virginia	*Washington Post*
6/29/14	Utah's Chaffetz takes a tour of the liberal side	*The Salt Lake Tribune*
7/1/14	Grocery store breaks ground in a Houston food desert	*Houston Business Journal Online*
7/16/14	Gardens aim to eliminate "food deserts"	Associated Press Newswires
7/23/14	Students living on campus struggle to find groceries	*University of Arizona News*
7/27/14	When did "hungry" become "food insecure"?	*Charleston Gazette-Mail*
8/20/14	Health begins at home	*The Philadelphia Daily News*
9/4/14	Florida officials map hunger in new online program	Associated Press Newswires
9/4/14	Food Inequality	*Lancaster New Era*
9/9/14	Shopping for a grocer: NYCHA seeks supermarket for food-deprived Rockaway	*New York Daily News*
9/15/14	Recent editorials published in Nebraska newspapers	The Associated Press
9/15/14	State map, database highlight hunger-prone areas of Collier, south Lee	*Naples Daily News*
9/25/14	BJCTA unanimously passes "mobile food market" participation	*Birmingham Business Journal Online*
9/26/14	New Walmart in east Tampa to help turn food desert into oasis	*Tampa Bay Times*
9/28/14	Food desert finds relief	*Tampa Bay Times*
10/7/14	Safeway's Palisades plans at issue in Tuesday D.C. Council vote	*Washington Post*
11/4/14	NYLS starts public interest law center and externship	*New York Law Journal*
11/26/14	Fast food in low-income areas contributes to obesity	*The Daily Cougar*
11/28/14	Building an oasis in Bankhead	*The Atlanta Journal - Constitution*
12/3/14	South Austin contains food deserts, healthy choices scarce	U-Wire
12/18/14	Farm truck foods to get rolling this spring	*Pittsburgh Post-Gazette*
12/19/14	City's hungriest real estate investor plans grocery store in West Oakland food desert	*San Francisco Business Times Online*
12/31/14	In Sacramento, fighting hunger requires more than charity	NPR: *All Things Considered*

Date	Title	Source
1/13/15	Food deserts increase in Erie County	Associated Press Newswires
1/23/15	Group eyes new grocer for town	*Charleston Gazette*
2/22/15	Town pulls together to open grocery store	*Charleston Gazette*
3/6/15	Shoppers Food sets up shop in vacant Stop Shop Save in North Baltimore	*Baltimore Business Journal Online*
3/7/15	Food insecurity in Richmond, state is subject of documentary	*Washington Times*
3/8/15	Starving for nutrition: Poor diets and inaccessibility to healthy foods are creating a crisis of chronic disease	*The Atlanta Journal - Constitution*
3/9/15	Lincoln college neighborhood sees void as food store closes	Associated Press Newswires
3/10/15	Save-A-Lot store opening in April to replenish "food desert" in south Raleigh	*Triangle Business Journal Online*
3/11/15	Eating habits set early in life, hard to change	*The Atlanta Journal - Constitution*
3/21/15	See no junk, buy no junk	*New York Times*
4/8/15	Alderson's new grocery store offers fresh, local produce	*Charleston Gazette-Mail*
4/8/15	Greensboro gives $250K to open food co-op in empty area	*The Washington Times*
4/14/15	What Gwyneth Paltrow's food stamp challenge gets totally wrong about poverty	*Washington Post*
4/21/15	Food security and poverty tourism	*Princeton University News*
4/25/15	West Virginia's hunger for grocery stores not just the East End, much of West Virginia classified as a "food desert"	*Charleston Gazette*
5/1/15	Grocery stores locate where the market is	*Charleston Gazette*
5/1/15	*PBS NewsHour* for May 1, 2015	PBS
5/3/15	Interview with Wisconsin congressman Paul Ryan	CBS News
5/4/15	Filling up on food co-ops	*Crain's New York Business*
5/4/15	Six miles separate cornucopia, desert	*Dayton Daily News*
5/5/15	Food choices worlds apart	*Dayton Daily News*
5/8/15	Living in the Spring Hill food desert volunteers working to provide access to fresh, healthy foods	*Charleston Gazette*
5/9/15	Giving the poor easy access to healthy food doesn't mean they'll buy it	*New York Times*
5/13/15	Grocery store held up over road funding	*The Atlanta Journal - Constitution*
5/31/15	Healthy food initiative seeks OK	*Dayton Daily News*
6/5/15	Alleviate food deserts by planting crops	*The Santa Fe New Mexican*

Date	Title	Source
6/7/15	Fresh fare: Since it hit the road last year, the mobile fresh bus has more than doubled its stops	*The Orange County Register*
6/7/15	When the grocer is gone, rural markets closing stores as customers drive to bigger locales	*Charleston Gazette*
6/10/15	City eyes incentives for grocers to address food problems	*Baltimore Business Journal*
6/10/15	UnitedHealthcare fights food insecurity with donation to Second Harvest Food Bank of Northwest North Carolina	Business Wire
6/21/15	Promoting nutritious food choices	*The Boston Globe*
6/26/15	Truman Medical Center sets aside plans for grocery	*Kansas City Star*
7/4/15	CNN Special: Feeding America's most vulnerable children	CNN
7/8/15	Farmers in the city	*The Record*
7/12/15	Do "Food Deserts" Cause Unhealthy Eating?	*The Wall Street Journal Online*
7/12/15	Town's store an oasis in a spreading food desert	*Star-Tribune*
7/17/15	West Dayton leaders seek help for redevelopment	*Dayton Daily News*
7/23/15	Dishing up cooking tips, tricks	*Spokesman Review*
8/1/15	Access to local groceries is key to staying healthy	*Star-Tribune*
8/2/15	Good Groceries, Healthy People	*Star-Tribune*
8/2/15	Seeds of change: A farm grows in Chester	*The Philadelphia Inquirer*
8/10/15	As grocery wars heat up, some areas go without	*Houston Business Journal Online*
8/21/15	Some areas of Houston flush with grocery stores; others go without	*Houston Business Journal Online*
9/20/15	Step 1 for nutrition: Access to healthy, fresh food	*Charleston Gazette*
9/24/15	"By nourishing plants, you're nourishing community"	CNN Wire
9/25/15	Closing the gap: Innovative solutions to hunger cropping up in food deserts	*The Georgetown Voice*
10/9/15	Millvale hires first sustainability coordinator	*Pittsburgh Post-Gazette*
10/25/15	Nearly half of Pittsburghers live in a food desert	*Pittsburgh Post-Gazette*
10/27/15	Some must get groceries by bus: Garfield residents cope as they wait for store to reopen	*Pittsburgh Post-Gazette*
10/30/15	HBJ 40 Under 40 Class of 2015 explain their "knockout moments"	*Houston Business Journal*
11/3/15	Grocery improved residents' diet	*Pittsburgh Post-Gazette*
11/3/15	"To market, to market" a new program, Fresh Access, returns farmers market availability to low-income consumers	*Pittsburgh Post-Gazette*

Date	Title	Source
11/7/15	Eating healthy The Hill's market begins to make a difference	*Pittsburgh Post-Gazette*
11/10/15	Restaurants abound in Oakland but where to buy groceries	*Pittsburgh Post-Gazette*
11/17/15	Pathmark closure jars East Harlem	*The Wall Street Journal Online*
11/18/15	Students, community combat hunger and homelessness in Dayton	*Flyer News*
12/2/15	Creating oases in New York City's "food deserts"	*The Wall Street Journal*
12/7/15	10 new Nevada supermarkets but none in food desert areas	Nevada NPR
12/7/15	Grocery chains leave food deserts barren	*Chicago Tribune*
12/7/15	Grocery store chains avoid opening in Alabama food deserts	Associated Press Newswires
12/7/15	Lake County rife with food deserts	*Times of Northwest Indiana*
12/7/15	Many RI neighborhoods still lack easy access to grocers	Associated Press Newswires
12/7/15	None of Utah's new supermarkets filled a food desert	*The Salt Lake Tribune*
12/7/15	Supermarkets not being built in Connecticut "food deserts"	*The Oklahoman*
12/7/15	Supermarkets still struggle to open in NJ "food deserts"	*Courier-Post*
12/10/15	Cooking classes being held in convenience stores	Associated Press Newswires
12/10/15	Retailers encouraged to make healthy food be more than a mirage	*St. Louis Post-Dispatch*
12/25/15	Working harder to supply food deserts	*Tampa Bay Times*
1/6/16	*PBS NewsHour* for January 6, 2016	PBS
1/7/16	Offering grace in a metro-area food desert	*The Atlanta Journal - Constitution*
1/17/16	Pushing the produce	*The Philadelphia Inquirer*
1/25/16	Feds tap Gary for urban agriculture program	*Times of Northwest Indiana*
1/27/16	Wal-Mart's shutdown creates new food deserts	Associated Press Newswires
2/1/16	Downtown Long Beach closes grocery store doors	*Daily 49er*
2/12/16	New community farmhouse will help diminish the "food desert" in Buffalo	*Buffalo News*
3/9/16	Toilet paper illustrates the cruel paradox that it's expensive to be poor	*Washington Post*
3/11/16	Take home pottery, help end hunger in Unity	*Bangor Daily News*
3/24/16	Creating asphalt wastelands in the name of fighting food deserts	*The Philadelphia Inquirer*

Date	Title	Source
3/24/16	This Phoenix garden introduces homegrown fruit, veggie plants to battle food desert	*Phoenix Business Journal Online*
3/31/16	Deserted in North Tulsa	*The Collegian*
4/3/16	Food co-op grocery proposed	*Dayton Daily News*
4/7/16	How one man single-handedly opened the only grocery store in one of New Orleans' poorest wards	*The Washington Post*
4/14/16	Minnesota among worst states for fresh food access	*Minneapolis/St. Paul Business Journal Online*
4/15/16	Resident on the East Side cannot afford fresh produce in grocery stores	*The Griffin*
4/20/16	Fresh food makes its way to Sandtown in year following unrest	*Baltimore Business Journal*
4/25/16	N.Y.C.-newcomer meal service Freshly expands to 28 states	*New York Business Journal Online*
4/29/16	Greensboro's fight for food security continues	*The Guilfordian*
5/4/16	Garfield Park Farmers Market brings a community together	*NUVO Newsweekly*
5/15/16	Emory doctor finds inspiration in food desert's grim health statistics	*The Atlanta Journal-Constitution*
5/15/16	Mapping San Diego's "food desert" spots	*The San Diego Union-Tribune*
5/17/16	Poverty numbers paint "bleak picture" in Manatee	*Herald Tribune*
5/19/16	Hunger is no game; fighting food deserts in Indianapolis	*NUVO Newsweekly*
5/26/16	Where the restaurants aren't—and why	*The Boston Globe*
6/1/16	Grocery store planned for "food desert" in west Ocala	*Ocala Star-Banner*
6/6/16	In a Pr. George's "food desert," an oasis of fresh produce	*The Washington Post*
6/13/16	SNAP rule would worsen food deserts	*The Hill*
6/24/16	Corner markets enlisted in healthy foods initiative	*Dayton Daily News*
6/27/16	Camco library to take food literacy on the road	*Courier-Post*
6/28/16	Mobile farmers market to serve "food desert" communities in west S.L.	*Deseret News*
6/30/16	SLC's food deserts need a longterm solution	*The Salt Lake Tribune*
7/6/16	Man goes on grocery store crusade for East Central	*The Spokesman*
7/14/16	Access to food a problem in Fox Valley	*USA TODAY*
7/15/16	Healthy communities' efforts boost economic opportunities too	*Daily Bulletin Columns*

Date	Title	Source
7/15/16	Internet shopping could help the poor with access to healthy food	Washington Post
7/23/16	Fight for E. Harlem store	New York Daily News
7/27/16	McDonald's, eat your heart out	L.A. Biz
8/8/16	Ensuring the integrity of the food stamp program	Washington Post
8/24/16	Stonehill College takes its discount "Mobile Market" to Brockton	The Boston Globe
8/28/16	Food deserts still a problem in Nebraska, but no easy fixes	The Washington Times
9/7/16	Charleston mayor deals with loss of downtown grocery store	Associated Press Newswires
9/12/16	Colorado Springs council hears proposal to allow residents to sell produce, "cottage foods"	The Gazette
9/25/16	Grocery store dietician Danielle Sanislow hits the aisles to help you eat right	The Philadelphia Daily News
9/30/16	Atlanta may seek $30K to plant fruit, nut trees	The Atlanta Journal - Constitution
10/6/16	Newly planted orchard could bear fruit within six months	Sarasota Herald-Tribune
10/17/16	Struggling to turn profit in food deserts	Dow Jones Institutional News
10/17/16	The battle against food deserts rages on	The Wall Street Journal
11/20/16	Group tackling food access in Alabama	The Washington Times
11/22/16	Farm partners with Indianapolis center to feed neighborhood	The Washington Times
12/9/16	Maryland nonprofit aiding development of local grocery store	Wichita Business Journal Online
12/31/16	Fears of food desert in high-end SoHo arise as grocery closes	The New York Times
1/3/17	N. Mpls finally to get supermarket	Star-Tribune
1/11/17	Food stamp recipients will soon be able to order groceries online	Washington Post
1/22/17	North Market serves up community goodness	Star-Tribune
1/29/17	H-E-B, partners to help "food desert"	Austin American-Statesman
2/8/17	Ekistics still committed to State Center despite legal wrangling	Baltimore Business Journal Online
3/18/17	Site chosen for grocery store in northwest Dayton	Dayton Daily News
3/21/17	If Dallas really wants to spend $3 million feeding food deserts, look no further than the corner store	Dallas News
3/26/17	Battling city's food deserts: Urban agriculture director brings produce to those in need	The Atlanta Journal - Constitution

Date	Title	Source
3/30/17	Providing access to healthy food is a community responsibility	LNP
4/5/17	Much of Vinton County will still be a food desert despite new grocery store	U-Wire
4/5/17	Price Rite grocery store opens in city "food desert"	*Daily Orange*
4/12/17	Food desert residents hunger for change	*Gay City News*
4/19/17	Lexington looks to eliminate "food deserts"	*The Dispatch*
4/19/17	Why LA's tech community is trying to hack hunger	CNN Wire
5/2/17	Want healthy food? In much of Mass., it's hard to get	*The Boston Globe*
5/3/17	"Food deserts" leave many hungering for better grocery access	*The Boston Globe*
5/7/17	Hoping to make food deserts bloom again	*Star-Tribune*
5/9/17	Jackson Cash & Carry, Doe's Eat Place and Baptist Health Merger	*Jackson Free Press*
5/19/17	Kendall Yards grocery store will feature chefs, local products and urban vibe	*The Spokesman-Review*
5/22/17	Pugh says tax incentives needed to lure retailers to blighted areas	*Baltimore Business Journal Online*
5/28/17	Grocery store on wheels delivers to "food deserts"	*Star-Tribune*
6/1/17	Oklahoma legislature passes bill to help eliminate food deserts	*Oklahoma Gazette*
6/10/17	A fight for health, bite by bite	*Daytona Beach News*
6/12/17	Charter school's healthy snack store serves students in food desert	*Chicago Tribune*
6/16/17	Little Red Hen making a big difference in Delridge community	*Westside Seattle*
6/18/17	A mobile oasis in a "food desert"	*Hendersonville Times News*
6/20/17	Conflict over city and county rules adds tension to farmers market	WBTV
6/29/17	Ultra Foods closing in Calumet Park leaves void	*Chicago Tribune*
7/5/17	Taking stock of Manhattan supermarkets	*New York Press*
7/12/17	These Fulton food deserts get temporary farmers markets in July	*The Atlanta Journal - Constitution*
7/15/17	In Maryland, rescuing food that might otherwise be wasted	*Baltimore Sun*
7/17/17	Beech Grove Marsh to re-open as Safeway	*The Indy Channel*
7/18/17	Baltimore health department gets $150,000 grant to expand healthy local stores program	*Baltimore Sun*
7/18/17	Making local and nutritional choices affordable for all of Georgia's families	*The Telegraph*

Date	Title	Source
7/21/17	Democrats in U.S. Congress urge review of Amazon's Whole Foods deal	Reuters
7/27/17	Urban Greens Market returns to Glendale, Poplar Grove	*Deseret News*
8/3/17	A renaissance of the neighborhood"	*The Washington Post*
8/4/17	Sens. Moran, Warner introduce first comprehensive Senate bill to encourage food service providers to help eradicate food deserts	FARS News Agency
9/9/17	North Side welcomes its first grocery co-op	*Star-Tribune*
9/22/17	Cost of healthy foods may explain heart risks linked to "food deserts"	Reuters Health E-Line
9/24/17	Dayton co-op grocery store gets $220K donation	*Dayton Daily News*
9/24/17	Project seeks to put end to "food desert"	*Dayton Daily News*
10/10/17	Southeastern Ohio food desert is about to get a grocery store	NPR: *Morning Edition*
10/29/17	New grocery store in McArthur will help alleviate Vinton County's "food desert"	U-Wire
10/31/17	Bill Clinton to visit St. Louis Wednesday	*St. Louis Business Journal Online*
11/2/17	Program launched to supply Alabama food deserts with fresh food	*Birmingham Business Journal Online*
11/20/17	How "food swamps" make us fat	*The Boston Globe*
12/14/17	Dayton grocery plan gets big boost	*Dayton Daily News*
12/21/17	New grocery for Jacobsville a matter of "great urgency"	*Evansville Courier & Press*
12/26/17	Fixing America's food deserts alone won't fix our terrible diets	*The Denver Post*
12/27/17	Wave of closures in NWI has raised concerns about food, pharmacy deserts	*The Times of Northwest Indiana*

Notes

1. I use pseudonyms without last names to protect the confidentiality of the food desert residents I interviewed privately. All other names of public figures and elected officials of Greenville include their last names and are real.

2. I use the terms *grocery store* and *supermarket* as synonymous throughout the book, but technically they are not. Traditionally, grocery stores sell dried and canned good staples, while supermarkets also sell fresh fruits, vegetables, baked goods, meats, and other items. It is the incorporation of services once offered in stand-alone butcher shops, bakeries, pharmacies, and so on that transform a grocery store into a supermarket.

3. Rural areas have food deserts, too, but for different reasons that require different remedies. The USDA identifies poor rural areas with low rates of vehicular access as food deserts when a grocery store is more than ten miles away.

4. According to 2019 Census estimates, thirty-three million people live in the 475 US cities with a population between fifty thousand and one hundred thousand. Roughly the same number live in the 18 US cities with a population over seven hundred fifty thousand.

5. My claims regarding the frequency of articles on food deserts published over the years is based on a search of the Academic Search Premier database. Specifically, the search was for the term *food desert(s)* to appear in either the title or the abstract of a peer-reviewed article in a scholarly journal. Other academic

databases yield slightly different results based on the menu of journals from which they draw.

6. For more on natural experiments, see Petticrew et al. (2005).

7. The USDA Economic Research Service (n.d.) no longer offers a singular definition of food deserts; instead, it offers a variety of options to identify "low-income" and "low-access" areas on its web-based "Food Environment Atlas," http://www.ers.usda.gov/data-products/food-environment-atlas.aspx.

8. For an overview of problems inherent in many food desert studies, see Hillier et al. (2011).

CHAPTER 2. A CONCEPT CATCHES FIRE

1. To see the TED: Ideas Worth Spreading (2013) video, go to https://www.ted.com/talks/ron_finley_a_guerilla_gardener_in_south_central_la?language=en.

2. See chapter 1 for a more thorough overview of academic studies on food deserts from 2007 to 2019.

3. For more on how media frames matter, see Tierney (2003) for an example of how media accounts in the aftermath of 9/11 repeated the "panic myth" that the public will automatically become hysterical in response to a new terrorist attack and be unable to evacuate or avoid danger. These media frames, with no empirical basis, largely shaped American Red Cross policy and educational campaigns for years to follow.

4. For more on the strengths and weaknesses of media content analysis, see Earl et al.'s article "The Use of Newspaper Data in the Study of Collective Action" (2004).

5. Because newswire stories are often reprinted in multiple outlets, duplications were deleted from the sample.

6. Because Maywood Market opened before 2011, this particular media account is not included in the data set in the appendix. As of publication date, it can still be found at https://abc7chicago.com/archive/7394893/.

7. Notably absent from media accounts of food deserts is any type of discussion about other forms of access. While scholars analyze access in many forms—cultural, economic, educational—news stories almost exclusively use the term as it relates to geography.

8. Although this article does not name the authors of the study referenced, it is most likely Boone-Heinonen et al. (2011) which was published on July 11, 2011, and found that supermarket availability was unrelated to diet quality.

9. A 2018 study of Supplemental Nutrition Assistant Program (food stamps) participants found that convenience stores account for only between 1 and 2 percent of their daily caloric intake (Taillie et al. 2018).

10. For more on the perspective of food pantry and soup kitchen operators' on the dilemma of whether to serve healthy food versus or what clients want to eat, see chapter 6.

11. For an overview of the evolution of crime mapping technology and practices, see Weisburd and Lum (2005); Wilson (2007).

CHAPTER 3. PERCEPTION, MONEY, AND TRANSPORTATION

1. As an example of how food related practices are entangled within the "everyday realities" of households, see Smith et al. (2014) on how eating behaviors went unchanged in the aftermath of the 2008 recession. Despite serious economic upheavals, rates of cooking at home and eating away from home stayed stable.

2. "Public assistance" here includes Supplemental Nutrition Assistance Program benefits (SNAP), Women and Infant Children nutrition benefits (WIC), Temporary Assistance for Needy Families (TANF), Section 8 housing vouchers, and/or Supplemental Security Income.

3. Because home cooking is in the "private sphere" of family life, it is still generally considered "women's work." Professional cooking, however, is in the "public sphere" and still generally considered "men's work"—thus the stereotypes of home "cooks" (women) and professional "chefs" (men) help explain the persistent gender inequality of domestic food preparation (Harris and Giuffre 2015; Trubek 2017).

4. Of course, not everything about the past was perceived as "better." Pre–civil rights Greenville, South Carolina was a harshly segregated place, where even a few retail amenities like a grocery store did not outweigh the effects of racism in the American South. For more on the history of Greenville in particular, see Huff (1995).

5. A number of stores in the Greenville area have used variations on this name at one point or another. To clarify, the historic grocery store that served primarily the Black community was called "Kash and Karry." Today, there is a "Kash & Karry" small convenience store in West Greenville that is generally seen as a venue for beer, cigarettes, and lottery tickets. In Southernside, there is also a "Kash & Karry" pharmacy that stands in the same location of the historic grocery store, but has no connection other than its name.

6. Subjective perceptions of the food environment can also render some options invisible. For example, even though there was a full-size Latino supermarket (La Unica) closer to the neighborhoods than the most visited shopping destination (a Walmart Supercenter), none of my interviewees ever reported shopping there except one who identified as both Black and Latina.

7. For more on the changing business model of grocery stores and how it con-tributed to the development of food deserts, see Deener (2017).

8. For more on the problems with how the poverty threshold is calculated, see Blank (2008). For more on updated calculations on the minimum amount needed to support a Thrifty Food Plan, see Carlson et al. (2007).

9. For precise categories and definitions of the varying degrees of food inse-curity, see Barrett (2010).

10. For more on the role that personal connections can play in alleviating food insecurity, See Morton et al. (2005).

11. For more research on the agency and resiliency in areas with limited food offerings, see Reese (2019).

12. For more on how to conceptualize the distance between home and store, see Papas et al.'s discussion of "destination accessibility" (2007: 139).

13. This percentage is similar to Dubowitz et al.'s finding (2015a) that only 17 percent of study participants living in a food desert ($N = 831$) used public transportation to shop for food.

14. For more on the historical evolution of food deserts, see Deener (2017) and Eisenhaur (2001).

15. Because of gentrification, the demographics of the Southernside and West Greenville neighborhoods are changing on a yearly basis. This figure is from the 2014 American Community Survey five-year estimates, the year I began my research on food deserts in those areas.

CHAPTER 4. SOCIAL CAPITAL, HOUSEHOLD DYNAMICS, TASTE

1. Other academic studies of food deserts have addressed the concept of social capital, but only indirectly. The study of the Pittsburgh supermarket intervention—where they calculated the impact of a new store on eating habits—did measure the number of children in the household, the years lived in the neighborhood, and respondents' overall "neighborhood satisfaction" (Dubowitz et al. 2015a). These variables set the groundwork for how invested people are in the place they live, but they are too superficial to uncover the ways that food des-ert residents nurture and activate the resources in their community.

2. There are many resources that constitute social capital, such as informa-tion channels, norms, and sanctions. For more, see Coleman (1988).

3. In most states, unprepared food items sold in grocery stores are exempt from state sales tax.

4. For more on food pantries and how they rely on organizations that "rescue" soon-to-be-expired food from grocery stores, see chapter 6.

5. One study of eating practices found that the overall nutritional quality of household diets improves as the number of family meals consumed together per week increased (Newman et al. 2015).

6. For similar findings, see Vaughn et al.'s article entitled: "Where Do Food Desert Residents Buy Most of Their Junk Food? Supermarkets" (2016).

7. The amount of time spent on food preparation declined until the 1990s, with a slight uptick after 2003. The only group to markedly increase their time in the kitchen are highly educated men, but not enough to erase the gender gap in cooking: women still spend more than twice as much time preparing food (Taillie et al. 2018).

8. Sociologist Karen Cerulo applies a similar logic to the ways culture offers us a framework to interpret our sensations. In her research, she analyzes how people decipher the meaning of particular smells. This "olfactory work" also involves a "partnership of brain, body, and cultured environment" (2018: 362).

9. Whereas sociologists once equated cultural capital with "highbrow" tastes that were prohibitively expensive, it is generally agreed today that cultural capital is deployed through a combination of "omnivorous" tastes, both highbrow and lowbrow (Peterson and Kern 1996).

10. Access to healthy foods is only one of the variables, external to the individual, that influence the values that we hold. It is the most salient in regard to food-related values, which is why I focus on it here, but it is not the only one. Other aspects of our social location also explain which values we cite to explain our actions, like socioeconomic status, occupation, gender, religion, and age cohort (Longest, Hitlin, and Vaisey: 2013).

11. For more on the impracticality of the home cooked meal in today's economic context, see Bowen, Brenton, and Elliot (2019).

CHAPTER 5. THE "HEALTHY FOOD" FRAME

1. Grocery delivery services and "meal kit" subscriptions services can also enable cooking from scratch, but these also add to the cost—making them unlikely food desert solutions given the economic constraints of their residents.

2. Frame alignment includes four different processes to make social movement interests more congruent and complementary with those of others. These include frame bridging, frame amplification, frame extension, and frame transformation. For more, see (Snow, Rochford, et al. 1986).

3. There was also a full-size Latino supermarket in the area, but as shown in the discussion on residents' perception of their food environment, it was effectively invisible to residents of Southernside and West Greenville; none reported shopping at them.

4. I use pseudonyms without last names to protect the confidentiality of the food desert residents I interviewed privately. All other names of public figures and elected officials of Greenville include their last names and are real.

5. Afterward, I checked my fieldnotes from West Greenville neighborhood meetings for the past few years. This woman had not attended any of them. This evening, she was among a dozen other first-time attendees. The meeting had been advertised on social media and drew a bigger crowd than usual. Her comment speaks to the effectiveness of the "healthy food" frame when it comes to recruiting new allies.

6. I heard a number of interviewees claim that local pizza vendors would not deliver to their addresses; however, when I called local outlets, they denied this, so I am not able to confirm residents' suspicions definitively.

7. For more on the impact of "urban renewal" in the Sunbelt, see Abbot (1981).

8. I also investigated another possible culprit for the concentrated poverty in the neighborhoods: large-scale "urban renewal" housing projects built by local governments nationwide to rehouse poorer, displaced residents (for more, see Massey and Denton 1993: 55–58). These initiatives, funded by the housing acts of 1949 and 1954, acquired and cleared blighted structures in a manner that would seemingly explain the disappearance of housing in the Southernside and West Greenville neighborhoods. However, while there was one 282-unit public housing tower constructed in an adjacent neighborhood in Greenville, it could not account for the full depopulation of the West Greenville and Southernside neighborhoods.

9. Reese, in her book, *Black Food Geographies*, argues that the term *food desert* itself masks how "the increasingly corporatized food system is not simply unequal; it is a byproduct of how structural racism touches every aspect of life— even where our food resources are located" (2019:7).

10. For a historical perspective on how consuming "healthy food" was framed as essential to citizenship in the United States and the impetus behind the development of federal nutritional guidelines, see Biltekoff (2013).

11. Mass incarceration is a more recent social problem being reframed as a health problem (Dumont et al. 2012; Wildeman and Wang 2017).

12. Rosenberg and Cohen offer a similar analysis when they outline the unintended costs of the "food access narrative": "shifting attention from the more fundamental upstream causes of malnourishment and health disparities: social inequality, race, gender, class oppression, and poverty" (2018: 1120).

13. For more on the types and objectives of food-related social movements in America today, see Broad (2015: 33–59).

CHAPTER 6. THE PROBLEM SOLVERS

1. The actual number of farms in the area is much greater. According to the 2012 Census of Agriculture (USDA 2012), Greenville county has over one

thousand farms with an average size of sixty-six acres. This does not include farms in adjacent counties also within an hour's drive. However, to be conservative, I am only including active farms in Greenville county that also have principal operators who claim farming as their primary occupation. This is the most conservative estimate. Thus, at a minimum, there are three hundred working farms within an hour's drive of the city of Greenville.

2. From 2011 through 2017, 22.6 percent of media accounts of food deserts—in the database I compiled from a FACTIVA search—discussed local farms and farmers markets as a potential solution. For more, see chapter 2. Articles in the database can be found in the appendix.

3. During their interview, the directors of Greenville's farmers market reported the program's moderate success; over $10,000 in EBT payments were accepted over the entire fourteen-week season the year before. Because EBT payments can come from TANF payments, not all were participants in the "Healthy Bucks" program. Also, with an average of two thousand shoppers each market session. The proportion of EBT payments relative to non-EBT payments was very small.

4. Local farmers at the Greenville market were trained on how to accept the vouchers, but I observed a bit of confusion and delays at the adjacent tables during my time working for Greenbrier. Additionally, select vendors at the downtown market also accepted payment from Women and Infant Children (WIC) food vouchers and a "Senior Voucher" provided by the South Carolina Department of Social Services. However, vendors had to go through an even more rigorous training program to be eligible to receive these payments, so only five out of seventy-five did so.

5. For more on the economics of Community Supported Agriculture, see Brown and Miller (2008).

6. Also, see Robinson et al. (2016) for a summary of the origins of the contemporary mobile farmer's markets across the country as well as the limitations of small-scale operations retail food operations—even if subsidized by grants—to produce a significant impact on local food environments.

7. For more on this intensive urban agriculture technique, see Stone (2016).

8. Community gardens can vary in scope and purpose. For an overview, see Ferris, Norman, and Sempik (2001).

9. For more on the double burden faced by food pantries and soup kitchens to prevent hunger *and* offer more nutritional food, see Sisson and Lown (2011).

10. For more on Fare and Square's business operation, see Benshoff (2016).

11. As explained in chapter 5, neighborhood residents were concerned about vagrancy and loitering at nearby gas stations. While it still sold beer, the regional chain made one change to its offerings for its store near Southernside: it agreed to not sell single beers to reduce loitering.

12. I calculated this figure at a local workshop on "Farm Planning and Maximum Budget." One presenter offered the group an accounting spreadsheet

detailing the economics of cultivating roughly 1.5 acres of land—a common size for a small-scale direct-to-consumer vegetable growing operations. His stall was one of the most popular at the downtown farmers market each week. He also sold CSA subscriptions that offered twelve weekly boxes of fresh produce for $300 a season (paid up front). At the end of each season, despite his gross sales of over $100,000, he was still only able to pay himself a salary of $29,000.

13. For more on the sporadic and "windfall" consumer spending practices of the poor, see Pugh (2004).

14. By convenience foods, I mean dishes prepared by others and consumed either away from home (e.g., restaurant, fast-food venue) or brought into the home to be eaten at a later time (e.g., take-out, delivery service). These include hot and cold bar items from grocery stores as well as almost-ready-to-eat items that require minimal assembly and preparation. I use the word *assemble* because actions like preparing sandwiches, boiling instant soups, or putting frozen dinners into the oven are not really "cooking" in the true sense of the word. Cooking involves heating or otherwise transforming raw ingredients into a more edible and palatable state.

CHAPTER 7. A PATH FORWARD

1. The most notable exceptions are qualitative investigations conducted near Washington, D.C. (Reece 2019) and Raleigh, North Carolina (Bowen, Brenton, and Elliot 2019).

2. In 2019, a similar Baltimore program subsidized fares to grocery stores with the Lyft ride sharing service (Richman 2019).

EPILOGUE

1. The following statistics presented are taken from American Community Survey five-year estimate data collected by the US Census Bureau.

2. For more on Unity Park, go to unityparkgreenville.com.

3. For more on the Greenville Housing Fund, go to greenvillehousing fund.com.

References

Abbott, Carl. 1981. *The New Urban America: Growth and Politics in Sunbelt Cities*. Chapel Hill: University of North Carolina Press.

ABC7 Chicago. 2010. "Full-Service Grocery Store to Open in Maywood." Retrieved June 16, 2021 (https://abc7chicago.com/archive/7394893/).

Abeykoon, A. M. Hasanthi, Rachel Engler-Stringer, and Nazeem Muhajarine. 2017. "Health-Related Outcomes of New Grocery Store Interventions: A Systematic Review." *Public Health Nutrition* 20(12):2236–48.

Ackoff, Sophie, Andrew Bahrenburg, and Lindsey Lusher Shute. 2017. *Building a Future with Farmers II: Results and Recommendations from the National Young Farmer Survey*. Hudson, NY: National Young Farmers Coalition.

Adams, Jean, Joel Halligan, Duika Burges Watson, Vicky Ryan, Linda Penn, Ashley J. Adamson, and Martin White. 2012. "The Change4Life Convenience Store Programme to Increase Retail Access to Fresh Fruit and Vegetables: A Mixed Methods Process Evaluation." *PLOS ONE* 7(6):e39431.

Allcott, Hunt, Rebecca Diamond, Jean-Pierre Dubé, Jessie Handbury, Ilya Rahkovsky, and Molly Schnell. 2019. "Food Deserts and the Causes of Nutritional Inequality." *The Quarterly Journal of Economics* 134(4):1793–1844.

An, Ruopeng, and Roland Sturm. 2012. "School and Residential Neighborhood Food Environment and Diet among California Youth." *American Journal of Preventive Medicine* 42(2):129–35.

Anderson, Elijah. 1990. *Streetwise: Race, Class, and Change in an Urban Community*. Chicago: University of Chicago Press.

Anzman, Stephanie L., Brandi Y. Rollins, and Leann L. Birch. 2010. "Parental Influence on Children's Early Eating Environments and Obesity Risk: Implications for Prevention." *International Journal of Obesity* 34:1116–24.

Bainbridge, Judith. 2017. "In 2005, MLK Day Finally Recognized in Greenville County." *Greenville News*, March 12.

Barbieri, Carla, and Patience M. Mshenga. 2008. "The Role of the Firm and Owner Characteristics on the Performance of Agritourism Farms." *Sociologia Ruralis* 48(2):166–83.

Barrett, Christopher B. 2010. "Measuring Food Insecurity." *Science* 327(5967): 825–28.

Baskar, Pranav. 2020. "Coronavirus FAQ: Is It Safe to Get on the Bus (or Subway)?" NPR.Org, August 28.

Bassuk, Ellen L., Lenore Rubin, and Alison Lauriat. 1984. "Is Homelessness a Mental Health Problem?" *American Journal of Psychiatry* 141(12):1546–50.

Baumann, Shyon, Michelle Szabo, and Josée Johnston. 2019. "Understanding the Food Preferences of People of Low Socioeconomic Status." *Journal of Consumer Culture* 19(3):316–39.

Bayor, Ronald H. 1988. "Roads to Racial Segregation Atlanta in the Twentieth Century." *Journal of Urban History* 15(1):3–21.

Beauchamp, Gary K., and Julie A. Mennella. 2009. "Early Flavor Learning and Its Impact on Later Feeding Behavior." *Journal of Pediatric Gastroenterology and Nutrition* 48:S25–30.

Beaulac, Julie, Elizabeth Kristjansson, and Steven Cummins. 2009. "A Systematic Review of Food Deserts, 1966–2007." *Preventing Chronic Disease* 6(3):A105.

Becker, Howard S. 1953. "Becoming a Marihuana User." *American Journal of Sociology* 59(3):235–42.

Bell, Judith, Gabriella Mora, Erin Hagan, Victor Rubin, and Allison Karphyn. 2013. *Access to Healthy Food and Why It Matters: A Review of the Research*. Oakland, CA, & Philadelphia, PA: Policy Link and The Food Trust.

Benshoff, Laura. 2016. "A Nonprofit Grocer Tries to Sell More Healthful Food without Going Under." National Public Radio, July 6.

Berger, Dan. 2009. "Constructing Crime, Framing Disaster: Routines of Criminalization and Crisis in Hurricane Katrina." *Punishment & Society* 11(4):491–510.

Berry, Wendell. 1977. *The Unsettling of America: Culture and Agriculture*. San Francisco: Sierra Club Books.

Biles, Roger. 2000. "Public Housing and the Postwar Urban Renaissance, 1949–1973." In *From Tenements to the Taylor Homes: In Search of an Urban*

Housing Policy in Twentieth-Century America, edited by J. F. Bauman, R. Biles, and K. M. Szylvian, 143–63. University Park: Pennsylvania State University Press.

Biltekoff, Charlotte. 2013. *Eating Right in America: The Cultural Politics of Food and Health*. Durham, NC: Duke University Press Books.

Bitler, Marianne, and Steven J. Haider. 2011. "An Economic View of Food Deserts in the United States." *Journal of Policy Analysis and Management* 30(1):153–76.

Blank, Rebecca M. 2008. "Presidential Address: How to Improve Poverty Measurement in the United States." *Journal of Policy Analysis and Management* 27(2):233–54.

Block, Jason P., and S. V. Subramanian. 2015. "Moving Beyond 'Food Deserts': Reorienting United States Policies to Reduce Disparities in Diet Quality." *PLOS Medicine* 12(12):e1001914.

Bluestone, Barry, and Bennett Harrison. 1982. *The Deindustrialization of America: Plant Closings, Community Abandonment, and the Dismantling of Basic Industry*. New York: Basic Books.

Bonilla-Silva, Eduardo. 2014. *Racism without Racists: Color-Blind Racism and the Persistence of Racial Inequality in the United States*. Lanham, MD: Rowman & Littlefield.

Boone-Heinonen, Janne, Penny Gordon-Larsen, Catarina I. Kiefe, James M. Shikany, Cora E. Lewis, and Barry M. Popkin. 2011. "Fast Food Restaurants and Food Stores: Longitudinal Associations with Diet in Young to Middle-Aged Adults: The CARDIA Study." *Archives of Internal Medicine* 171(13): 1162–70.

Bourdieu, Pierre. 1984. *Distinction: A Social Critique of the Judgement of Taste*. Cambridge, MA: Harvard University Press.

Bowen, Sarah, Joslyn Brenton, and Sinikka Elliott. 2019. *Pressure Cooker: Why Home Cooking Won't Solve Our Problems and What We Can Do about It*. New York: Oxford University Press.

Breyer, Betsy, and Adriana Voss-Andreae. 2013. "Food Mirages: Geographic and Economic Barriers to Healthful Food Access in Portland, Oregon." *Health & Place* 24:131–39.

Brinkley, Catherine, Charlotte Glennie, Benjamin Chrisinger, and Jose Flores. 2019. "'If You Build It with Them, They Will Come': What Makes a Supermarket Intervention Successful in a Food Desert?" *Journal of Public Affairs* 19(3):e1863.

Broad, Garrett. 2016. *More Than Just Food: Food Justice and Community Change*. Oakland: University of California Press.

Brown, Allison. 2002. "Farmers' Market Research 1940–2000: An Inventory and Review." *American Journal of Alternative Agriculture* 17(4):167–76.

Brown, Cheryl, and Stacy Miller. 2008. "The Impacts of Local Markets: A Review of Research on Farmers Markets and Community Supported Agriculture (CSA)." *American Journal of Agricultural Economics* 90(5): 1298–1302.

Bucher, Tamara, Clare Collins, Megan E. Rollo, Tracy A. McCaffrey, Nienke De Vlieger, Daphne Van der Bend, Helen Truby, and Federico J. A. Perez-Cueto. 2016. "Nudging Consumers towards Healthier Choices: A Systematic Review of Positional Influences on Food Choice." *British Journal of Nutrition* 115(12):2252–63.

Bullard, Robert Doyle, Glenn Steve Johnson, and Angel O. Torres. 2004. *Highway Robbery: Transportation Racism and New Routes to Equity.* Cambridge, MA: South End Press.

Bureau of Labor Statistics. 2016. "American Time Use Survey." Retrieved July 16, 2018 (https://www.bls.gov/tus/home.htm).

Burns, Amy Clarke. 2015. "Q&Amy: Pete Hollis Property Ripe for Development." *Greenville News*, June 22.

Callum-Penso, Lillia. 2014. "Upstate Groups Nourish Food Deserts." *Greenville News*, December 2.

Carlson, Andrea, Mark Lino, WenYen Juan, Kenneth Hanson, and P. Peter Basiotis. 2007. *Thrifty Food Plan, 2006.* CNPP-19. Washington, DC: U.S. Department of Agriculture, Center for Nutrition Policy and Promotion.

Carlson, Steven J., Margaret S. Andrews, and Gary W. Bickel. 1999. "Measuring Food Insecurity and Hunger in the United States: Development of a National Benchmark Measure and Prevalence Estimates." *Journal of Nutrition* 129(2):510S–516S.

Caspi, Caitlin E., Glorian Sorensen, S. V. Subramanian, and Ichiro Kawachi. 2012. "The Local Food Environment and Diet: A Systematic Review." *Health & Place* 18(5):1172–87.

Centers for Disease Control and Prevention. 2019. "Intimate Partner Violence." Retrieved January 25, 2020 (https://www.cdc.gov/violenceprevention/intimatepartnerviolence/index.html).

Cerulo, Karen A. 2018. "Scents and Sensibility: Olfaction, Sense-Making, and Meaning Attribution." *American Sociological Review* 83(2):361–89.

City of Greenville. 2014. *RFP No. 14-3461: Acquisition and Development of the Former Green Plaza.* Greenville, SC.

Clayton, Joseph. 2020. "COVID-19 and Our Food: Temporary Change or a New Normal?" *Food Dive*, November 4.

Cleveland, David A., Nora M. Müller, Alexander C. Tranovich, D. Niki Mazaroli, and Kai Hinson. 2014. "Local Food Hubs for Alternative Food Systems: A Case Study from Santa Barbara County, California." *Journal of Rural Studies* 35:26–36.

Coello, Sara. 2020. "SNAP Benefits Increased 40 Percent to Curb Coronavirus Hardships." *Post and Courier*. Retrieved November 19, 2020 (https://www .postandcourier.com/health/covid19/snap-benefits-increased-40-percent-to -curb-coronavirus-hardships/article_5d43a89e-84a7-11ea-ba17 -cfb6bdd9b55b.html).

Cohen, Lizabeth. 2003. *A Consumers' Republic: The Politics of Mass Consumption in Postwar America*. New York: Knopf.

Cole, Luke W., and Caroline Farrell. 2006. "Structural Racism, Structural Pollution and the Need for a New Paradigm." *Washington University Journal of Law & Policy* 20(1):265–82.

Coleman, James S. 1988. "Social Capital in the Creation of Human Capital." *American Journal of Sociology* 94:S95–120.

Connor, Eric. 2017. "Historic Marker Will Commemorate Poinsett Mill." *Greenville News*, August 11.

———. 2019. "Unity Park: How History Will Help Shape a Greenville Crown Jewel and Who Will Benefit." *Greenville News*, April 15.

Connerly, Charles E. 2002. "From Racial Zoning to Community Empowerment: The Interstate Highway System and the African American Community in Birmingham, Alabama." *Journal of Planning Education and Research* 22(2):99–114.

Cordain, Loren. 2010. *The Paleo Diet Revised: Lose Weight and Get Healthy by Eating the Foods You Were Designed to Eat*. New York: Houghton Mifflin Harcourt.

Cummins, Steven, Ellen Flint, and Stephen A. Matthews. 2014. "New Neighborhood Grocery Store Increased Awareness of Food Access but Did Not Alter Dietary Habits or Obesity." *Health Affairs* 33(2):283–91.

Cummins, Steven, and Sally Macintyre. 1999. "The Location of Food Stores in Urban Areas: A Case Study in Glasgow." *British Food Journal* 101(7):545–53.

———. 2002. "'Food Deserts'—Evidence and Assumption in Health Policy Making." *BMJ* 325(7361):436–38.

Dahlberg, Linda L., and James A. Mercy. 2009. "History of Violence as a Public Health Problem." *American Medical Association Journal of Ethics* 11(2):167–72.

Daniel, Caitlin. 2016. "Economic Constraints on Taste Formation and the True Cost of Healthy Eating." *Social Science & Medicine* 148:34–41.

Davis, Angelia. 2018. "Racial Restrictions in Old Property Deeds Have Shaped Today's Neighborhoods in Upstate South Carolina." *Greenville News*, July 6.

Deener, Andrew. 2017. "The Origins of the Food Desert: Urban Inequality as Infrastructural Exclusion." *Social Forces* 95(3):1285–309.

Department of For-Hire Vehicles. 2019. "Mayor Bowser Expands Taxi-to-Rail Transportation Options for East of the River Neighborhoods." Retrieved

January 25, 2020 (https://dfhv.dc.gov/release/mayor-bowser-expands-taxi -rail-transportation-options-east-river-neighborhoods).

Diamond, Jared M. 1997. *Guns, Germs, and Steel: The Fates of Human Societies.* New York: W. W. Norton & Company.

DiSantis, Katherine Isselmann, Amy Hillier, Rio Holaday, and Shiriki Kumanyika. 2016. "Why Do You Shop There? A Mixed Methods Study Mapping Household Food Shopping Patterns onto Weekly Routines of Black Women." *International Journal of Behavioral Nutrition and Physical Activity* 13:11.

Donahue, Marie, and Stacy Mitchell. 2018. *Dollar Stores Are Targeting Struggling Urban Neighborhoods and Small Towns. One Community Is Showing How to Fight Back.* Washington, DC: Institute for Local Self-Reliance.

Drewnowski, Adam, Anju Aggarwal, Philip M. Hurvitz, Pablo Monsivais, and Anne V. Moudon. 2012. "Obesity and Supermarket Access: Proximity or Price?" *American Journal of Public Health* 102(8):e74–80.

Drewnowski, Adam, and Nicole Darmon. 2005. "Food Choices and Diet Costs: An Economic Analysis." *Journal of Nutrition* 135(4):900–904.

D'Rozario, Denver, and Jerome D. Williams. 2005. "Retail Redlining: Definition, Theory, Typology, and Measurement." *Journal of Macromarketing* 25(2):175–86.

Dubowitz, Tamara, Madhumita Ghosh-Dastidar, Deborah A. Cohen, Robin Beckman, Elizabeth D. Steiner, Gerald P. Hunter, Karen R. Flórez, Christina Huang, Christine A. Vaughan, Jennifer C. Sloan, Shannon N. Zenk, Steven Cummins, and Rebecca L. Collins. 2015a. "Diet and Perceptions Change with Supermarket Introduction in a Food Desert, but Not Because of Supermarket Use." *Health Affairs* 34(11):1858–68.

Dubowitz, Tamara, and La'Vette Wagner. 2019. "The Hill District Is Losing More Than a Supermarket." *Pittsburgh Post-Gazette,* March 31.

Dubowitz, Tamara, Shannon N. Zenk, Bonnie Ghosh-Dastidar, Deborah A. Cohen, Robin Beckman, Gerald Hunter, Elizabeth D. Steiner, and Rebecca L. Collins. 2015b. "Healthy Food Access for Urban Food Desert Residents: Examination of the Food Environment, Food Purchasing Practices, Diet and BMI." *Public Health Nutrition* 18(12):2220–30.

Dumont, Dora M., Brad Brockmann, Samuel Dickman, Nicole Alexander, and Josiah D. Rich. 2012. "Public Health and the Epidemic of Incarceration." *Annual Review of Public Health* 33(1):325–39.

Earl, Jennifer, Andrew Martin, John D. McCarthy, and Sarah A. Soule. 2004. "The Use of Newspaper Data in the Study of Collective Action." *Annual Review of Sociology* 30(1):65–80.

Eisenhauer, Elizabeth. 2001. "In Poor Health: Supermarket Redlining and Urban Nutrition." *GeoJournal* 53(2):125–33.

Elbel, Brian, Alyssa Moran, L. Beth Dixon, Kamila Kiszko, Jonathan Cantor, Courtney Abrams, and Tod Mijanovich. 2015. "Assessment of a Government-Subsidized Supermarket in a High-Need Area on Household Food Availability and Children's Dietary Intakes." *Public Health Nutrition* 18(15):2881–90.

Elitzak, Howard, and Abigail Okrent. 2018. "New U.S. Food Expenditure Estimates Find Food-Away-From-Home Spending Is Higher Than Previous Estimates." US Department of Agriculture: Economic Research Service, November 5. Retrieved March 3, 2020 (https://www.ers.usda.gov/amber -waves/2018/november/new-us-food-expenditure-estimates-find-food-away -from-home-spending-is-higher-than-previous-estimates/).

Elliott, Charlene. 2011. "'It's Junk Food and Chicken Nuggets': Children's Perspectives on 'Kids' Food' and the Question of Food Classification.'" *Journal of Consumer Behaviour* 10(3):133–40.

Escaron, Anne L., Ana P. Martinez-Donate, Ann Josie Riggall, Amy Meinen, Beverly Hall, F. Javier Nieto, and Susan Nitzke. 2016. "Developing and Implementing 'Waupaca Eating Smart': A Restaurant and Supermarket Intervention to Promote Healthy Eating through Changes in the Food Environment." *Health Promotion Practice* 17(2):265–77.

Farmer, Paul. 2005. *Pathologies of Power: Health, Human Rights, and the New War on the Poor.* Berkeley: University of California Press.

Feng, Jing, Thomas A. Glass, Frank C. Curriero, Walter F. Stewart, and Brian S. Schwartz. 2010. "The Built Environment and Obesity: A Systematic Review of the Epidemiologic Evidence." *Health & Place* 16(2):175–90.

Ferris, John, Carol Norman, and Joe Sempik. 2001. "People, Land and Sustainability: Community Gardens and the Social Dimension of Sustainable Development." *Social Policy & Administration* 35(5):559–68.

Fitzmaurice, Connor, and Juliet B. Schor. 2019. "Homemade Matters: Logics of Opposition in a Failed Food Swap." *Social Problems* 66(1):144–61.

Franklin, Brandi, Ashley Jones, Dejuan Love, Stephane Puckett, Justin Macklin, and Shelley White-Means. 2012. "Exploring Mediators of Food Insecurity and Obesity: A Review of Recent Literature." *Journal of Community Health* 37(1):253–64.

Freud, Sigmund. 1949/1989. *An Outline of Psycho-Analysis.* The Standard Edition. edited by J. Strachey. New York: W. W. Norton & Company.

Fryar, Cheryl D., Jeffery P. Hughes, Kiersten A. Herrick, and Namanjeet Ahluwalia. 2018. *Fast Food Consumption among Adults in the United States, 2013–2016. NCHS Data Brief, No 322.* Hyattsville, MD: National Center for Health Statistics.

Gerstel, Naomi, and Dan Clawson. 2018. "Control over Time: Employers, Workers, and Families Shaping Work Schedules." *Annual Review of Sociology* 44(1):77–97.

Gilbert, E. W. 1958. "Pioneer Maps of Health and Disease in England." *Geographical Journal* 124(2):172–83.

Gluckman, Peter D., and Mark A. Hanson. 2009. "Developmental and Epigenetic Pathways to Obesity: An Evolutionary-Developmental Perspective." *International Journal of Obesity* 32(S7):S62–71.

Goffman, Erving. 1974. *Frame Analysis: An Essay on the Organization of Experience.* Cambridge, MA: Harvard University Press.

Gordon-Larsen, Penny, Janne Boone-Heinonen, and Barry M. Popkin. 2012. "Supermarkets: Components of Causality for Healthy Diets—Reply." *Archives of Internal Medicine* 172(2):195–97.

Hamm, Michael W., and Anne C. Bellows. 2003. "Community Food Security and Nutrition Educators." *Journal of Nutrition Education and Behavior* 35(1):37–43.

Han, Euna, Lisa M. Powell, Shannon N. Zenk, Leah Rimkus, Punam Ohri-Vachaspati, and Frank J. Chaloupka. 2012. "Classification Bias in Commercial Business Lists for Retail Food Stores in the U.S." *International Journal of Behavioral Nutrition and Physical Activity* 9:46.

Harcourt, Bernard E. 2005. *Illusion of Order: The False Promise of Broken Windows Policing.* Cambridge, MA: Harvard University Press.

Harries, Caroline, Julia Koprak, Candace Young, Stephanie Weiss, Kathryn M. Parker, and Allison Karpyn. 2014. "Moving from Policy to Implementation: A Methodology and Lessons Learned to Determine Eligibility for Healthy Food Financing Projects." *Journal of Public Health Management and Practice* 20(5):498–505.

Harris, Deborah A., and Patti Giuffre. 2015. *Taking the Heat: Women Chefs and Gender Inequality in the Professional Kitchen.* New Brunswick, NJ: Rutgers University Press.

Harris, Jennifer L., Jennifer L. Pomeranz, Tim Lobstein, and Kelly D. Brownell. 2009. "A Crisis in the Marketplace: How Food Marketing Contributes to Childhood Obesity and What Can Be Done." *Annual Review of Public Health* 30:211–25.

Harrold, Judy, ed. 2015. *Ball Blue Book: Guide to Preserving.* 37th edition. Rye, NY: Jarden Home Brands.

Hillier, Amy, Carolyn C. Cannuscio, Allison Karpyn, Jacqueline McLaughlin, Mariana Chilton, and Karen Glanz. 2011. "How Far Do Low-Income Parents Travel to Shop for Food? Empirical Evidence from Two Urban Neighborhoods." *Urban Geography* 32(5):712–29.

Hochschild, Arlie Russell. 1983. *The Managed Heart: Commercialization of Human Feeling.* Berkeley, CA: University of California Press.

———. 1990. "Ideology and Emotion Management: A Perspective and Path for Future Research." In *Research Agendas in the Sociology of Emotions*, edited by T. D. Kemper, 117–42. Albany: State University of New York Press.

———. 1997. *The Time Bind: When Work Becomes Home and Home Becomes Work.* New York: Henry Holt and Company.

Huff, Archie Vernon. 1995. *Greenville: The History of the City and County in the South Carolina Piedmont.* Columbia: University of South Carolina Press.

Inagami, Sanae, Deborah A. Cohen, Brian Karl Finch, and Steven M. Asch. 2006. "You Are Where You Shop: Grocery Store Locations, Weight, and Neighborhoods." *American Journal of Preventive Medicine* 31(1):10–17.

Jackson, Sherry. 2013. "'Baby BI-LO' on North Main Closing." *Upstate Business Journal.* Retrieved January 24, 2020 (https://upstatebusinessjournal.com /baby-bi-lo-north-main-closing/).

Johnson, Steven. 2006. *The Ghost Map: The Story of London's Most Terrifying Epidemic--and How It Changed Science, Cities, and the Modern World.* New York: Riverhead Books.

Johnston, Josée, and Shyon Baumann. 2015. *Foodies: Democracy and Distinction in the Gourmet Foodscape.* Second edition. New York: Routledge.

Jones, Marian Moser. 2015. "Creating a Science of Homelessness During the Reagan Era." *The Milbank Quarterly* 93(1):139–78.

Kasarda, John D. 1989. "Urban Industrial Transition and the Underclass." *The ANNALS of the American Academy of Political and Social Science* 501(1):26–47.

Kato, Yuki. 2013. "Not Just the Price of Food: Challenges of an Urban Agriculture Organization in Engaging Local Residents." *Sociological Inquiry* 83(3):369–91.

Katz, Donald B., and Brian F. Sadacca. 2011. "Taste." in *Neurobiology of Sensation and Reward, Frontiers in Neuroscience,* edited by J. A. Gottfried. Boca Raton, FL: CRC Press.

Khan, Shamus. 2015. "Not Born This Way." *Aeon.* Retrieved January 2, 2018 (https:// aeon.co/essays/why-should-gay-rights-depend-on-being-born-this-way).

Khan, Shamus Rahman. 2011. *Privilege: The Making of an Adolescent Elite at St. Paul's School.* Princeton, NJ: Princeton University Press.

Kolb, Kenneth H. 2014. *Moral Wages: The Emotional Dilemmas of Victim Advocacy and Counseling.* Oakland, CA: University of California Press.

Koop, C. Everett. 1982. *"Family Violence: A Chronic Public Health Issue": Lecture to the Western Psychiatric Institute.* Pittsburgh, PA.

Kulish, Nicholas. 2020. "'Never Seen Anything Like It': Cars Line Up for Miles at Food Banks." *New York Times,* April 8.

Landrum, Cindy. 2017. "'Homeless Triangle' Salvation Army Agrees to Increase Patrols, Reduce Community Lunches to Two Days per Week." *Greenville Journal.* Retrieved June 25, 2018 (https://greenvillejournal.com/2017/09/07 /mediation-yields-ideas-ease-tensions-greenvilles-homeless-triangle/).

———. 2019. "Who Is Lila Mae Brock and Why Is the City Commissioning a Statue of Her?" *Greenville Journal,* January 3.

Lawless, Kristin. 2018. *Formerly Known as Food: How the Industrial Food System Is Changing Our Minds, Bodies, and Culture.* New York: St. Martin's Press.

LeDoux, Timothy F., and Igor Vojnovic. 2013. "Going Outside the Neighborhood: The Shopping Patterns and Adaptations of Disadvantaged Consumers Living in the Lower Eastside Neighborhoods of Detroit, Michigan." *Health & Place* 19:1–14.

Lloyd, Richard. 2012. "Urbanization and the Southern United States." *Annual Review of Sociology* 38(1):483–506.

Longest, Kyle C., Steven Hitlin, and Stephen Vaisey. 2013. "Position and Disposition: The Contextual Development of Human Values." *Social Forces* 91(4):1499–1528.

Martin, Katie S., Debarchana Ghosh, Martha Page, Michele Wolff, Kate McMinimee, and Mengyao Zhang. 2014. "What Role Do Local Grocery Stores Play in Urban Food Environments? A Case Study of Hartford-Connecticut." *PLOS ONE* 9(4):e94033.

Massey, Douglas S., and Nancy A. Denton. 1993. *American Apartheid: Segregation and the Making of the Underclass.* Cambridge, MA: Harvard University Press.

McDermott, Andrew J., and Mark B. Stephens. 2010. "Cost of Eating: Whole Foods versus Convenience Foods in a Low-Income Model." *Family Medicine* 42(4):280–84.

Mennella, Julie A., Coren P. Jagnow, and Gary K. Beauchamp. 2001. "Prenatal and Postnatal Flavor Learning by Human Infants." *Pediatrics* 107(6):e88.

Mikkelsen, Leslie, and Sana Chehimi. 2007. *The Links between the Neighborhood Food Environment and Childhood Nutrition.* Oakland, CA: Prevention Institute.

Miller, Char. 2003. "In the Sweat of Our Brow: Citizenship in American Domestic Practice During WWII—Victory Gardens." *Journal of American Culture* 26(3):395–409.

Mitchell, Anna B. 2019. "Rail Lines Divide Greenville's Southernside—Footbridge Could Bring Community Together." *Greenville News*, September 24.

Mohl, Raymond. A. 2000. "Planned Destruction: The Interstates and Central City Housing." In *From Tenements to the Taylor Homes: In Search of an Urban Housing Policy in Twentieth-Century America*, edited by J. F. Bauman, R. Biles, and K. M. Szylvian, 226–45. University Park: Pennsylvania State University Press.

Morland, Kimberly, Ana V. Diez Roux, and Steve Wing. 2006. "Supermarkets, Other Food Stores, and Obesity: The Atherosclerosis Risk in Communities Study." *American Journal of Preventive Medicine* 30(4):333–39.

Morland, Kimberly, Steve Wing, and Ana Diez Roux. 2002. "The Contextual Effect of the Local Food Environment on Residents' Diets: The

Atherosclerosis Risk in Communities Study." *American Journal of Public Health* 92(11):1761–68.

Morton, Lois Wright, Ella Annette Bitto, Mary Jane Oakland, and Mary Sand. 2005. "Solving the Problems of Iowa Food Deserts: Food Insecurity and Civic Structure." *Rural Sociology* 70(1):94–112.

Moss, Michael. 2014. *Salt Sugar Fat: How the Food Giants Hooked Us.* Reprint edition. New York: Random House.

Newman, Sarah L., Rachel Tumin, Rebecca Andridge, and Sarah E. Anderson. 2015. "Family Meal Frequency and Association with Household Food Availability in United States Multi-Person Households: National Health and Nutrition Examination Survey 2007–2010." *PLOS ONE* 10(12):1–13.

New York Times. 2011. "The Truth Behind Stop-and-Frisk." September 2.

NourishLife. 2010. "Michael Pollan: Supermarket Secrets." Retrieved January 23, 2020 (https://www.youtube.com/watch?v=snP4o-unOoA).

Oleschuk, Merin. 2019. "Gender, Cultural Schemas, and Learning to Cook." *Gender & Society* 33(4):607–28.

Papas, Mia A., Anthony J. Alberg, Reid Ewing, Kathy J. Helzlsouer, Tiffany L. Gary, and Ann C. Klassen. 2007. "The Built Environment and Obesity." *Epidemiologic Reviews* 29(1):129–43.

Parker, Traci. 2015. "Southern Retail Campaigns and the Struggle for Black Economic Freedom in the 1950s and 1960s." In *Race and Retail: Consumption Across the Color Line*, edited by M. Bay and A. Fabian, 87–108. New Brunswick, NJ: Rutgers University Press.

Parks, Lisa Fujie, Larry Cohen, and Nicole Kravitz-Wirtz. 2007. *Poised for Prevention: Advancing Promising Approaches to Primary Prevention of Intimate Partner Violence.* Oakland, CA: Prevention Institute.

Payne, Gayle Holmes, Holly Wethington, Lauren Olsho, Jan Jernigan, Rosanne Farris, and Deborah Klein Walker. 2013. "Implementing a Farmers' Market Incentive Program: Perspectives on the New York City Health Bucks Program." *Preventing Chronic Disease* 10.

Perrucci, Carolyn C., Robert Perrucci, Dena B. Targ, and Harry R. Targ, eds. 1988. *Plant Closings: International Context and Social Costs.* London: Aldine Transaction.

Peterson, Richard A., and Roger M. Kern. 1996. "Changing Highbrow Taste: From Snob to Omnivore." *American Sociological Review* 61(5):900–907.

Petticrew, Mark, Steven C. J. Cummins, Catherine Ferrell, Anne Findlay, Cassie Higgins, Caroline Hoy, Ade Kearns, and Leigh Sparks. 2005. "Natural Experiments: An Underused Tool for Public Health?" *Public Health* 119(9):751–57.

Piedmont Health Foundation. 2017. *Winter Report 2017: Greenlink Operations.* Greenville, SC: Piedmont Health Foundation.

Pinstrup-Andersen, Per. 2009. "Food Security: Definition and Measurement." *Food Security* 1(1):5–7.

Pollan, Michael. 2007. *The Omnivore's Dilemma: A Natural History of Four Meals*. New York: Penguin.

———. 2009. *In Defense of Food: An Eater's Manifesto*. New York: Penguin Books.

Portinari, Folco. 1989. "Slow Food Manifesto." *Slowfood USA*. Retrieved January 16, 2019 (https://www.slowfoodusa.org/manifesto/).

Pugh, Allison J. 2004. "Windfall Child Rearing: Low-Income Care and Consumption." *Journal of Consumer Culture* 4(2):229–49.

Putnam, Robert D. 2000. *Bowling Alone: The Collapse and Revival of American Community*. New York: Simon and Schuster.

Ralli, Tania. 2005. "Who's a Looter? In Storm's Aftermath, Pictures Kick Up a Different Kind of Tempest." *New York Times*, September 5.

Redman, Russell. 2020. "Pandemic Sways Most Americans to Eat at Home More Often." *Supermarket News*, September 11.

Reese, Ashanté M. 2019. *Black Food Geographies: Race, Self-Reliance, and Food Access in Washington, D.C.* Chapel Hill, NC: University of North Carolina Press.

Reicks, Marla, Amanda C. Trofholz, Jamie S. Stang, and Melissa N. Laska. 2014. "Impact of Cooking and Home Food Preparation Interventions among Adults: Outcomes and Implications for Future Programs." *Journal of Nutrition Education and Behavior* 46(4):259–76.

Richman, Talia. 2019. "Baltimore Residents Who Live in Food Deserts Can Now Take a Subsidized Lyft Ride to Grocery Store." *Baltimore Sun*, November 18.

Robinson, Jonnell A., Evan Weissman, Susan Adair, Matthew Potteiger, and Joaquin Villanueva. 2016. "An Oasis in the Desert? The Benefits and Constraints of Mobile Markets Operating in Syracuse, New York Food Deserts." *Agriculture and Human Values* 33(4):877–93.

Rosenberg, Nathan A., and Nevin Cohen. 2018. "Let Them Eat Kale: The Misplaced Narrative of Food Access Colloquium: Taking a Bite out of the Big Apple: A Conversation about Urban Food Policy." *Fordham Urban Law Journal* 45(4):1091–120.

Rozin, Paul, Jonathan Haidt, and Katrina Fincher. 2009. "From Oral to Moral." *Science* 323(5918):1179–80.

Ruhlman, Michael. 2017. *Grocery: The Buying and Selling of Food in America*. New York: Abrams Press.

Sadler, Richard C., Jason A. Gilliland, and Godwin Arku. 2013. "A Food Retail-Based Intervention on Food Security and Consumption." *International Journal of Environmental Research and Public Health* 10(8):3325–46.

Sampson, Robert J., and Stephen W. Raudenbush. 1999. "Systematic Social Observation of Public Spaces: A New Look at Disorder in Urban Neighborhoods." *American Journal of Sociology* 105(3):603–51.

Sampson, Robert J., Patrick Sharkey, and Stephen W. Raudenbush. 2008. "Durable Effects of Concentrated Disadvantage on Verbal Ability among

African-American Children." *Proceedings of the National Academy of Sciences* 105(3):845–52.

Schneider, Felicitas. 2013. "The Evolution of Food Donation with Respect to Waste Prevention." *Waste Management* 33(3):755–63.

Schor, Juliet B. 1992. *The Overworked American: The Unexpected Decline Of Leisure.* Reprint edition. New York: Basic Books.

Scribner, R. 1996. "Paradox as Paradigm: The Health Outcomes of Mexican Americans." *American Journal of Public Health* 86(3):303–5.

Shah, Dhavan V., Douglas M. McLeod, Eunkyung Kim, Sun Young Lee, Melissa R. Gotlieb, Shirley S. Ho, and Hilde Breivik. 2007. "Political Consumerism: How Communication and Consumption Orientations Drive 'Lifestyle Politics.'" *ANNALS of the American Academy of Political and Social Science* 611(1):217–35.

Simmet, Anja, Julia Depa, Peter Tinnemann, and Nanette Stroebele-Benschop. 2017. "The Nutritional Quality of Food Provided from Food Pantries: A Systematic Review of Existing Literature." *Journal of the Academy of Nutrition and Dietetics* 117(4):577–88.

Simon, Bryant. 2011. "'A Down Brother': Earvin 'Magic' Johnson and the Quest for Retail Justice in Los Angeles: After the 1992 Riots, L.A.'s Beloved Laker Allied with Starbucks and Other Corporate Dining and Entertainment Outfits to Revive South Central. Why Did He Fail?" *Boom: A Journal of California* 1(2):43–58.

Singh, Maanvi. 2015. "Why A Philadelphia Grocery Chain Is Thriving in Food Deserts." National Public Radio, May 14.

Sisson, Lisa G., and Deborah A. Lown. 2011. "Do Soup Kitchen Meals Contribute to Suboptimal Nutrient Intake & Obesity in the Homeless Population?" *Journal of Hunger & Environmental Nutrition* 6(3):312–23.

Smith, Lindsey P., Shu Wen Ng, and Barry M. Popkin. 2013. "Trends in US Home Food Preparation and Consumption: Analysis of National Nutrition Surveys and Time Use Studies from 1965–1966 to 2007–2008." *Nutrition Journal* 12:45.

———. 2014. "Resistant to the Recession: Low-Income Adults' Maintenance of Cooking and Away-from-Home Eating Behaviors during Times of Economic Turbulence." *American Journal of Public Health* 104(5):840–46.

Snow, David A., Susan G. Baker, Leon Anderson, and Michael Martin. 1986. "The Myth of Pervasive Mental Illness among the Homeless." *Social Problems* 33(5):407–23.

Snow, David A., and Robert D. Benford. 1988. "Ideology, Frame Resonance, and Participant Mobilization." *International Social Movement Research* 1:197–217.

Snow, David A., E. Burke Rochford, Steven K. Worden, and Robert D. Benford. 1986. "Frame Alignment Processes, Micromobilization, and Movement Participation." *American Sociological Review* 51(4):464–81.

Stern, Dalia, Jennifer M. Poti, Shu Wen Ng, Whitney R. Robinson, Penny
Gordon-Larsen, and Barry M. Popkin. 2016. "Where People Shop Is Not
Associated with the Nutrient Quality of Packaged Foods for Any Racial-
Ethnic Group in the United States." *The American Journal of Clinical
Nutrition* 103(4):1125–34.
Stone, Curtis. 2016. *The Urban Farmer: Growing Food for Profit on Leased and
Borrowed Land*. Gabriola Island, BC, Canada: New Society Publishers.
Styles, Madison. 2018. "Plan to Build Burger King in the West End Brings
Concerns to the Community." *FOX Carolina*. Retrieved June 17, 2021
(https://www.foxcarolina.com/news/plan-to-build-burger-king-in-the-west
-end-brings-concerns-to-the-community/article_98b174c0-8372-5adc-ac9e
-efcbf5c9366a.html).
Taillie, Lindsey Smith, Anna H. Grummon, and Donna R. Miles. 2018. "Nutri-
tional Profile of Purchases by Store Type: Disparities by Income and Food
Program Participation." *American Journal of Preventive Medicine*
55(2):167–77.
TED: Ideas Worth Spreading. 2013. *Rod Finley: A Guerrilla Gardener in South
Central LA*.
Tierney, Kathleen. 2003. "Disaster Beliefs and Institutional Interests: Recycling
Disaster Myths in the Aftermath of 9-11." In *Terrorism and Disaster: New
Threats, New Ideas*, edited by Lee Clarke, 33–51. Research in Social Problems
and Public Policy. Bingely, UK: Emerald Group Publishing.
Tierney, Kathleen, Christine Bevc, and Erica Kuligowski. 2016. "Metaphors
Matter: Disaster Myths, Media Frames, and Their Consequences in Hur-
ricane Katrina:" *ANNALS of the American Academy of Political and Social
Science* 604(1):57–81.
Treuhaft, Sarah, and Allison Karpyn. 2010. *The Grocery Gap: Who Has Access
to Healthy Food and Why It Matters*. Oakland, CA & Philadelphia, PA: Policy
Link and The Food Trust.
Triangle Business Journal Online. 2015. "Save-A-Lot Store Opening in April to
Replenish 'Food Desert' in South Raleigh." March 10.
Trubek, Amy B. 2017. *Making Modern Meals: How Americans Cook Today*.
Oakland: University of California Press.
Turner, Ariel. 2019. "Nautic Brewing to Open on Edge of Proposed Unity Park
Site." *Upstate Business Journal*, February 27.
US Census Bureau. 2016. "The Majority of Children Live with Two Parents,
Census Bureau Reports." November 17, 2016. Retrieved January 24, 2020
(https://www.census.gov/newsroom/press-releases/2016/cb16-192.html).
———. 2018. Households by Size: 1960 to Present. Historical Household Tables.
(https://www.census.gov/data/tables/time-series/demo/families/households
.html).

US Department of Agriculture. 2012. "2012 Census of Agriculture." Retrieved January 25, 2020 (https://www.nass.usda.gov/Publications/AgCensus/2012/#full_report).

US Department of Agriculture, Economic Research Service. n.d. "Food Environment Atlas." Retrieved January 23, 2020 (www.ers.usda.gov/foodatlas/).

US Department of Health and Human Services. 1986. *Surgeon General's Workshop on Violence and Public Health*. HRS-D-MC 86-1. Leesburg, Virginia.

———. 2011. "CED Grant Awards FY 2011, Office of Community Services, Administration for Children and Families." Retrieved September 17, 2016 (http://www.acf.hhs.gov/ocs/resource/fy-2011-ced-funding).

US Department of Health and Human Services, Office of Community Services. 2016. "Healthy Food Financing Initiative." . Retrieved October 4, 2017 (https://www.acf.hhs.gov/ocs/programs/community-economic-development/healthy-food-financing).

Valdez, Zulema. 2011. The New Entrepreneurs: How Race, Class, and Gender Shape American Enterprise. Stanford, CA: Stanford University Press.

Vaughan, Christine A., Deborah A. Cohen, Madhumita Ghosh-Dastidar, Gerald P. Hunter, and Tamara Dubowitz. 2017. "Where Do Food Desert Residents Buy Most of Their Junk Food? Supermarkets." *Public Health Nutrition* 20(14):2608–16.

Wang, Haoluan, Feng Qiu, and Brent Swallow. 2014. "Can Community Gardens and Farmers' Markets Relieve Food Desert Problems? A Study of Edmonton, Canada." *Applied Geography* 55:127–37.

Weisburd, David, Gerben J. N. Bruinsma, and Wim Bernasco. 2009. "Units of Analysis in Geographic Criminology: Historical Development, Critical Issues, and Open Questions." in *Putting Crime in Its Place: Units of Analysis in Geographic Criminology*, edited by D. Weisburd, W. Bernasco, and G. J. N. Bruinsma, 3–31. New York: Springer New York.

Weisburd, David, and Cynthia Lum. 2005. "The Diffusion of Computerized Crime Mapping in Policing: Linking Research and Practice." *Police Practice and Research* 6(5):419–34.

White House Task Force on Childhood Obesity. 2010. *Solving the Problem of Childhood Obesity within a Generation: White House Task Force on Childhood Obesity Report to the President*. Washington, DC.

Widener, Michael J., Steven Farber, Tijs Neutens, and Mark W. Horner. 2013. "Using Urban Commuting Data to Calculate a Spatiotemporal Accessibility Measure for Food Environment Studies." *Health & Place* 21:1–9.

Wildeman, Christopher, and Emily A. Wang. 2017. "Mass Incarceration, Public Health, and Widening Inequality in the USA." *The Lancet* 389(10077):1464–74.

Willis, Jeffrey R. 2003. *Remembering Greenville: Photographs from the Coxe Collection*. Charleston, SC: Arcadia.

Wilson, James Q., and George L. Kelling. 1982. "Broken Windows: The Police and Neighborhood Safety." *The Atlantic*, March.

Wilson, Ronald E. 2007. "The Impact of Software on Crime Mapping: An Introduction to a Special Journal Issue of Social Science Computing Review on Crime Mapping." *Social Science Computer Review* 25(2):135–42.

Wilson, William J. 1987. *The Truly Disadvantaged: The Inner City, the Underclass, and Public Policy*. Chicago: University of Chicago Press.

———. 2009. *More Than Just Race: Being Black and Poor in the Inner City*. New York: W. W. Norton.

Woodhall-Melnik, Julia, and Flora I. Matheson. 2017. "More Than Convenience: The Role of Habitus in Understanding the Food Choices of Fast Food Workers." *Work, Employment and Society* 31(5):800–815.

Wrigley, Neil, Daniel Warm, Barrie Margetts, and Amanda Whelan. 2002. "Assessing the Impact of Improved Retail Access on Diet in a 'Food Desert': A Preliminary Report." *Urban Studies* 39(11):2061–82.

Yao, Mengni, Amy Hillier, Elizabeth Wall, and Katherine I. DiSantis. 2019. "The Impact of a Non-Profit Market on Food Store Choice and Shopping Experience: A Community Case Study." *Frontiers in Public Health* 7(78).

Index

Founded in 1893,
UNIVERSITY OF CALIFORNIA PRESS
publishes bold, progressive books and journals
on topics in the arts, humanities, social sciences,
and natural sciences—with a focus on social
justice issues—that inspire thought and action
among readers worldwide.

The UC PRESS FOUNDATION
raises funds to uphold the press's vital role
as an independent, nonprofit publisher, and
receives philanthropic support from a wide
range of individuals and institutions—and from
committed readers like you. To learn more, visit
ucpress.edu/supportus.